Chilton's

Repair and Tune-Up Guide

for the

BMW

Illustrated

PRODUCED BY THE AUTOMOTIVE BOOK DEPARTMENT

CHILTON BOOK COMPANY

PHILADELPHIA NEW YORK LONDON

Published in Philadelphia by Chilton Book Company,
and simultaneously in Ontario, Canada,
by Thomas Nelson & Sons, Ltd.

Manufactured in the United States of America

Library of Congress Catalog Card Number 78-143690
ISBN 0-8019-5576-9

ACKNOWLEDGMENTS

Chilton Book Company expresses appreciation to these firms for their generous assistance:

ARNOLT CORPORATION
Warsaw, Indiana

CHAMPION SPARK PLUG COMPANY
Toledo, Ohio

GEON
Woodbury, New York

GOODYEAR TIRE & RUBBER COMPANY
Akron, Ohio

HOFFMAN MOTORS CORPORATION
New York, New York

Contents

BMW Distributors

HOFFMAN MOTORS CORPORATION
375 PARK AVENUE
NEW YORK, NEW YORK 10022
212–759-5120

HOFFMAN MOTORS CORPORATION
1862 SOUTH LA CIENEGA BLVD.
LOS ANGELES, CALIFORNIA 90035
213–274-8231

HOFFMAN MOTORS CORPORATION
3334 RICHMOND AVENUE
HOUSTON, TEXAS 77006
713–526-5533

MANHEIM BMW SALES & SERVICE
MILL & WOLF STREETS
MANHEIM, PENNSYLVANIA 17545
717–665-2020

ELSCO CORPORATION
1843 EAST ADAMS STREET
JACKSONVILLE, FLORIDA 32202
904–353-5988

ARCHIE D. WALKER JR.
MOTORS, INC.
7419 WASHINGTON AVENUE, SOUTH
EDINA, MINNESOTA
612–473-4284

Chapter 1
Identification and Maintenance

BMW Models

The Bavarian Motor Works of Munich, Germany has a 50-year tradition of building engines with from one to twenty-four cylinders. The company was formed as the Bavarian Aircraft Works on March 7th, 1916. BMW engines have set speed and endurance records in the air, on the water, and on the ground. The first production jet aircraft was built by BMW in 1944.

The first motor vehicle to bear the white and blue BMW insignia of the whirling propellor was the BMW motorcycle, introduced in 1923. This machine used a horizontally opposed two cylinder engine and shaft drive, features which are retained in present day BMW motorcycles.

Car production was begun in 1928. The present, highly successful series of BMW automobiles was initiated in 1959, with the BMW 1500.

In 1967, the company introduced the BMW 1600 and 1800 Series, and later the 2002. All have in-line 4-cylinder water cooled engines with displacements upward from 120 cu. in.

In 1969, to satisfy the demand for a larger car that combines the ultimate in passenger comfort with the maneuverability of a sports sedan, BMW introduced the revolutionary 6-cylinder 2500 and 2800. These are full size, elegantly styled cars using fine materials, and are very fast, with amazing acceleration and cruising speeds of 130 miles per hour. General specifications for these cars can be found in this book; however, no repair procedures are available as yet.

In 1969, BMW produced 148,079 vehicles, of which 65,837 were exported.

How to Take Care of Your BMW

Model Identification

The manufacturer's plate, chassis number and engine number are the means of identifying your car, and must be quoted in all correspondence with the dealer when requesting information or ordering spare parts.

The Manufacturer's Plate is located at the back of the engine compartment on the right. The Chassis Number is also located at the back of the engine compartment next to the lock. The Engine Number is on the rear left hand side of the crankcase.

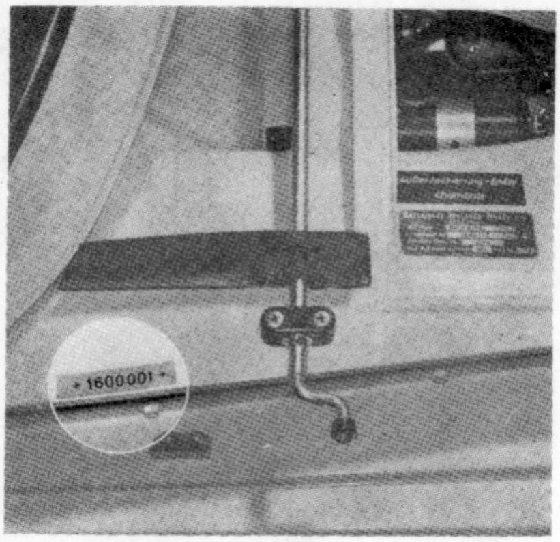

Engine compartment, with Chassis number, left, and Manufacturer's Plate number upper right.

Engine number is located on rear left side of crankcase.

Running-in Period — 2002, 1600

Engines of the 2002 and 1600 Series have no governors. Maximum speed limits should be observed for the first 1200 miles, for maximum economy and life expectancy. The maximum speeds in each year should only be maintained for short periods while running in.

Maximum Speeds for First 600 Miles (1000 km)

	BMW 2002	*BMW 1600*
1st Gear	20 mph	20 mph
2nd Gear	40 mph	35 mph
3rd Gear	55 mph	55 mph
4th Gear	75 mph	70 mph

Maximum Speeds for the Second 600 Miles

	BMW 2002	*BMW 1600*
1st Gear	20 mph	20 mph
2nd Gear	40 mph	40 mph
3rd Gear	65 mph	60 mph
4th Gear	85 mph	80 mph

Maximum Cruising Speeds

BMW 2002	*BMW 1600*
106 mph	97 mph

Maximum Speeds After Running-in is Complete

	BMW 2002	*BMW 1600*
1st Gear	28 mph	26 mph
2nd Gear	51 mph	48 mph
3rd Gear	79 mph	74 mph
4th Gear	106 mph	100 mph

During the running-in period up to 320 miles, avoid heavy brake applications especially from high speeds, and do not subject the brakes to extended hard usage.

Fuel and Oil

BMW engines require high octane (95) fuel. In using lower octane ratings, knocking or "pinging" can be avoided by keeping the engine turning at 2500 rpm or above, by shifting down in good time and accelerating gently.

Average fuel consumption is affected by many factors, including load, road and weather conditions, driving methods, tire pressures and traffic flow.

After driving in slow moving traffic for long periods, let the car's engine "take a deep breath" by traveling for a mile or so at fairly high engine speeds. This will disperse any carbon deposits that may have accumulated.

Engine oil consumption also depends upon a variety of factors. BMW engines are designed to take full advantage of the highly refined oils available today. Neither the engine, gearbox, nor final drive oils should require any additives. Also, do not change to a different brand of oil unless a complete oil change, including the oil filter, is undertaken.

Check the oil at the start of a trip and at re-fueling stops. If necessary, add oil to bring level to upper mark on dipstick. It is useless to overfill the engine and can even cause harm in certain circumstances. The quantity of oil represented by the distance between the upper and lower marks on the dipstick is 3.2 pints. The oil level should never fall below the lower mark. Do not take off filler cap while engine is running.

Model	Engine			Horsepower (SAE)		Carb. Type	Brakes F/R Disc (DS) Drum (DM)	Elec. Sys. (V.)	Track F/R (In.)	Wheel-base (In.)	Overall Dimensions (Approx. In.)			Wt. (Lbs.)	Tire Size (In.)	Tire Pres. (PSI)*** Std./Rad.	
	No. of Cyl.	Cap. (Cu. In./C.C.)	Comp. Ratio (:1)	BHP	@RPM						Lgth.	Width	Ht.			F	R
1500	4	91/1490	8.8	90	5900	SOLEX 36PDSI	DS/DM	6	52/54	100	177	67	57	2073	6.00-14, 165SR14	24/26	24/26
1600	4	96/1573	8.6	94	5700	SOLEX 36PDSI	DS/DM	6	52/54	100	177	67	57	2073	6.00S-14, 165SR14	24/26	24/26
1600 2 Door	4	96/1573	8.6	96	5800	SOLEX 38PDSI	DS/DM	6**	52/52	99	166	63	55	2070	6.00S-13, 165SR13	24/26	24/26
1600TI	4	96/1573	9.5	118	6200	2 SOLEX 40PHH	DS/DM	12	52/52	99	166	63	55	2070	165SR13	24/26	24/26
1800, 1800A	4	108/1773	8.6	102	5800	SOLEX 38PDSI	DS/DM	6	52/54	100	177	67	57	2073	6.00S-14, 165SR14	24/26	24/26
1800/69	4	108/1766	8.6	102	5800	SOLEX 38PDSI	DS/DM	12	52/54	98	177	67	57	2073	6.00S-14, 165SR14	24/26	24/26
1800TI	4	108/1773	9.5	124	5800	2 SOLEX 40PHH	DS/DM	6	52/54	100	177	67	57	2073	6.00S-14, 165SR14	24/26	24/26
2002, 2000CA	4	121/1990	8.5	113	6000, 5800-CA	SOLEX 40PDSIT* or 40PDSI	DS/DM	12	52/52	99,100	166, 178	63, 66	55, 53	2200	165SR13 6.955-14, 175SR (or HR) 14	24/26	24/26
2000, 2000A	4	121/1990	8.5	113	6000	SOLEX 40PDSIT* or 40PDSI	DS/DM	12	52/54	100	177	67	57	2300	175H14, 1755R (or HR) 14	24/26	24/26
2000TI, 2000CS	4	121/1990	9.3	135	5800	2 SOLEX 40PHH	DS/DM	12	52/54	100	177, 178	67, 65	57, 53	2300	6.95H-14, 175SR (or HR) 14	24/26	24/26
2500	6	152/2494	9.0	170	6000	2 ZENITH 35/40INAT	DS/DS	12	57/58	106	185	69	55	2950	DR70X14	27/29	26/28
2800	6	170/2788	9.0	192	6000	2 ZENITH 35/40INAT	DS/DS	12	57/58	106	185	69	57	2950	DR70X14	27/29	26/28
2800CS	6	170/2788	9.0	192	6000	2 ZENITH 35/40INAT	DS/DM	12	57/55	103	183	66	54	2866	DR70X14	27/29	26/28

*With automatic choke. **Later models have a 12-volt system. ***For continuous use above 150 KPh (93 mph), add 3 PSI.

After long periods of running at high speeds, allow the engine to idle for a short time before switching it off. This frees pockets of heat in the cooling system and prevents loss of water.

Inspection and Service

Your BMW should be inspected and serviced at regular intervals as outlined in the owner's manual using only recommended procedures and materials. Oil in the crankcase should be checked at each re-fueling or at least every 300 miles. BMW recommends a minimum of twice yearly inspections, even if the mileage between service periods has not yet reached the correct figure. Consult the Maintenance Schedule and the Lubrication Chart for recommended procedures and intervals. Consult the capacities chart for refill capacities. Both the lubrication chart and the capacities chart give recommended lubricant viscosities.

Lubrication

Change engine oil in the BMW 2002 and 1600 models (after the prescribed initial service period for new engines) every 4000 miles during the summer months and every 2000 miles during the remainder of the year. If the car is used for frequent short trips, change the oil every month. Engine oil level is accurately shown on the dipstick only when the engine is warm but not running — preferably after sitting a while to allow oil to drain into sump. Change engine oil while it is warm. Change oil filter element at each oil change.

Capacities

	Crankcase		*Transmission*		*Rear Axle*		*Fuel*		
Model	*Cap. (Pts) (Add .53 for Filter)*	*Max. Oil Press. (PSI)*	*Cap. (Pts)*	*Vis. (SAE)*	*Cap. (Pts)*	*Vis. (SAE)*	*Tank Cap. (Gals)*	*Pump Press. (PSI @1000 RPM)*	*Cooling Capacity (Pts) (Including Heater)*
1500	8.6	71-85	2.64	80	1.9	90	14.5	2.99-3.56	14.6
1600	8.6	71-85	2.64	80	1.9	90	14.5	2.99-3.56	14.6
1600-2 Door	8.6	71.85	2.1	80	1.9	90	12.2	2.99-3.56	14.6
1600TI	8.6	71-85	2.1	80	1.9	90	12.2	2.99-3.56	14.6
1800, 1800A	8.6	71-85	2.1*, Note 1	80 ATF TYPE A	1.9 Note 2	90	14.5	2.99-3.56	14.6
1800/69	8.6	71-85	2.1	80	1.9 Note 2	90	14.5	2.99-3.56	14.6
1800TI	8.6	71-85	2.1*	80	1.9	90	14.5	2.99-3.56	14.6
2002	8.6	71-85	2.1	80	1.9	90	12.2	2.99-3.56	14.6
2000, 2000A	8.6	71	2.1, Note 1	80, ATF TYPE A	1.9 Note 2	90	14.5	2.99-3.56	14.6
2000TI	8.6	71	2.1	80	1.9 Note 2	90	14.5	2.99-3.56	14.6
2000CS	8.6	71	2.1	80	1.9 Note 2	90	14.5	2.99-3.56	14.6
2000CA	8.6	71	Note 1	ATF TYPE A	1.9 Note 2	90	14.5	2.99-3.56	14.6
2500	10.6						19.7	–	25.4
2800	10.6						19.7	–	25.4
2800CS, CA	10.6						15.4	–	25.4

Note 1 – ZF automatic transmission capacity is 10 Pts at initial filling and 3.2 Pts. at oil change.
Note 2 – Capacity is 2.74 Pts when the short neck rear axle is used on these models.
*2.64 Pts for long neck gearbox.

Lubrication chart

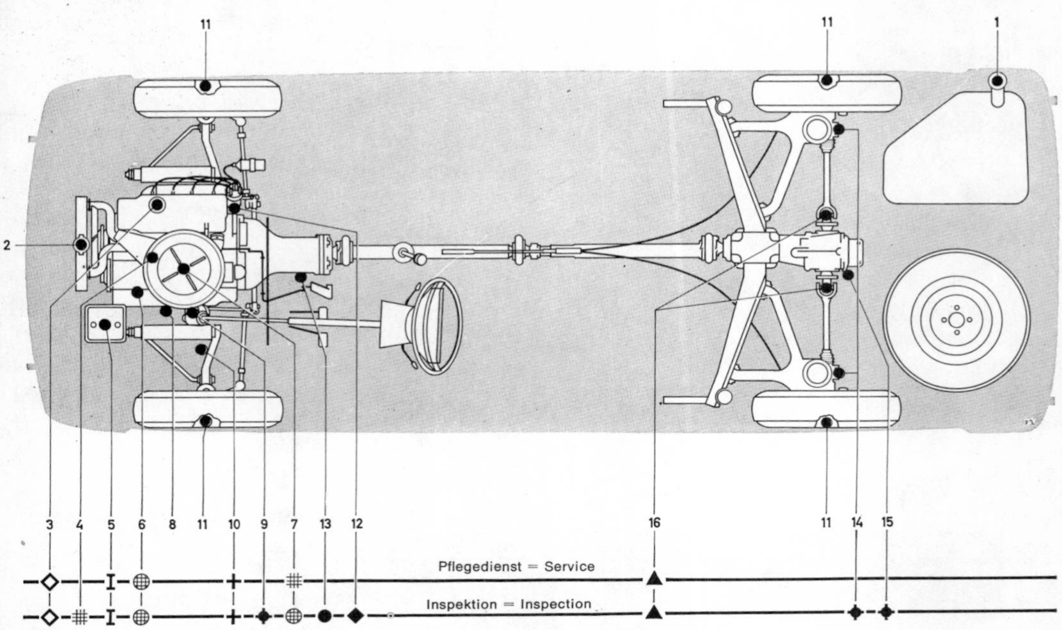

BMW 2002 lubrication chart.

Key to Lubrication Chart

1. Fuel filler	Branded super grade fuel
2. Radiator filler (Coolant outlets are situated at the bottom left of the radiator and the bottom right of the engine block)	Check frost- resistance before and during the cold season.
3. Engine oil filler	◆ Branded HD engine oil ◇ indicates oil change
4. Fuel pump fine mesh filter	# indicates filter cleaning
5. Battery	I Distilled water
6. Engine oil filter	⊕ indicates filter renewal
7. induction air filter	# indicates filter cleaning ⊕ indicates filter renewal
8. Engine oil level dipstick	Check oil level regularly
9. Steering box (permanently filled)	✦ Branded hypoid gear oil SAE 90
10. Hydraulic brake fluid reservoir	+ ATE brake fluid, blue
11. Wheel bearings (examine every 60 000 km/40 000 miles)	▲ Branded multi-purpose grease with drip point 180° C (356° F)
12. Oil nipple for ignition distributor	◆ Branded HD oil, as engine oil
13. Gearbox (change oil every 24 000 km/16 000 miles)	● Branded gearbox oil, SAE 80 (or, if not available, HD engine oil SAE 30)
14. Half shaft sliding joints (change oil every 24 000 km/16 000 miles) (not used on nomaintenance half-shafts)	✦ Branded hypoid gear oil, SAE 90
15. Final drive	✦ Branded hypoid gear oil, SAE 90
16. Half-shaft universal joint grease nipples (not used on nomaintenance half-shafts)	▲ Branded multi-purpose grease with drip point 180° C (356° F)

Important instruction to service stations

Strengthened points for single column car lifts with 4 lifting points:

Outer extremity of body under fold directly adjacent to the reinforced points for the car's own jack.

For lifts with 3 lifting points:

At front below the two floor section struts, in line with the front door pillars.

At rear, in the centre of the V-shaped box-section carrier, close to the propeller shaft flange.

Warning: Never jack up directly on to the final drive.

ENGINE OIL

Temperatures		*Viscosity*
Above 50°F.		SAE 30,
		SAE 20W40
	or	SAE 20W50
Below 50°F.		SAE 20
	or	SAE 10W30

Change gearbox oil while it is warm. Unscrew first the drain plug and then the oil filler plug on the left hand side of the gearbox to assist draining. When fully drained, firmly replace drain plug. Fill to underside of filler aperture. Both drain and filler plugs have conical threads, and

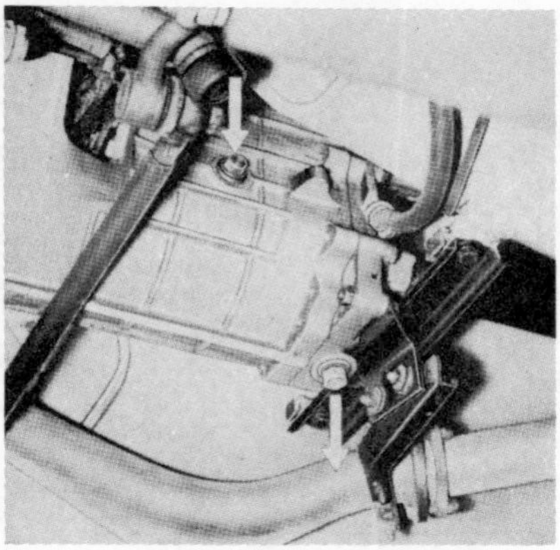

Gearbox filler and drain plugs.

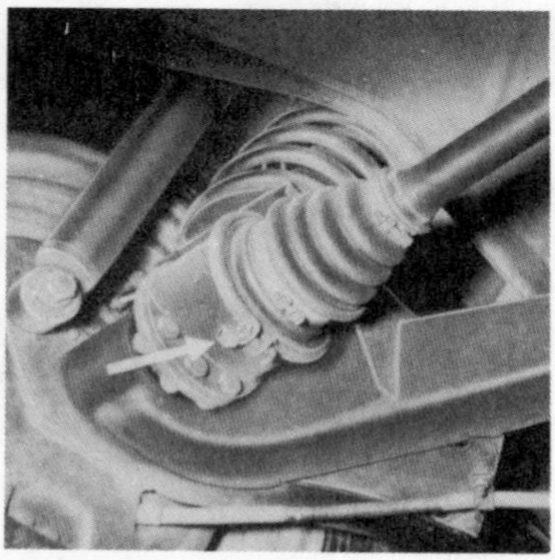

Filler/drain plug of half-shaft sliding joint.

therefore should not be replaced with plugs having metric threads.

Change oil in half-shaft sliding joints unless they are of the no-maintenance type. Turn rear wheel until combined filler/drain plug is pointing down, then unscrew plug and allow oil to drain. To refill joint, turn wheel again until orifice points upward at 45 degrees and fill to lower edge of orifice. Capacity is 6.3 ounces.

Change oil in rear while it is warm. Unscrew oil drain plug and then oil filler plug on the left side of the casing. Clean plugs and replace drain plug. Fill to lower edge of filler orifice with hypoid gear oil SAE 90. Capacity for all models is 1.9 pints.

Lubricate half shaft universal joints if they are not the maintenance-free type, with multi-purpose grease.

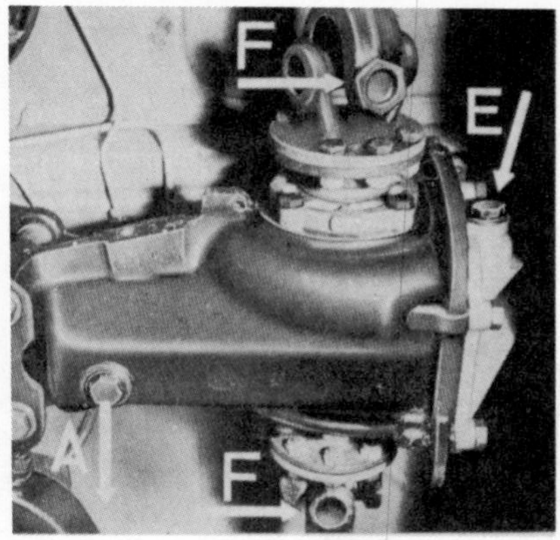

Hypoid rear drain plug (A), filler plug (E) and half-shaft universal joints (F).

Oil level should be up to lower edge of filler orifice. Steering box oil level should be checked but no oil change is required. Fill to lower edge of orifice with hypoid gear oil SAE 90. Capacity is 10.5 ounces.

Lubricate carburetor linkage with one or two drops of engine oil while moving throttle controls. Disconnect ball joints, fill cups with high temperature grease and reconnect.

Lubricate distributor by applying a light coat of high temperature grease to the cam. Do not allow grease or dirt to contaminate the breaker points. Remove rotor and add two drops of engine oil to the felt pad in the shaft. Apply two drops of oil to outer nipple of distributor shaft (above distributor clamp). Retighten nipple.

Maintenance Checks

Clutch Adustment

Check clutch operating clearance at the thrust rod on lower left side of clutch housing. To reset to the prescribed clearance of .12″ (3 mm), loosen locknut, turn adjusting nut, then re-tighten locknut.

Cooling System Care

Check water level occasionally. Always do this when the engine is cold and there is no pressure in the system. The water level should be no higher than .75″ (2 cm) below the base of the filler orifice.

Replace radiator coolant at least every two years, when the entire cooling system should be flushed with clean water. The recommended coolant is a mixture of 40%

Clutch adjusting and locking nuts.

ethylene glycol and 60% water. To drain the cooling system, open the drain plug at the bottom left side of the radiator, and the plug at the right rear side of the engine block. While draining set the heater temperature control to "warm".

Effective cooling system protection against rust requires at least a 25% solution (+ 10°F.) of the recommended antifreeze through summer and winter. If water only is used, a water pump lubricant and a heavy duty cooling system protector should be added. Methanol or alcohol alone are not recommended for the cooling system. These agents with their low boiling points evaporate (boil off) in a short time. Ethylene glycol antifreeze compounds have boiling points close to 400°F., well above the heat range of water cooled engines. Antirust and lubrication additives are helpful in lubricating the water pump and protecting metal parts . The rust and foam inhibitors used in antifreeze lose their power with aging, particularly in older engines, with greater rust deposits. Antifreeze itself eventually loses its protective properties and becomes an irritant to the cooling system. Replace at recommended intervals.

Antifreeze is harmful to the oil system of the engine. If cooling system fluid has leaked into the engine oil, ethylene-glycol-monobutyl-cellusolve, available from jobbers is recommended for flushing the system.

Water condensation in the engine is often caused by limited use of the car. If an engine only runs two or three miles before being shut down, it does not maintain its proper operating temperature long enough to evaporate water that may be present in the crankcase. Regular oil changes will help eliminate water accumulation. Also check the thermostat for too quick opening. If necessary, change thermostat for hotter engine operation.

Fan Belt Adjustment

A tight fan belt will cause rapid wear of the alternator and water pump bearings. A loose fan belt will slip and wear excessively, causing noise, engine overheating and fluctuating alternator output. Fan belt tension is correct when light finger pressure deflects the belt .2-.4", or when a pull of 17 to 24 lbs. (8-11 kg) is required to slide the pulley. An oily or frayed fan belt should be replaced. Remove belt by loosening alternator mounting bolts. Tension new belt by positioning alternator. Then tighten mounting bolts.

Air Induction Valve

The automatic air induction pre-heat valve is located in a housing to the right of the radiator. Every 8000 miles, the lever should be placed in the winter (W) position and the valve's freedom of movement checked. If necessary, oil the valve. In the "W" position air drawn in at the front of the car is mixed with air preheated around the exhaust manifold in a ratio dependent on outside and engine temperatures, until it reaches approximately 86°F. At approximately this same outside temperature, the pre-heat supply hose is completely closed and the car obtains all its induction air supply from the fresh air hose. In summer, the lever should be used to set the valve to the "S" position. The cover plate can be removed for inspection purposes.

Drum Brake Adjustment

Disc brakes require no adjustment, but cars with drum brakes have two eccentric adjustment cams for separate adjustment of the two shoes. Turn the left cam counterclockwise and the right cam clockwise to tighten until wheel cannot be turned. Then back off the cams about ⅛ turn until the wheel moves freely.

Exhaust Emission Control System

Fresh air flow is directed by a V-belt driven air pump to injector tubes located

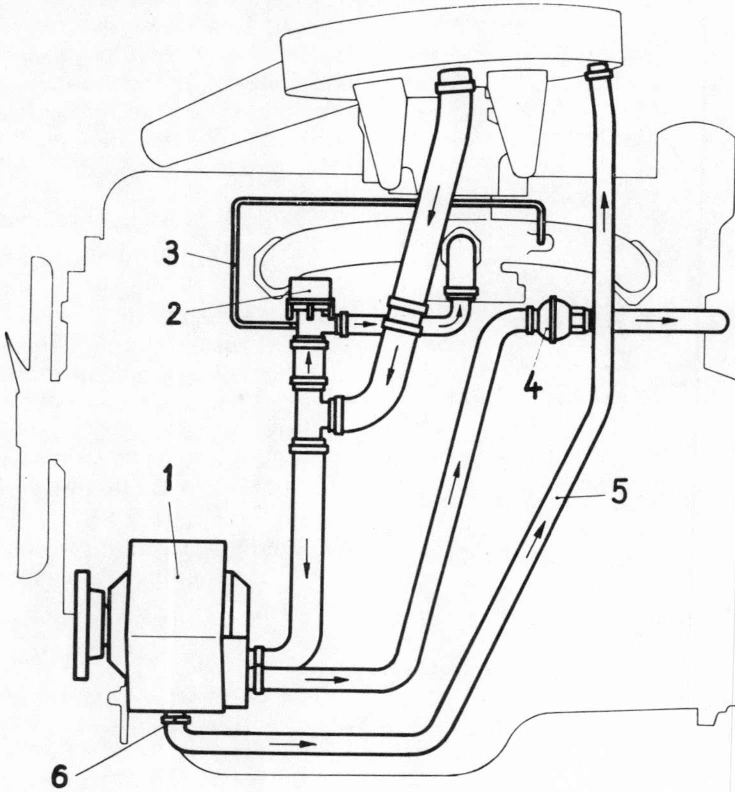

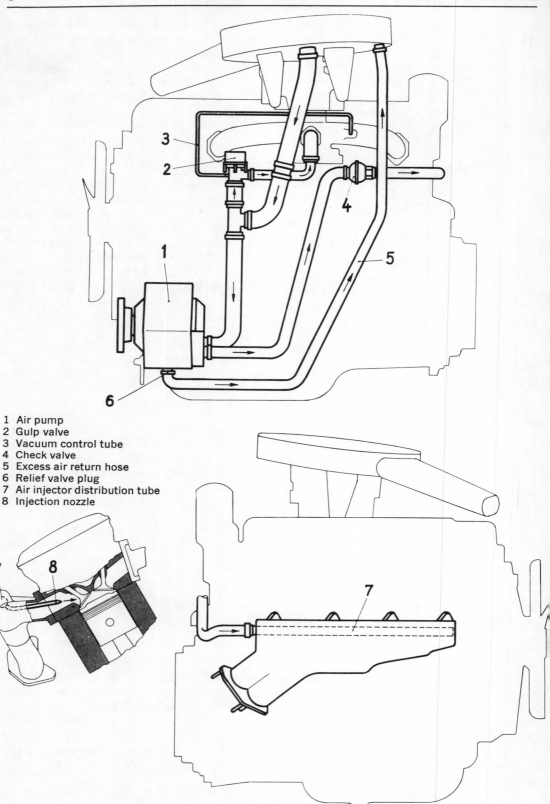

1 Air pump
2 Gulp valve
3 Vacuum control tube
4 Check valve
5 Excess air return hose
6 Relief valve plug
7 Air injector distribution tube
8 Injection nozzle

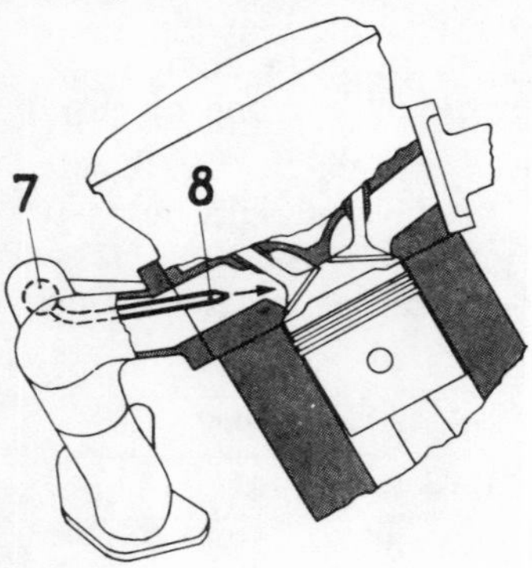

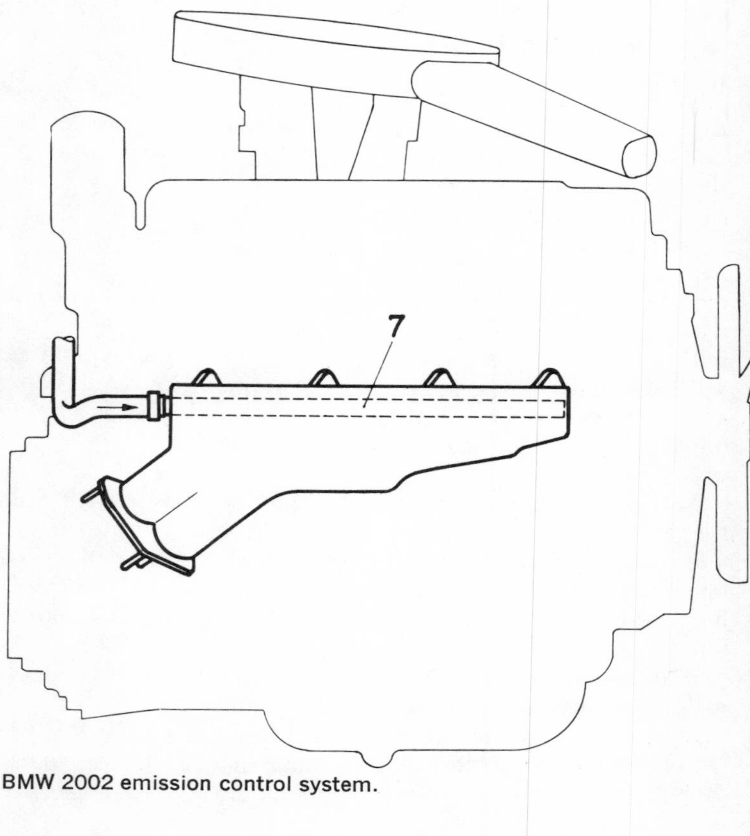

BMW 2002 emission control system.

in each exhaust port immediately behind the exhaust valve. Since exhaust gases at this point are above ignition temperatures, mixture with an excess of oxygen is all that is required to start burning action. This oxidizes the noxious hydrocarbons and changes most of the carbon monoxide to harmless carbon dioxide.

Components of the emission control system such as the air pump, check valve, and gulp valve are maintenance-free. But the air pump V-belt tension should be ⅛″ to ⅜″ slack under thumb pressure and should be adjusted if required. Do not use a pry bar for adjustment. Tighten by hand to avoid pump housing distortion. Inspect hoses, bolts, and nuts of the system for tightness.

Ignition timing of emission controlled engines is checked and if necessary reset as follows with the engine running at normal operating temperature using a timing light and a tachometer.

1. Remove vacuum advance hose from distributor. Set idle speed to exactly 2000 rpm by adjusting idle screw. Direct strobe light at timing mark (steel ball in rim of flywheel) through opening in clutch housing. Some engines have three timing marks on the crankshaft pulley. These are clockwise, OT-top dead center, Z-mark for rough initial static timing, Z-mark for timing at 2000 rpm. There is a corresponding mark on the timing chain cover.

2. If marks do not line up, loosen clamp on distributor housing and turn until marks are aligned. Re-check engine speed and reset to 2000 rpm if required. Re-tighten distributor housing clamp and re-connect vacuum hose to distributor. Timing procedures for engine without exhaust emission control are given in Chapter 5.

Adjust idling of emission controlled engines as follows:

1. Disconnect air hose leading from air pump to exhaust manifold at the pump.

2. Set engine idle speed to 1000 rpm with engine at normal operating temperature.

3. Turn idle mixture adjustment screw (with air hose removed) to obtain 6-8% CO. (If exhaust tester does not give a CO indication, adjust to 75.5% combustion efficiency). Repeat steps 2 and 3 until the specified values have been achieved.

4. Reconnect air hose to pump.

Idle adjustment procedures for engines without emission control are given in Chapter 2.

Electrical Maintenance

Fuses

Fuses are mounted in a clear plastic box located under the hood to the rear. The blown fuse can easily be seen through the container. Never replace a blown fuse with one of higher rating. Always try to find the reason the fuse blew. By-passing a blown fuse with a piece of wire entails a fire risk.

Brake Warning Light

The BMW has a dual, independent hydraulic brake system feeding the front and rear wheels. Failure of either one of the systems leaves the other still operative. A warning light on the instrument panel

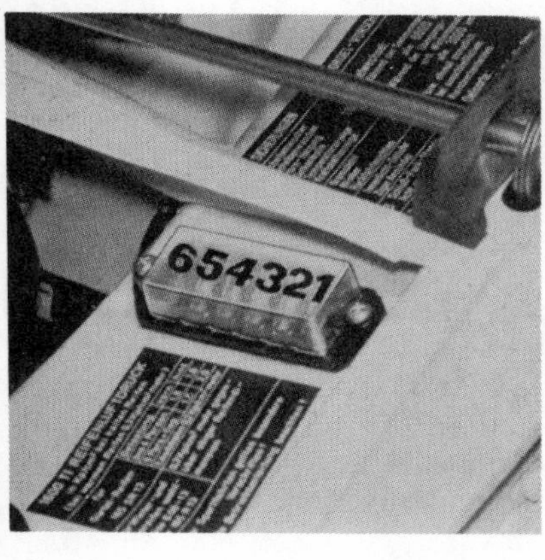

No.	Fuse (to DIN 72581)	Item
1	8 A	Front parking lights, left and right
2	8 A	License plate lights, right tail light
3	8 A	Instrument lights, left tail light
4	8 A	Interior light, clock, cigar lighter
5	8 A	Stop and turn lights, backup lights
6	16 A	Heater blower, horn, wiper motor, washer unit, fuel and temperature gauges, oil pressure and brake warning lights

Fuse numbers and sizes, and the circuits they control.

comes on to warn the operator that one of the systems has failed. To test the warning light bulb, turn on ignition switch and press the small button on the instrument panel. Replace the bulb if it does not light.

Battery Care

Batteries should be checked periodically for adequate electrolyte level, proper output and good connections. Add nothing but distilled water, and fill when necessary to about 3/16″ above the plates.

Inspect the battery case for cracks and weakness. A leaky battery should be replaced. Check the specific gravity of the battery electrolyte with a hydrometer. Readings from a fully charged battery will depend on the make but will be in the range of 1.260 to 1.310 times as heavy as pure water at 80°F. NOTE: *all cells should produce nearly equal readings.* If one or two cell readings are sharply lower, the cells are defective, and if they continue to be low after charging, the battery must be replaced.

As a battery releases its charge, sulphate ions in the electrolyte become attached to the plates — reducing the density of the fluid. The specific gravity of the electrolyte varies not only with the percentage of acid in the liquid, but also with the temperature. As temperature increases, the electrolyte expands so that specific gravity is reduced. As temperature drops, the electrolyte contracts and specific gravity increases. To correct readings for temperature variation, add .004 to the hydrometer reading for every 10°F that the electrolyte is above 80°F, and subtract .004 for every 10°F that the electrolyte is below 80°F. The drawing shows the total correction to make for any temperature above or below 80°F.

The state of charge of the battery can be determined roughly from the following specific gravity readings:

Hydrometer Readings	*Condition*
1.260-1.310	Fully charged
1.230-1.250	¾ charged
1.200-1.220	½ charged
1.170-1.190	¼ charged
1.140-1.160	Almost discharged
1.110-1.130	Fully discharged

Make a light-load voltage test to detect weak cells. First draw off the transient surface charge by operating the starter for three seconds and then turning on the low beam lights. After one minute, test each cell (with lights still on) with the voltmeter. A fully charged battery will have no cell voltage below 1.95 volts and no cell will vary more than .05 volts from the others. A greater variation at full charge indicates a defective cell.

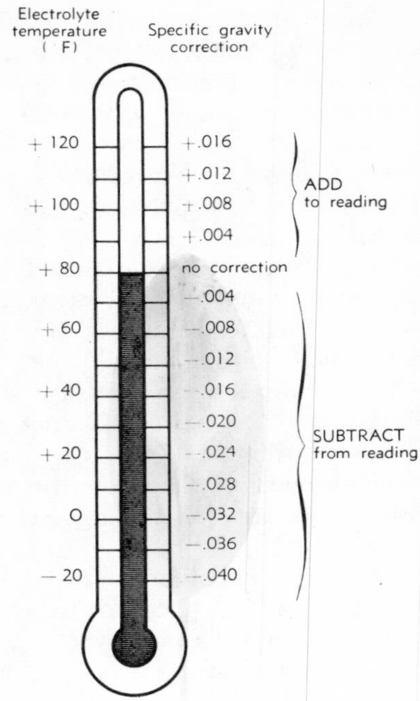

Temperature affects the specific gravity readings of batteries.

Another battery check requires connecting a charger for three minutes under 40 amperes for a 12-volt battery. Read the battery voltage with the charger still operating. Voltage over 15.5 volts indicates a defective battery. If battery voltage is under this limit and individual cell readings are within 0.1 volt, the battery is usable.

Charging a weak battery is best done by a slow-charge method. If quick charging is attempted, check the cell voltages and the color of the electrolyte a few minutes after charge is started. If cell voltages are not uniform or if electrolyte is discolored with brown sediment, quick charging should be stopped in favor of a slow charge. In either case, do not let electrolyte temperature exceed 120°F.

If high electrical circuit voltage is suspected, the voltage regulator might be cutting in abnormally due to corroded or loose battery connections. The symptoms are hard starting, full ammeter charge and lights flaring brightly. After cleaning, coat battery terminals with petroleum jelly (vaseline) to prevent recurrence of problem.

Overcharging is a common cause of battery failure. A symptom of overcharging is a frequent need for addition of water to the battery. The generating system should be corrected immediately to prevent internal battery damage.

Tire Care Suggestions

Pressures

Proper tire pressure assures maximum riding comfort with reasonable tire life. Check the pressure of tires when they are cold. Inadequate pressure will increase running resistance, raise fuel consumption and accelerate tire wear. Rotate tires for longer, more even wear.

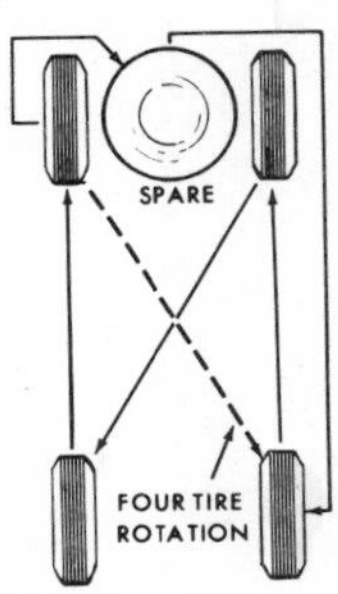

Broken line shows tire rotation pattern when not using spare.

Solid line shows tire rotation pattern using all five tires.

Balance

Wheel and tire balance is more important in extending tire life than casual drivers realize. Imbalance is the principal cause of tramp, car shake, pounding and riding roughness. It often contributes to steering misalignment and damage. Original balance of the tire and wheel is gradually lost as the tires wear. Severe acceleration, braking, cornering and slide-slipping upset wheel balance in even less time. Wheels also need balancing after punctures are repaired. Check wheel balance each time the tires are rotated — every 8,000 miles — for maximum tire and front-end life.

Tread Wear

Check tire tread wear by placing the top edge of a penny in a tread groove. If the top of Lincoln's head is completely exposed the tire should be replaced or recapped. Ninety percent of tire failure occurs in the last 10% of tread life.

Tread design affects acceleration, speed, cornering, braking, heat dissipation, wear, noise and related factors. The tread pattern should be checked periodically for uneven or premature wear.

Suggested First Inspection after 1000 Miles—2002, 1600

1. Change engine oil and filter element.
2. Change oil in gearbox.
3. Change oil in rear.
4. Check oil level of half-shaft sliding joints.
5. Check steering box oil level.
6. Check radiator water level, connections, antifreeze.
7. Check brake fluid level, connections.
8. Clean fuel pump filter, tighten screws.
9. Tighten carburetor screws and nuts.
10. Check air pre-heat valve.
11. Check fan belt tension.
12. Lubricate distributor.
13. Tighten engine bolts, torque cylinder head bolts.
14. Check valve clearances, ignition point gap and dwell angle.
15. Tighten bolts and nuts on front axle, steering, gearbox, drive shafts, rear axle and brakes.
16. Tighten body and exhaust system bolts.
17. Check steering play.
18. Check brake system.
19. Check clutch clearance.
20. Check front wheel bearing play.
21. Check tire pressures.
22. Check wheel balance.
23. Check headlight adjustment.
24. Check carburetor adjustment.

Suggested Maintenance Schedule—2002, 1600

Procedure	*Frequency — Thousands of Miles* 0.3	4.0	8.0	16.0
Check engine oil level	●			
Check tire pressures	●			
Check battery	●			
Check radiator coolant level	●			
Change engine oil and filter		●		
Lubricate drive shaft and half-shaft universal joints		●		
Clean air filter element		●		
Check brake fluid, inspect connections		●		
Check carburetor adjustment		●		
Check gearbox oil level			●	
Check rear oil level			●	
Check half-shaft sliding joint oil level			●	
Check steering box oil level			●	
Clean battery terminals			●	
Clean fuel pump bowl and filter			●	
Check air pre-heat valve			●	
Check V-belt tension			●	
Lubricate distributor			●	

Procedure	*Frequency — Thousands of Miles* 0.3	4.0	8.0	16.0
Lubricate carburetor linkage			●	
Replace spark plugs[1]			●	
Tighten engine bolts, torque cylinder head bolts			●	
Check valve clearances			●	
Replace air filter element			●	
Check steering and track rod joints			●	
Check rear and half-shafts			●	
Tighten front axle, steering, gearbox, half-shafts, rear axle, brakes, bolts and nuts			●	
Check disc brake pads			●	
Adjust drum brakes			●	
Check front wheel bearings			●	
Rotate tires and check condition			●	
Balance wheels			●	
Check clutch clearance			●	
Check distributor points			●	
Change gearbox oil				●
Change half-shaft sliding joint oil				●

1 Check spark plug gaps frequently (about every 3000 miles).

Chapter 2

Troubleshooting Checks

Locating No-Start Problems

One frequent cause of the engine not starting is carburetor flooding. To check this out, press accelerator clear to floor and hold there while attempting to start engine. If engine does not start, the trouble is elsewhere.

When the cause of engine failure is unknown, the most efficient way to get the engine running again is to follow a series of troubleshooting checks that break no-start problems into four areas — engine-cranking, ignition, fuel, and compression. Locating no-start trouble is easily done by following this simple sequence.

1. First try to crank the engine with the starter. Slow engine cranking, or none at all indicates that the trouble is in the battery, cables, switches or starter. Detailed testing to find the specific defect is provided in the next section of this chapter, *Testing No-Start Components,* ENGINE CRANKING SYSTEM CHECKS.

2. If engine cranking checked out normally, disconnect a wire from a spark plug, hold it (avoid shock by wearing glove) about ¼ to ½″ from the plug terminal, and have the engine cranked over with the ignition switch on. Check for strong, evenly-timed arcs. The ignition system must supply (often through worn parts) an amount of voltage necessary to form a bright spark at the electrode gap. If there is no spark or if the arc pulse is irregular or weak, the problem is in the ignition system. Special testing for ignition trouble is described in the next section under IGNITION CHECK.

3. With cranking and ignition successfully checked, remove the air cleaner for access to the carburetor. Work the throttle linkage up and down. A stream of fuel should spurt from the accelerator jets. If no fuel ejects into the carburetor throat after repeated throttle pumping, there is a defect in the fuel system. A less common malfunction is continuous flooding of the carburetor. If the carb throat is soaked with gasoline and fumes are profuse, have the engine cranked and check for fuel streaming from the main jet into the intake manifold. This check reveals another type of fuel system trouble. Extensive testing procedures are presented in the next section, under FUEL SYSTEM CHECKS.

4. The last no-start troubleshooting check is for an infrequent, yet sometimes elusive problem — no compression. In most cases compression failures show up in one or two cylinders and are normally not severe enough to prevent starting. However, "blow-by" into the intake manifold due to a burnt or improperly seated valve

can impede the flow of gas vapor into the cylinders and prevent starting. Complete compression failure can be caused by a burnt valve, jumped timing chain, stripped timing gear, a broken camshaft, or possibly, the improper mating of timing gears in a newly rebuilt engine. Check for compression by removing a spark plug, sealing the piston chamber with a thumb, cork or other object, and having the engine cranked over. Good compression will gently pop the thumb from the opening. No-compression troubles are analyzed in another section, *Hard Starting, Poor Performance — Tuning*.

Testing No-Start Components

Once the no-start problem has been localized to one of the areas — engine cranking, ignition, fuel, compression — special testing within that area can directly identify the malfunction while saving expense and valuable time. Each of the units below has a step-by-step troubleshooting test procedure to eliminate the suspicion of working parts and to determine the exact trouble.

Engine Cranking System Checks

The engine-cranking network includes the battery, cables, switches and starter. The battery and cables are checked first because they are the storehouse and supply of all electrical power, feeding the starter motor, ignition system, lights, and accessories.

Turn on the headlights and crank the engine with the starter. If the lights dim sharply and the cranking slows drastically, either the battery cables are making poor contact or the battery itself is nearly discharged. If the headlights stay bright but the starter turns slowly, the starter cables or switches may be faulty or the starter defective. If the starter does not turn, the solenoid may be defective.

Check the difference in voltage readings taken at the battery and at the starter, while the starter is cranking the engine, to determine the voltage drop through the cables and solenoid. A test for the solenoid is given under "checking switches."

Checking Cables

Check the connections by carefully working a screwdriver between each cable connector and its terminal post. WARNING:

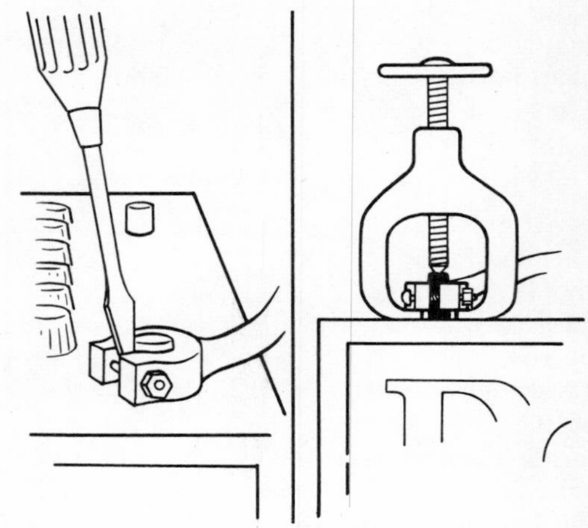

Test the cable connections with a screwdriver (left). Remove corroded connector with puller (right).

hammering, jarring or prying against the terminal may loosen and short-out the battery plates. If the engine cranking improves, the trouble is the connection. Sometimes an imperfect connection can be identified simply by "smoke" or vapor rising from corrosion in that area when the starter switch is actuated.

Cleaning cables and terminals should be done with utmost care to prevent damage to the battery. If a cable cannot be removed by hand easily after the clamp bolt is loosened, a small screw-type puller should be used. Thorough wire brushing or application of a strong baking soda solution will successfully clean terminals and connectors. CAUTION: *cleaning solutions will damage the battery cells if allowed to seep through the vented caps.*

Battery Test

If engine cranking is still unsuccessful after checking out the cable connections, the battery may be discharged. A hydrometer reading can be used to quickly tell if any cells are dead. A battery that is normal (though discharged) will have nearly equal specific gravity readings for each cell. (Readings of a fully charged battery range from 1.280 to 1.310, depending on the make.) But if one or two cells have a reading far lower than the others, there is an electrical short circuit within the battery. Tips for charging batteries properly are given in Chapter 1 under Battery Care.

Once it has been determined that the battery is discharged, the generator and regulator must be checked for proper charging rate as described in Chapter 5—Electrical Systems.

Checking Switches

After the battery and cables have been checked, the starting system switches should be tested.

(Test 1) First, bypass the starter-switch by running a jumper cable or other heavy-gauge lead directly from the hot terminal of the fully charged battery to the input terminal of the solenoid. DANGER: *rings, watches and other metal in contact with the hand can cause severe burns with accidental battery-voltage contact. A heavy-cloth glove offers good protection against burns caused by sudden overheating of the jumper cable.* If the starter motor turns when electrical contact is made, the malfunction is in the starter switch or its wiring. If there is no starter response or just a click in the solenoid, make a second test.

(Test 2) Cautiously touch the hot cable directly to the starting motor input lead. This bypasses the solenoid. In a clutch-type starter assembly, the starter should spin but will not engage the flywheel when the solenoid is omitted from the circuit. If the starter spins, the trouble is in the solenoid unless in the previous test the solenoid had clicked. The solenoid serves two simultaneous functions—switching power into the starting motor and engaging the starter-clutch assembly. If the solenoid clicked in the first test and the starting motor spun free in the second test, the solenoid is good and the trouble may be a jammed starter or frozen engine. If starter gear is jammed against flywheel, place gear shift lever in high gear and gently rock car back and forth. Getting no response with the hot lead on the starter terminal indicates that the problem is in the starting motor itself.

Starter Check

The intensity of the spark at the contact of the hot cable with the starter terminal may help determine the fault in the motor. A bright, nearly-welding intensity flash indicates that there is a short circuit within the starting motor. A weak spark or none at all points to a poor connection of the motor brushes with the commutator. The brushes could be completely worn. The brush springs could be broken. The commutator could have burnt spots or be dirty or oily.

Chapter 5 discusses procedures for overhaul and test of electrical equipment.

Ignition Check

Troubleshooting the ignition system for a no-start problem involves checking through the primary and secondary ignition circuits from the battery to the spark plugs. Locating the fault can be done quickly by following the easy tests below.

The initial test for troubleshooting the ignition system is to check for the strength of the arc between a disconnected spark plug wire and its terminal ¼ to ½″ away. A poor spark indicates ignition system trouble. (Locating No-Start Problems.)

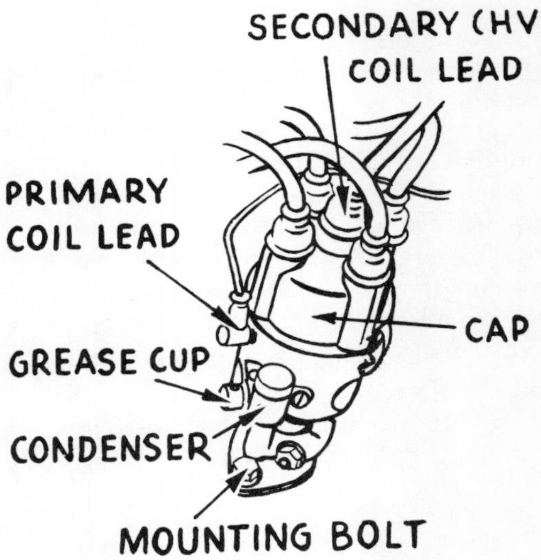

Distributor components.

Testing Ignition Switch

Ignition switch failures are the most frequent so are wisely checked first. Find the wire from the ignition switch that leads to the ignition coil, disconnect it at the coil and turn on the ignition. Touch the detached wire momentarily to a ground. Watch for a faint spark. No spark indicates a failure in the switch or in wiring or connections between the battery and the coil. If the wire did spark when touched to a ground, reconnect it to the coil before proceeding.

Checking Coil Circuit

The coil, which supplies high tension electrical current to the distributor cap and from there to the spark plugs, is energized and timed by the contact points inside the distributor. Therefore, checking the coil also requires testing the points.

First remove the distributor cap. Check it and the distributor rotor (on the shaft below the cap) for fractures and worn metal parts. Check the center carbon contact (button) in the distributor cap. The button should extend from the cap, be clean and have no cracks.

Turn the engine by hand slowly (grasping the fan belt and pulley) until the contact points are fully open. After removing the high-tension coil lead from the distributor cap (center wire), turn on the ignition switch. With a small screwdriver, firmly short-circuit the movable contact point to the fixed contact point while holding the disconnected high-tension wire approximately ¼″ from a ground. (Avoid shock by wearing glove). Repeated make and break of the circuit with the screwdriver should give an intermittent spark from the high-tension wire to ground. A weak spark, or none at all, means there are bad points, condenser or ignition coil, or faulty wiring between the distributor points and the coil.

Inspection of Contact Points

While the contact points are still positioned fully apart, make checks to determine if they should be cleaned or replaced or if the condenser is bad.

First, inspect the points for pits and discoloration. Second, with the ignition switch on, slide a screwdriver slowly down the side of the movable contact almost to the base of the distributor. As the screwdriver gets closer, electricity should arc to the base. If there is no spark or the spark is not strong and distinct, the problem is in the condenser or in the distributor wiring.

Next, have the engine cranked by the starter while closely observing the opening and closing of the contact points. An arc should occur between the points just as they begin to break contact. Again the spark must be strong and distinct, and yellow to white color. Poor arcing or bluish color shows that the points should be cleaned or replaced or the condenser is "open". No arcing indicates that the wiring within the distributor is faulty or the condenser is shorted.

If these two tests show no sparking across the contact points, inspect the primary and ground wiring in the distributor.

Primary Circuit Wiring Check

The coil primary wire that attaches (within the condenser) to the contact-point assembly terminal sometimes becomes twisted, frayed, or shorted (often intermittently) to the housing. Another problem could be a broken ground (pigtail) wire between the contact-point assembly plate and the distributor housing. Closely inspect the wiring for faults.

Condenser Check

Detach and isolate the condenser case from the distributor while leaving the condenser lead on its terminal. Hand-turn the engine to open the points fully and then short-out the movable contact point by slowly sliding the screwdriver (against the contact) down toward the distributor base. If a spark occurs across the gap between the screwdriver and ground, the condenser has a short-circuit and must be replaced. To test a condenser is difficult and perhaps not worth the time. It is best to replace a suspected condenser.

Fuel System Checks

Troubleshooting the fuel system for an unknown starting problem normally requires a check of the carburetors, fuel pump, tank and lines for fuel restriction. A less common no-start problem is chronic carburetor flooding.

Checking Carburetors

In the previous section *(Locating No-Start Problems)*, the throttle linkage was worked up and down by hand to check fuel injection into the carb throat by the accelerator jet. No-start fuel problems are most often caused by no gasoline reaching the carburetors.

In rare instances, stale gasoline will prevent starting. To test for stale fuel, prime the engine by squirting fresh gas into the carb throat. If the engine then kicks over — analyze the gas in the tank by removing a small sample to a distant safe area, and cautiously attempt to ignite it.

If there is no fuel at the carburetor, check the tank, lines and fuel pump. First, look for an improperly vented cap.

Fuel Pump Test

If lacking gas at the carburetor, disconnect the fuel pump outlet line. WARNING: *to safeguard against dangerous sparks, first remove the high tension wire from the coil.* Cranking the engine should force fuel out of the line in steady spurts. A further test is to disconnect the input line of the fuel pump, hold a thumb on the input fitting while cranking the engine, and test for suction from the pump. No suction indicates that the fuel-pump diaphragm is leaking — maybe perforated — or that the diaphragm linkage is worn. Check the crankcase for gasoline. Often a ruptured diaphragm will leak fuel into the engine. A broken or worn camshaft or cam lobe could also be the defect.

Fuel pressure is determined by the degree of compression of the diaphragm spring in the fuel pump. A weak spring causes low fuel pressure; extreme spring tension creates pressures that are too high. Excessive pump pressure causes carburetor flooding and, in almost all cases, leads to dilution of oil around the cylinder rings. Insufficient pump pressure causes lean combustion mixture and results in a rough running engine, meager power output, and misfiring at high rpm.

BMW fuel pumps maintain pressures varying from 2.13 to 3.6 PSI, depending on the model, at normal engine operating speeds.

To check fuel pump pressure, insert a T-joint in the fuel line at the pump outlet to the carburetor and connect a pressure gauge rated from 0-7 PSI to the T-joint.

The pumping capacity can be adjusted by varying the length of stroke of the pump diaphragm. The stroke is determined by the wear of the diaphragm linkage, wear of the cam lobe, and the distance the pump actuating rod is spaced from the cam lobe. The length of stroke amounts to only a few tenths of a millimeter in normal operation but this must be precise to ensure peak fuel pump performance. Stroke is

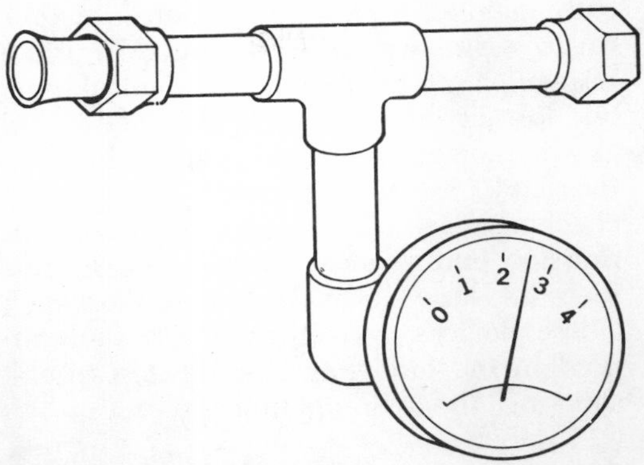

Measuring fuel pump pressure.

adjusted by adding or removing gaskets at the flange. The pressure, which should not exceed 4 PSI, can be lowered by installing one or more additional gaskets between the pump flange and the block.

Checking Tank and Lines

Good suction at the pump input, but no output, indicates a restricted fuel line to the tank, air leak in the line, or a clogged tank filter. Tighten all fuel line connections from the pump to the tank and recheck fuel pump operation. If there is still no pressure, drain tank, blow compressed air through the line from the fuel pump end, and then remove tank and flush.

Test for Vapor Lock

Fuel lines in areas exposed to excessive heat should be insulated because gasoline vaporizes when heated. The vapor bubbles prevent fuel flow to the carburetors and thus starve the engine for gas. If vapor forms and stalls the engine, let it cool before trying to restart it. Then, pour cold water on the fuel pump, and start the engine.

Hard Starting, Poor Performance—Tuning

Many who have the "If it works, don't fool with it" attitude find that when they have car trouble, it is a major and expensive problem. A wiser approach that assures maximum car enjoyment is to keep an alert eye and ear on the car's daily performance. In addition, a semi-annual tune-up (Spring, Autumn) most economically maintains good performance. A thorough tune-up should include close inspection of the major mechanical parts and lubricating system of the engine as well as the normal electrical and fuel system overhaul. Ideal instruments for quickly checking mechanical engine parts are compression and vacuum gauges and a short piece of hose (a makeshift stethoscope). These devices and other simple tools are used in the following step-by-step trouble shooting and tune-up procedures.

Spark Plugs and Wiring Check

After removing the spark plugs, carefully inspect them for cracked or broken porcelain and loose electrodes. Compare the condition of the spark plugs to that of the plugs illustrated to identify the cause of poor-performance. In general, the symptoms are indicated by the color of the plugs; tan or medium gray — proper carburetion, plug in good working order. Black — fuel mixture too rich, gap too wide, plug too cold. Light gray — fuel mixture too lean, plug loose or leaking, valves not closing fully, plug too hot. Oily plugs might indicate that oil has been sucked into combustion chamber due to worn cylinders, piston rings or improper crankcase venting. Also possible, if only one or two plugs are affected, is plug misfiring from a poor or broken electrical circuit.

Spark plugs with minor carbon and oxide deposits can be cleaned, adjusted and reinstalled. Clean the plugs in a sandblasting machine or carefully by hand with a fine wire brush taking care not to scratch the porcelain. Dry carbon dust is best blown off with compressed air; oily plugs can be washed clean with a solvent. Set the electrode gap by bending the outside electrode to the proper clearance. Never bend the center electrode. See General Tune-up Specifications chart for spark plug types and recommended gaps.

Spark plugs should not be reset more than once because the point-of-heat changes as the center electrode wears back toward the insulator. Place a new compression gasket on each plug and tighten with only enough force to crush the gasket (normally ½ turn after seated by hand). It is a good practice to tighten spark plugs with a torque wrench.

WIRING

Spark plug wiring should be removed, cleaned with a kerosene-moistened cloth, wiped dry and then carefully inspected for brittle, cracked, gummy or otherwise deteriorated insulation. Aged wiring permits electrical spark leakage . . . the cause of engine missing and crossfiring. Defective wiring should be replaced. Inspect and clean the wire terminals, spark plug terminals, and the distributor cap sockets to assure perfect electrical contact.

DISTRIBUTOR

After removing the distributor cap, inspect it for carbon paths which accumulate in areas of high voltage leakage. Discard the cap if any are present. Otherwise, clean the inside of the cap and check for cracks. Remove corrosion from the copper contacts and inspect the condition of the center (carbon) button. The button should extend from the cap, and be clean and without cracks. If any contacts are deeply scored, replace the cap. Inspect the distributor rotor for burns and, if necessary, replace it. With the rotor arm off, lubricate the distributor cam with non-corrosive high temperature grease. (NOTE: Do not allow grease or dirt to contaminate breaker points.)

Checking Points, Condenser, Connections

Carefully examine the contact (breaker) assemblies in the distributor for the following poor-performance conditions:

1. Points are blackened, pitted or worn excessively. (Points in extended service normally become dull-gray without losing efficiency.)

2. Movable contact-point arm has lost spring action.

3. Fiber rubbing block on breaker is badly worn or loose.

4. Coil primary wire (attached to the breaker assembly with the condenser) is twisted, frayed and shorted on the distributor plate.

5. Condenser lead connection is loose or damaged.

6. Ground wire (pigtail) between the breaker assembly plate and the distributor housing is frayed or loose.

Replace any distributor components that are faulty. Contact points that are slightly burned can be cleaned with a point file.

Model	Spark Plug Gap In. (mm.)						Distributor					Valves				Pressures	
	Bosch W200 T30	Beru 200/14/3A	Beru 230/14/3A	Champion N9Y	Bosch W215P21 (Platinum Tipped)	Bosch W235P21 (Platinum Tipped)	Point Gap In. (mm)	Dwell Angle°	Point Pressure oz.	Static Timing (Engine Cold)	Dynamic Timing	Clearance (In./mm Cold Engine)[2]	Int. Valve Opens @.02" (.5mm) Clearance	Int. Valve Closes @.011" (.28mm) Clearance	Cranking Com-pression (PSI)	Fuel Pump Pressure (PSI @ 1000 RPM)
1500	.024 +.004 (.6+.1)	.024 +.004 (.6+.1)		.024 +.004 (.6+.1)	.014 (.35)		.016 (.4)	60±1	15.9-19.5	3°BTDC		.0059-.0079 (.15-.20)	4°BTDC 52°ABDC	18° BTDC 66°ABDC	*	Solex PE 15059 2.99-3.56
1600	.024 +.004 (.6+.1)	.024 +.004 (.6+.1)		.024 +.004 (.6+.1)	.014 (.35)		.016 (.4)	60±1	15.9-19.5	3°BTDC	25°BTDC @1400 ±55 RPM[1]	.0059-.0079 (.15-.20)	4°BTDC 52°ABDC	18° BTDC 66°ABDC	*	Solex PE 15059 2.99-3.56
1600-2 Door	.024 +.004 (.6+.1)	.024 +.004 (.6+.1)		.024 +.004 (.6+.1)	.014 (.35)		.016 (.4)	60±1	15.9-19.5	3°BTDC	25°BTDC @1400 ±55 RPM[1]	.0059-.0079 (.15-.20)	4°BTDC 52°ABDC	18° BTDC 66°ABDC	*	Solex PE 15520 2.99-3.56
1600 TI	.024 +.004 (.6+.1)		.024 +.004 (.6+.1)		.014 (.35)		.016 (.4)	60±1	15.9-19.5	TDC	25°BTDC @2200 ±55 RPM	.0059-.0079 (.15-.20)	4°BTDC 52°ABDC	18° BTDC 66°ABDC	*	Solex PE 15520 2.99-3.56
1800, 1800A	.024 +.004 (.6+.1)		.024 +.004 (.6+.1)	.024 +.004 (.6+.1)		.014 (.35)	.016 (.4)	60±1	15.9-19.5	3°BTDC	25°BTDC @1400 ±55 RPM	.0059-.0079 (.15-.20)	4°BTDC 52°ABDC	18° BTDC 66°ABDC	*	Solex PE 15059 2.99-3.56
1800/69	.024 +.004 (.6+.1)		.024 +.004 (.6+.1)	.024 +.004 (.6+.1)		.014 (.35)	.016 (.4)	60±1	15.9-19.5	3°BTDC	25°BTDC @1400 ±55 RPM	.0059-.0079 (.15-.20)	4°BTDC 52°ABDC	18° BTDC 66°ABDC	*	Solex PE 15581 2.99-3.56
1800TI	.024 +.004 (.6+.1)		.024 +.004 (.6+.1)			.014 (.35)	.016 (.4)	60±1	15.9-19.5	3°BTDC[3]	25°BTDC @2200 ±55 RPM	.0059-.0079 (.15-.20)	4°BTDC 52°ABDC	18° BTDC 66°ABDC	*	Solex PE 15059 2.99-3.56
2002	.024 +.004 (.6+.1)		.024 +.004 (.6+.1)			.014 (.35)	.016 (.4)	60±1	15.9-19.5	3°BTDC	25°BTDC @1400 ±55 RPM	.0059-.0079 (.15-.20)	4°BTDC 52°ABDC	18° BTDC 66°ABDC	*	Solex PE 15517, 15574 2.99-3.56
2000, 2000A	.024 +.004 (.6+.1)		.024 +.004 (.6+.1)			.014 (.35)	.016 (.4)	60±1	15.9-19.5	3°BTDC	25°BTDC @1400 ±55 RPM	.0059-.0079 (.15-.20)	4°BTDC 52°ABDC	18° BTDC 66°ABDC	*	Solex PE 15517, 15574 2.99-3.56
2000 TI	.024 +.004 (.6+.1)		.024 +.004 (.6+.1)			.014 (.35)	.016 (.4)	60±1	15.9-19.5	TDC	25°BTDC @2200 ±55 RPM	.0059-.0079 (.15-.20)	4°BTDC 52°ABDC	18° BTDC 66°ABDC	*	Solex PE 15517, 15574 2.99-3.56
2000 CS	.024 +.004 (.6+.1)		.024 +.004 (.6+.1)			.014 (.35)	.016 (.4)	60±1	15.9-19.5	TDC	25°BTDC @2200 ±55 RPM	.0059-.0079 (.15-.20)	4°BTDC 52°ABDC	18° BTDC 66°ABDC	*	Solex PE 15517, 15574 2.99-3.56
2000 CA	.024 +.004 (.6+.1)		.024 +.004 (.6+.1)			.014 (.35)	.016 (.4)	60±1	15.9-19.5	3°BTDC	25°BTDC @1400 ±55 RPM	.0059-.0079 (.15-.20)	4°BTDC 52°ABDC	18° BTDC 66°ABDC	*	Solex PE 15517, 15574 2.99-3.56

[1]Models with emission control set at 2000 ±55 RPM. In all models firing order is 1-3-4-2.
[2]A cold engine is at 95°F or less.
[3]1800 TISA model is set at TDC.
*Good: above 149.3; normal: 135.1 to 149.3; poor: below 128.

Carbon fouled

Oil fouled

Electrodes worn

Heavily coated

Overheated

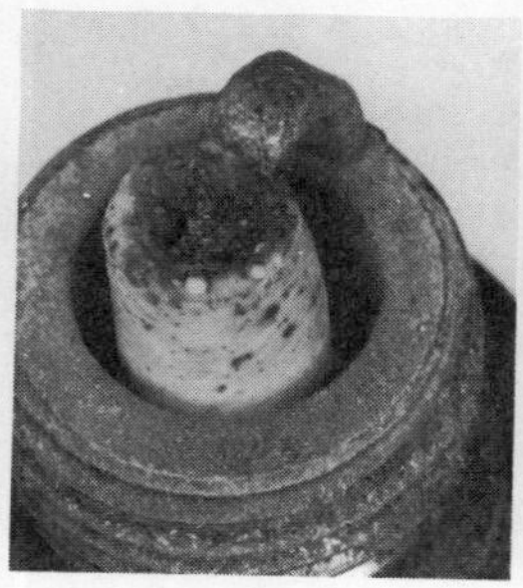

Melted

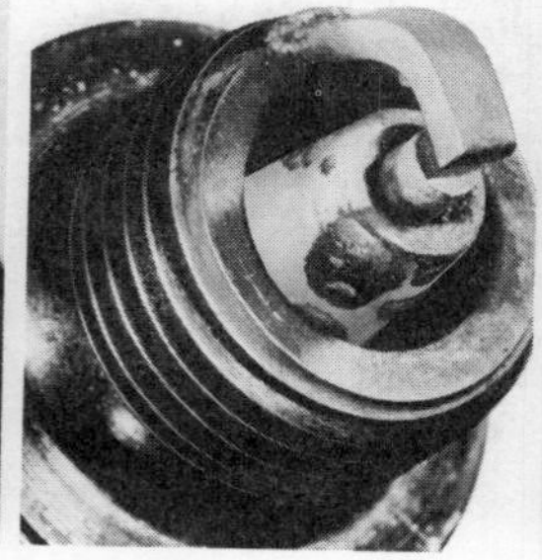

Splash fouled

Bent electrode

Carbon Fouled Plugs
If only one plug is carbon fouled and others are normal, check ignition wiring for a break or loose connections. A compression check might indicate mechanical trouble in that cylinder.
If all plugs are sooted, fuel mixture might be too rich, spark gap could be too large, or the plug heat value is too high.

Oil Fouled Plugs
Plugs may have been "drowned" with fuel during cranking. If choke operates properly, fouling could be caused by poor oil control. A hotter plug is needed.

Excessive Electrode Gap
If all plugs have brown-gray deposits and electrode wear from .008″ to .010″ greater than original gap, they are completely worn. Replace entire set.

Heavily Coated Plugs
Heavy deposits, if easily flaked off, result from scavenger additives used in some brands of fuel. Though this accumulation creates heat buildup, its chemical nature causes only minimum electrical shorting. Replacement plugs should have same heat range.

Chipped Insulator
If one or two plugs in a set have chipped insulator tips, severe detonation was the likely cause. Bending the center electrode during gapping can also crack the insulator. Replace with new plugs of the correct gap and heat range. Check for over-advanced timing.

Normal, Usable Plugs
Plugs with evenly-colored light tan or gray deposits and moderate electrode wear (.005 gap growth) can be cleaned, regapped, and reinstalled.

All Plugs Overheated
If set has dead white insulators and badly eroded electrodes (.001″ erosion per 1,000 miles), check ignition timing for over-advance. Install next colder heat range.

One Plug Badly Burned
If one plug in a set has melted electrodes, preignition was likely encountered in that cylinder; check for intake manifold air leaks and possible cross fire. Be sure the one plug is not the wrong heat range.

Mechanical Damage
A broken insulator and bent electrodes result from some foreign object falling into the combustion chamber. If valves overlap, objects can travel from one cylinder to another. Always clean out cylinders to prevent recurrence.

One or Two Plugs "Splashed" Fouled
Some plugs in a relatively new set may have splashed deposits. This may occur after a long-delayed tune-up when accumulated cylinder deposits are thrown against the plugs at high engine rpm. Clean and reinstall these plugs.

Bent Side Electrodes
Improperly gapping plugs will weaken side electrode and alter electrical performance of spark plug.

Common plug defects and causes.

Adjusting Point Gap

The breaker point gap must be correctly set before adjusting ignition timing. Turn the crankshaft until a cam lobe on the distributor shaft has fully raised the breaker arm. Loosen the breaker plate hold-down screw and, using a feeler gauge, adjust the breaker gap. Insert a screwdriver blade between the two small studs so that it engages with the slot in the breaker plate, then turn the blade to obtain the correct gap. Tighten the hold-down screw.

Coil and Polarity

Briefly inspect the coil housing for weak spots and cracks (especially around the tower) caused by high-voltage leaks or deterioration.

An ignition coil having reversed polarity could reduce spark plug efficiency as much as 25%, resulting in a drastic loss of power. A check to determine if the ignition polarity matches the battery circuit polarity can easily be made in any of three ways.

A. For negative ground systems, firmly attach a "high-reading" (few-thousand-volt) voltmeter positive lead to engine ground. Then momentarily touch the negative lead of the voltmeter to the secondary-circuit coil wire that leads to the distributor cap. A positive (up-scale) voltage reading indicates correct polarity. A negative (down-scale) reading shows a reversed polarity that will cause hard starting and premature wear of ignition components.

B. An optional test is to hold a soft-lead wood pencil in the gap between a disconnected spark plug wire and plug or ground. With the engine cranking, observe the direction of spark jump. "Flaring" of spark between the pencil and plug means that polarity is correct. Flaring on the wire side of the pencil means polarity is incorrect.

C. "Dishing" of the plug side-electrode indicates wrong polarity. If polarity is wrong, reverse the two primary leads at the ignition coil.

Setting Ignition Timing

If you have not set the breaker point gap, do so before proceeding. See paragraph, *Adjusting Point Gap*.

Next, turn the crankshaft until the Top

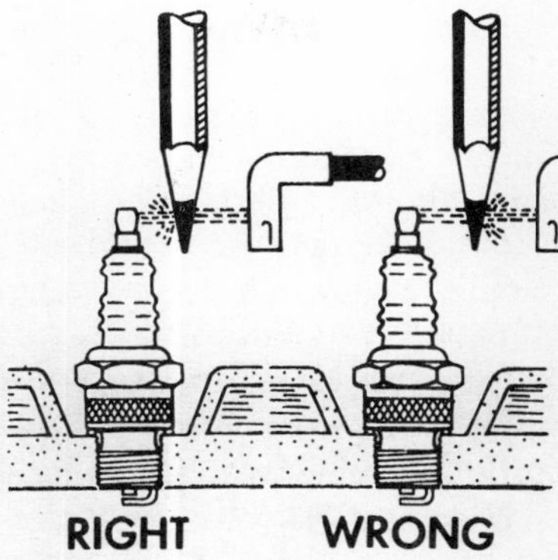

Coil polarity check.

Dead Center timing marks are properly aligned and the No. 1 cylinder is at Top Dead Center in firing position as described in Chapter 5. The distributor rotor should directly face the No. 1 cylinder spark plug-wire contact in the distributor cap, and the distributor should be positioned so that the points are just opening. There is a notch in the rim of the distributor at the No. 1 position.

Checking Vacuum

The vacuum gauge shows the difference in pressure between the inside and outside of the intake manifold. Since the atmospheric pressure varies with altitude and changes daily with the weather, the action of the vacuum gauge needle is more indicative than any specific pressure valve. In general, the vacuum reading is less for higher elevation and also shows a drop from an extreme high-pressure weather system to a stormy, low pressure system. Pressure measurement is in inches. A well-tuned engine will give a vacuum reading of 18-20″ at sea level.

Reading Vacuum

Attach the gauge to the intake manifold or on the engine side of the carburetor throttle butterfly. Warm the engine. Set the idle speed between 800 and 1000 rpm, remove the air filter (in case it is partially clogged) and check to see that the carburetor choke is open.

Make the first reading with the engine idling around 900 rpm. The needle should be steady and in the 18-20″ range. If the pointer remains steady but at a substantially lower pressure, the poor-performance problem affects power in all of the cylinders. It could be improper ignition or valve timing or an intake manifold leak. Improper valve timing normally gives the indicator a lower reading (7″-drop) than poor ignition timing (4″-drop). The size of a manifold leak determines where the indicator will stabilize. A severe warp or crack may reduce vacuum as much as 15″. If the vacuum indicator wavers or fluctuates at idle rpm, the poor-performance problem probably affects only one or two cylinders. Use the illustrated guide to interpret vacuum gauge readings.

Checking Compression

A second important instrument is the compression gauge, used to measure pressure differences between cylinders. Pressure variations of more than 20% between cylinders can cause loss of power and poor idling.

Warm the engine to operating temperature, remove all spark plugs, prop open the throttle linkage so air intake is not restricted and attach the compression gauge to the spark plug opening.

Crank engine with throttle open and note gauge pointer reading after fifth revo-

Vacuum tests to measure performance.

	Vacuum Reading	*Possible Reasons*	*Next Test*
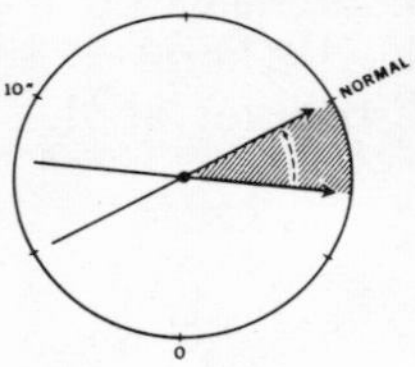	Steady gauge reading 18–20″ at all speeds. Throttle is released and engine speed quickly cuts from over 2000 rpm to idle. Needle jumps 2–5″ above normal and then quickly drops to normal without pause or hesitation.	Normal engine performance.	Vacuum okay. Go to compression tests.
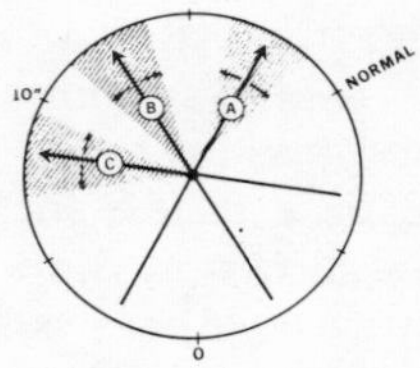	Steady low reading. Figure A. (less than 2″ drop)	Retarded ignition timing.	Loosen clamp, rotate distributor to reset timing. Check gauge improvement.
	Steady, very low reading. Figure B.	Late valve timing.	Check valve timing. Make compression tests.
	Steady, extremely low reading. (up to 15″ drop) Figure C.	Severely warped or cracked intake manifold. Bad carburetor-to-manifold gasket.	Inspect manifold. Squirt oil around seal to detect leak.
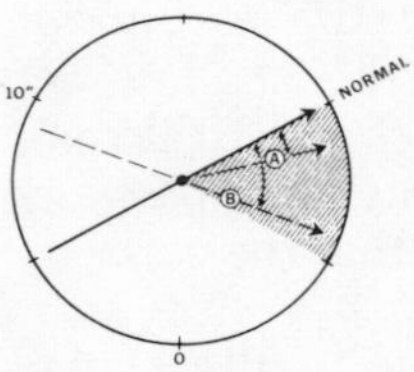	Pointer does not jump much above normal when throttle is quickly closed and engine speed is cut from above 2000 rpm to idle. Figure A.	Piston rings may be worn or defective and are blowing into crankcase.	Take compression test of cylinders to pinpoint trouble.
	Pointer jumps 2–5″ above normal upon quick deceleration but hesitates at higher pressure before returning to normal. Figure B.	Restricted exhaust system is causing backpressure on engine.	Check exhaust for dents, restrictions, clogged muffler.

	Vacuum Reading	*Possible Reasons*	*Next Test*
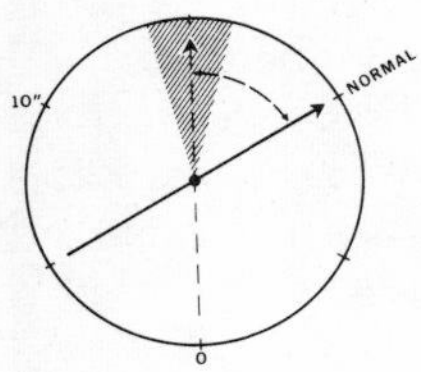	Pointer (rhythmically drops 1–7" below normal vacuum at regular intervals.	Leaking combustion chamber or valve; (ignition or plug failure involving one cylinder).	Make compression tests; (make ignition check).
	Pointer drops rapidly but intermittently (not every time) and then recovers.	Valve sticking at times won't close tight.	Note which valve sticks. Apply penetrating oil to one valve guide at a time. Problem will correct itself temporarily.
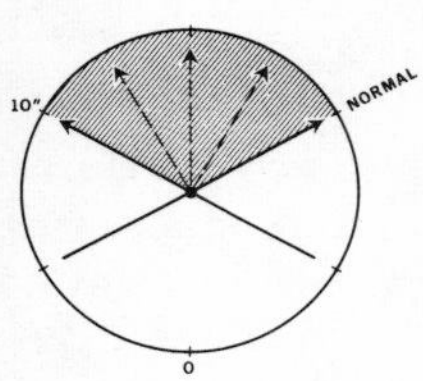	Pointer wavers rapidly between 10–20" at idle becoming worse with higher rpm.	Weak or broken spring causing valve to close slowly.	Remove valve covers; check condition of springs.
	Wavers irregularly at idle; fluctuates rapidly in smaller range at higher rpm.	Manifold leak at intake port—upsets and reduces cylinder draft.	Squirt oil around manifold; check vacuum increase when oil fills leak. Replace faulty gasket.
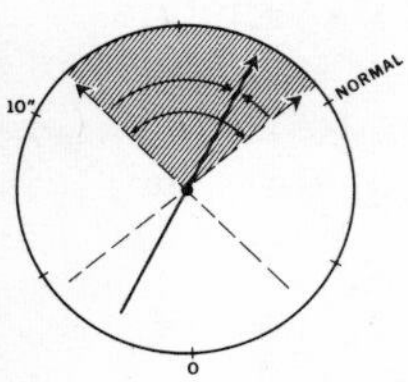	Drifts at idle; stabilizes at higher engine rpm.	Burnt valve; combustion chamber leak.	Make compression tests.
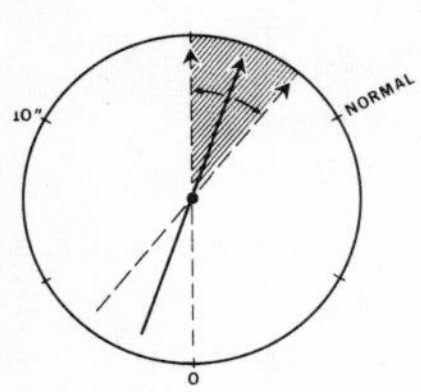	Wavers irregularly in one range despite engine speed.	Unbalanced carburetion; improper spark plug gap, ignition timing; poor valve seating.	Adjust carburetors; check plug gap; check distributor and advance spark; make compression tests.
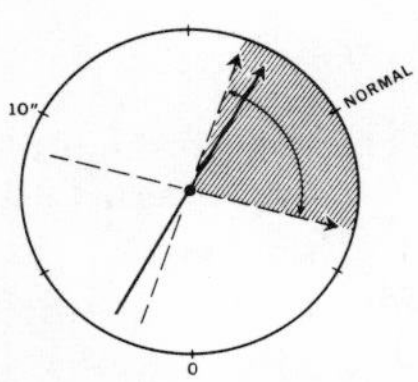	Vacuum averages lower than normal at idle, needle fluctuates almost 3" on both sides of normal.	Worn valve guides admitting air—upsetting carburetion.	Squirt oil on guide seals. Check vacuum improvement.

lution. Repeat procedure on each cylinder. All cylinders should be within ten pounds of each other and maintain the pressure given in the General Tuneup Specifications Table. One or two low readings in the cylinders indicate trouble with valves, rings, pistons, or combustion-chamber leaks. Low compression readings in all cylinders indicate incorrect valve timing.

To determine the fault, squirt about an ounce of light oil into the low-compression cylinder, replace the compression gauge, and crank the engine another five revolutions for the second reading. If compression increases substantially, the rings are worn or stuck and need replacing.

No increase in compression after adding oil to the cylinder narrows the trouble to improper valve seating, a cracked or broken piston, or a combustion-chamber leak between the head and the cylinder.

First, check out the possibility of a combustion chamber leak. Turn the engine while checking for hissing noises and perhaps a discharge of oil from the flange between the cylinder and the head. This indicates a poor seal between the cylinder head and the cylinder. A leaky head gasket can often be detected by loss of compression in two adjacent cylinders.

Detecting piston damage involves replacing all the spark plugs, starting the engine, and listening for a distinctive clicking noise at idle and upon acceleration. Combustion gasses (blow-by) will also escape into the crankcase through the piston crack. See TROUBLESHOOTING ENGINE NOISES, in this chapter.

Abnormal Oil Consumption

Another way to identify poor-performance troubles is by a check of oil consumption. Continual addition of oil, fouled spark plugs and blue-gray exhaust smoke are obvious signs.

Worn or broken piston rings permit oil to enter the combustion-chamber and reduce burning efficiency. In addition, poor rings permit combustion gasses to enter the crankcase. This hot "blow-by" changes the crankcase oil into vapor that escapes through the ventilating system. Blow-by, if excessive, could also pressurize the crankcase, forcing oil leakage through weak pan seals. Worn valve guides fail to keep oil out of the combustion-chamber, resulting in poor performance and excessive oil consumption.

Before assuming that engine wear is the cause of excessive oil usage, make a thorough inspection for external leaks. After placing clean paper underneath the engine, run it at a medium speed until the oil is hot. Stop the engine and check for oil drippings on the paper. Trace the leak to its cause and correct it. In many cases the leak is the sole cause of abnormal oil consumption. It has been estimated that a single drop of oil lost every 50 feet will amount to a full quart every 500 miles, an amount worth saving.

Greater oil consumption is normal if the oil used is too light or if the engine is run often at high speed. A break-in period for new rings also requires additional oil.

High Ring Friction

In a newly rebuilt engine, poor performance is sometimes due to too much ring friction. Firm expander springs often press the rings too tightly against the cylinder walls. Engine power and gas economy drop conspicuously.

Test for excessive ring friction by holding the throttle open to an engine speed of 1000 rpm. Then turn off the ignition. An engine with proper tension will slow to a stop and then roll back and forth momentarily. An engine with tight rings will stop suddenly without rolling.

Valve Clearance

Improper valve clearance adjustment results in loss of power and possible valve damage. Excessive clearance can be detected by noisy valves. Insufficient clearance causes valve burning and possible backfiring through the carburetor.

Basic valve-clearance adjustment for each cylinder is at the point where both valves are closed, TDC of the piston's compression stroke. Follow the firing order of the engine which is 1-3-4-2. Final adjustment of all valves is when the engine is at rest and cold.

Troubleshooting Engine Noises

If engine noises can be located and analyzed before the engine is disassembled, correcting the problem is much easier. Of course fine tuning is not possible until engine mechanical troubles are repaired. For locating noises, a piece of water hose of convenient length is a handy substitute for a stethoscope.

Valve Noises

Valve noise is a loud rhythmic clicking that varies directly with rpm, but occurs at half the beat of other engine noises because the cam shaft rotates at half engine speed. Remove the valve cover to help locate noises better. Set engine rpm to the speed where the noise is most pronounced. If needed, hold end of piece of hose close to cams and listen to one valve at a time until the noisemaker is identified.

Sticky valves and cams with excessive clearance have similar sounds although sticking-valve noises are normally intermittent. Check for excessive clearance by inserting a feeler gauge between the noisy valve stem and its rocker. If the noise stops, reset the clearance. Remember, valves will burn if clearance is reduced below factory specifications. Valve sticking becomes pronounced when the engine idles after having been run hard. As the idling engine cools to its normal operating temperature the sticking-valve noise lessens. When a valve sticks, the lost compression from improper closing makes the engine idle roughly.

Warped and burnt valves also cause the engine to run irregularly, especially under low-speed load. They sometimes click but more often make hissing, wheezing sounds through the exhaust manifold (exhaust valve) or back fire (intake valve) through the carburetor.

Broken springs and bent valve stems don't close valves properly and are noisy as well. Loose rocker arms transmit heavy rattling sounds.

Piston Noises

Generally, piston noises result from a piston slapping from side to side in its bore due to excessive clearance. However, if the piston noise is faint in a cold engine and disappears shortly after the engine reaches operating temperature, the condition might not be worth special attention.

Individual piston noises can be detected by shorting out one spark plug at a time while the engine is under partial load until the noise ceases. The piston makes no noise when its spark plug doesn't fire. A collapsed or badly worn piston makes a low-pitched, dull metallic noise when the engine is under a load. Broken rings or a cylinder ridge not removed when installing new rings will produce a steady, clicking, metallic noise at all engine speeds. Loose wrist pins give a sharp metallic knock that is more noticeable when the engine is idling. Speeding up the engine to about 1500 rpm and then releasing the throttle is another way to detect the wrist pin knock.

Crankshaft Noises

Crankshaft noises can be grouped into main bearing noise, connecting rod noise, and crankshaft end-play noise.

A loose main bearing gives a heavy bumping noise when the engine is under load. A loose connecting rod bearing has a steady rap after letting up slightly on the accelerator when car is driven about 50 mph. Shorting one spark plug at a time relieves pressure on each connecting rod bearing in turn and thereby deadens the noise of the defective bearing.

Excessive crankshaft end-play can be heard as a thud each time the clutch pedal is depressed. A rapping noise, when speeding and slowing the engine, indicates a loose flywheel.

Detonation

Detonation, an explosion rather than a smooth burning of the fuel in a cylinder, is caused by an imbalance of compression, heat, fuel, valves and timing. Detonation can be devastating to engine parts. Each of the following problems must be eliminated to prevent detonation.

A. Excessive cooling system temperature.
B. Insufficient spark plug heat range.
C. Over-advanced ignition timing.
D. Too-low fuel octane rating.
E. Lean carburetor/fuel mixture.
F. Stuck manifold heat control valve.

With the ignition system checked, the vacuum and compression readings interpreted, and engine noises investigated, the mechanic should have a good indication of any mechanical defects in the engine. These malfunctions should be corrected before attempting to tune the engine.

Fuel System

A final pre-tune-up step involves cleaning the carburetors, fuel filters and, if necessary, lines and tank.

Many fuel system problems result from

Piston damaged by inaudible detonation and preignition at high speeds.

accumulation of water, dirt, and gummy residues in the tank, lines and pump. Other problems are caused by restricted tank ventilation, leaking lines and connections, and worn out moving parts. These troubles, when identified before disassembly, can be eliminated efficiently.

Ideally, the carburetor should be taken apart, cleaned thoroughly, and reassembled with new gaskets and other non-metal parts. If complete disassembly is not feasible, it is recommended that the carburetor jets be removed from time to time and blown through with compressed air. Wash carburetor housing with solvent (engine cold) to remove dirt. Remove only one jet at a time for cleaning to prevent a mistake on replacement. NOTE: *the jets should not be cleaned with a sharp or abrasive object that might cause deformation of the close factory calibration.*

Checking Fuel-Air Mixture

Poor engine performance can be caused by fuel-air mixtures that are either too rich or too lean. Both are harmful to the engine. A lean mixture at high speeds over-heats the combustion chambers to the point where the valves might burn. A rich mixture washes lubricating oil from the cylinders, resulting in scuffed rings and scored cylinder walls.

Rub paper or cloth around the inside of the exhaust pipe, checking for carbon deposits. A rich mixture leaves a black residue. Choke off the carburetor while the warmed engine is running at 1500 rpm. (The palm of the hand can be used to restrict incoming air.) By reducing the air flow, the air-fuel mixture is normally enriched and the engine speeds up somewhat. If it doesn't speed up at all, the mixture adjustment is too rich; if it speeds up drastically, the mixture adjustment is *too lean.*

When the carburetor has a lean mixture, the engine pauses and then accelerates poorly with apparent sponginess (there might be backfiring). If a weak fuel pump or restricted gas line is the cause of the lean mixture, the engine runs out of fuel at higher engine speeds.

Rich mixture can be caused by high fuel pressure forcing the needle valve from its seat. The carburetor floods and performance breaks down.

A malfunctioning carburetor cannot be tuned, so should be overhauled.

Adjusting the Carburetor

Richness of idle speed mixture is determined by the setting of a volume control screw, allowing a very precise adjustment of fuel-air mixture; air intake is through a calibrated orifice located in the body of the carburetor in a recessed space beneath the venturi.

The engine must be warm, and the spark plugs and points in good condition. Gently screw the volume control screw in as far as it will go; then back it out about 2½ turns for a preliminary setting. With the engine idling:

1. Slightly tighten throttle stop screw to adjust idle speed to 700-800 rpm.
2. Loosen volume control screw until engine begins to idle roughly. Then tighten screw slowly until engine idles smoothly. The correct setting gives the fastest possible smooth idle.
3. Slowly loosen throttle stop screw to adjust engine idle to approximately 800 rpm. NOTE: *never completely tighten the volume control screw.* See Chapter 1 for carburetor adjustment on models with exhaust emission control.

Cleaning Fuel Filters

Loosen cover retaining screw and remove screen from the fuel pump. Wash screen and cover in solvent and blow dry with air. Replace gasket if necessary and reinstall screen, cover and bolt. Then start engine and check for leaks.

Cleaning Air Filters

To clean the dry paper filter, remove and tap lightly to loosen dirt, or blow out with compressed air. Restricted filters will adversely affect engine performance. If too dirty, replace element.

Oil-wetted metal-mesh air filters can be washed in solvent. Blow out with compressed air or let dry in open. Re-oil lightly prior to installation.

Cleaning Carburetor Parts

All carburetors have numerous small passages that can be fouled by carbon and gummy deposits. Metal parts should be soaked in carburetor solvent until thoroughly clean. However, the solvent will weaken or destroy cork, plastic and leather components. These parts should be wiped with a clean, lint-free cloth. While the carburetor is disassembled, check the bowl cover with a straight edge for warped surfaces.

The needle valves and seats should be closely inspected for wear and damage. Replace these parts when imperfect because their performance affects engine tuning most critically.

After cleaning the parts, blow air through the high and low speed jets to ensure that all passages are clear. Reassemble the carburetor, using new gaskets and other non-metal parts.

Lubricating Carburetor Linkage

Lubricate all pivot points with 1-2 drops of engine oil while moving throttle controls. Lubricate accelerator pump rods. Disconnect all ball joints, fill cups with grease, and reconnect. Move linkage back and forth to check for proper functioning.

Clutch Troubleshooting

Clutch slippage, chatter, and grabbing are most noticeable when accelerating from a standstill in first or reverse gears. Dragging of the clutch is obvious when shifting between gears, especially into and out of reverse.

DRAGGING — fails to release completely

a. Excessive linkage free play

b. Sticking or faulty pilot bearing

c. Damaged clutch plates (pressure and/or driven)

d. Release yoke off pivot ball-stud

e. Driven-plate hub binding on main drive gear spline.

SLIPPING — does not firmly engage

a. Insufficient linkage free play

b. Oil-soaked driven disc (correct oil leak before installing new assembly)

c. Worn or damaged driven disc

d. Warped pressure plate or flywheel

e. Weak diaphragm spring (replace cover assembly)

f. Driven plate not seated (make 20-50 normal starts)

g. Driven plate overheated (check lash after cooled)

GRABBING-CHATTER — intermittent seizing and slipping

a. Oil, spotted, burned or glazed facings

b. Worn splines on main drive gear or clutch disc

c. Loose engine or drive train mountings

d. Warped pressure plate, clutch disc or flywheel

e. Burned or smeared resin on flywheel or pressure plate (sand smooth if superficial, replace if burned or heat-checked)

RATTLING — transmission click

a. Release yoke loose on pivot ball-stud or in bearing groove (replace if necessary)

b. Oil in driven-disc damper (replace driven-disc)

THROW-OUT BEARING NOISE — clutch fully engaged

a. Improper linkage adjustment

b. Throw-out bearing binding on transmission bearing retainer (clean, lubricate, check for burrs, nicks)

c. Insufficient tension between release yoke and pivot ball-stud (yoke improperly installed and/or linkage spring weak)

TIGHT PEDAL — when depressed or returns sluggishly

a. Bind in linkage (lubricate and free up)

b. Weak pressure plate spring

c. Weak linkage spring

d. Driven disc worn

Manual Transmission Troubleshooting

NOISE — in forward speeds

a. Low lubricant level or incorrect lubricant

b. Transmission misaligned or loose

c. Mainshaft bearing or front main bearing worn or damaged

d. Countergear or bearings worn or damaged

e. Main drive gear or synchronizers worn or damaged

NOISE — in reverse

a. Reverse sliding gear or shaft, worn or damaged

HARD SHIFTING

a. Clutch improperly adjusted

b. Shift shafts or forks worn

c. Incorrect lubricant

d. Synchronizers worn or broken

JUMPING OUT OF GEAR

a. Partial engagement of gear

b. Transmission misaligned or loose

c. Worn pilot bearing

d. End play in main drive gear (bearing retainer loose or broken, loose or worn bearings on main drive gear and mainshaft)

e. Worn clutch teeth on main drive gear and/or on synchronizer sleeve

f. Worn or broken blocking rings

g. Bent mainshaft

STICKING IN GEAR

a. Clutch not released fully

b. Low lubricant level or incorrect lubrication

c. Defective (tight) main drive gear pilot bearing

d. Frozen blocking ring on main drive gear cone

e. Burred or battered teeth on synchronizer sleeve and/or main drive gear

Automatic Transmission Troubleshooting

SPEED AT SHIFT TOO HIGH:

a. Accelerator linkage incorrectly adjusted

b. Leakage in governor piston rings

c. Leakage past governor piston rings

d. Governor bushing jammed

SPEED AT SHIFT TOO LOW:

a. Accelerator linkage incorrectly adjusted

b. Governor bushing jammed

c. Throttle pressure too low

ACCELERATOR KICKDOWN NOT FUNCTIONING:

a. Accelerator linkage incorrectly adjusted

b. Throttle pressure valve sticking

SHIFT LEVER CANNOT BE MOVED TO P POSITION:

a. Shift linkage incorrectly adjusted

b. Parking lock mechanism defective

SHIFT LEVER CANNOT BE MOVED TO R POSITION:

a. Shift linkage incorrectly adjusted

VEHICLE WILL NOT MOVE FORWARD OR BACKWARD:

a. Shift linkage incorrectly adjusted

b. Oil level too low

c. Oil pressure too low

d. No drive to oil pump

e. Reducing passage in input shaft blocked

SLIPPING AT GEAR CHANGE POINTS:

a. Accelerator linkage disconnected

b. Oil pressure too low

WHINING VARYING WITH SPEED AND LOAD CHANGE:

a. Center bearing of drive shaft defective

HIGH-PITCHED WHISTLING NOISE IN NEUTRAL, DISAPPEARS ON ACCELERATION:

a. Torque converter plate whistling—hydraulic flow noise

Drive Shaft Troubleshooting

Defects in the drive shaft or drive shaft components are usually evidenced by vibration, thumping or clicking sounds. Vibration shows up as a growling noise which becomes louder as the speed increases and may be due to wear, a bent drive shaft, insufficient lubrication or improper assembly. No attempt should be made to repair a bent or damaged drive shaft. A new one should be installed. Worn universal joints usually cause a loud clicking sound if the car is driven slowly and accelerated and decelerated.

Front End Troubleshooting

When servicing steering and front suspension assemblies, it is advisable to check every front end part because all of the assemblies are so closely interrelated.

First, check the front end for worn or loose-fitting parts. Repair or replace what is faulty. Second, inspect and adjust the steering gear assembly. Third, set the front end alignment. And last, balance the wheels.

To detect front-end troubles quickly, follow these simple procedures:

1. With the front end jacked up, shake both wheels simultaneously to detect any looseness between them. Tie-rod and steering linkage joints sometimes loosen under severe road stresses. Check weaknesses further by shaking and prying against members connected to these joints.

2. Check out wheel suspension joints by having each wheel shaken up and down while the steering knuckle and control arm joints are observed for play.

3. Spin the wheels rapidly to test for deteriorated bearings. Listen for bearing noise and touch bumper to feel vibration that rough bearings create.

4. Rig a piece of chalk so it just clears the wheel rim and rotate the wheel to test for wheel runout. The chalk will mark misaligned, protruding rim areas. Repeat test on inside rim. Wheel should be straightened or replaced if runout exceeds 1/8″.

5. Lower front end to ground and bounce car to check for deteriorated shock absorbers.

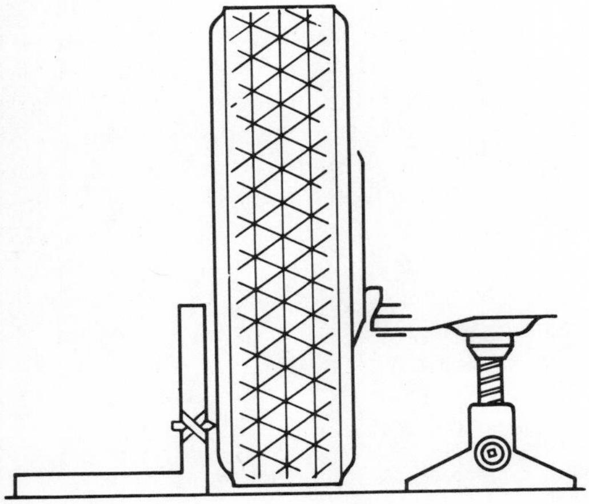

Testing for front wheel runout.

6. Check pre-owned cars for possible front end damage by measuring and comparing the wheelbase on both sides. Measure carefully from common points such as from the rear of the front-wheel rim to the rear of the back-wheel rim. If one side has a shorter or longer wheelbase than is listed in specifications, compare several measurements on both sides between various points until the dislocated part is found.

Diagonal measurements from right front to left rear wheels and from left front to right rear wheels will uncover a distorted chassis (if wheelbase measurements are equal). A twisted chassis will alter tracking and make front end alignment difficult if not impossible.

Vehicle Wandering

Vehicle wandering requires constant steering wheel correction, is annoying and also dangerous. It may be caused by incorrect caster or toe-in, too low tire pressure, excessive or insufficient play in the steering mechanism, worn or stiff steering rod ball joints, stiff control arm system, excessive play in rear end suspension.

Pulling To One Side

Check for uneven tire pressure, weak or uneven front springs, over-tightened wheel bearing, faulty wheel alignment, dragging brake, bent steering rod, or incorrect camber.

Hard Steering

Caused by too-low tire pressure, insufficiently lubricated steering gear or front end, excessive caster, damaged bearing in gear housing or steering column, damaged thrust bearing in steering knuckles, damaged front axle member or body.

Shimmy

Caused by wheels bent, misaligned or unbalanced, worn or warped brake drum, too-low tire pressure, damaged steering rod, loose or worn front wheel bearings.

Front End Alignment

Front end alignment centers on the precise geometric relationship of a number of parts — even when they are changing positions — that provides front wheel stability and control. These geometric angles include steering axis cant, caster, camber, included angle, toe-in, and toe-out (turning arc). Before any adjustment is made, the condition of the complete front end system should be checked following the procedures given in the previous paragraphs and any defects corrected. Check the air pressure in all the tires. Check that the front tires are worn evenly. If not, replace or rotate them with the rear tires. Front wheel alignment must always be adjusted in this order:

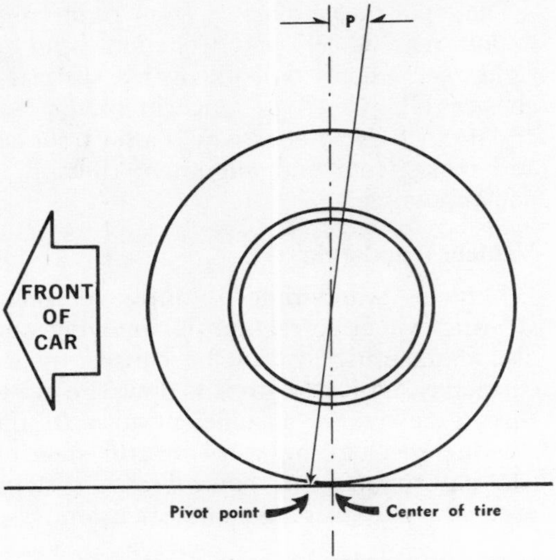

Front wheel caster. P = positive caster. The pivot point ahead of the center line of the tire holds the wheel stable.

1. Caster
2. Camber
3. Toe-In

Caster

Caster is the cant of the upper ball joint toward the rear of the car (positive). It gives the wheel another type of directional stability by moving the pivot point of the wheel forward of the tire's center. Positioning the pivot point ahead of center causes a drag on the bottom of the wheel (at the center) when it turns, thereby resisting the turn and tending to hold the wheel steady in whatever direction it has been going. The same principle of drag holds a weather vane pointer into the wind. The vane's bulky part seeks the point of minimum resistance behind the pivot.

Too slight a caster angle will cause the wheels to wander or weave at high speed and steer erratically when the brakes are applied. Too great a caster angle creates hard steering and shimmy at low speeds. Placing the weight of the car directly over the pivot point allows easiest steering and takes some load off the outside wheel bearings.

Camber

Camber is the angle that the centerline of the wheel makes with the vertical. The top of the wheel cants away from the car so that the center of the tire at the road lies at a point projected along the inclined axis of the upper and lower ball joints (steering axis cant).

Toe-Out

Toe-out (turning arc) is the difference in angle of the two wheels in a turn. As the front end turns, the outside wheel describes a larger circle than does the inside wheel. The turning angle of each is, therefore, not the same and the difference of the two angles is toe-out. If all previously discussed front end angles and measurements are correct and yet toe-out is wrong, one or both of the steering arms are bent.

Toe-In

Usually measured in inches, this is the amount that both wheels are closer together at the front than at the rear. Toe-in is related to wheel camber and compression forces on the steering linkage with forward speed. The greater the camber, the greater is the toe-in, usually. Set toe-in only after checking caster and camber.

Steering Axis Cant

Steering axis cant, or kingpin inclination as termed years ago when kingpins were standard, is the angle (from the vertical) at which the steering knuckle is attached to the upper and lower ball joints. The canted steering knuckle controls wheel directional stability by forcing the wheel to lift the chassis in order to turn from a straight ahead direction. As the steering arm releases its force over the wheel, the wheel returns to its straight ahead position under the force of the chassis weight. This inclination is not adustable.

Included Angle

This is found by adding the steering axis cant to the positive wheel camber. This total must be equal on both front wheels regardless of what individual differences exist in axis cant and camber between the wheels. If the included angles of the two sides are different, a wheel spindle might be bent, possibly from striking a curb sharply.

Chapter 3
Engine

The BMW 1500, 1600, 1800 and 2000 Series all have four-cylinder, in-line water cooled engines, with BHP ranging from 90 for the 1500, to 135 for the 2000 TI and 2000 CS cars. The 2500, 2800 and 2800 CS models use two double-barrel Zenith carburetors and six-cylinder, in-line water cooled engines to boost this horsepower to 170 for the 2500 and to 192 for the 2800 and 2800 CS models. All power plants are single overhead camshaft types.

Air filter removal. Filter mounting screws (1, 2), air intake hose clamp (3), heater tube (4), air preheater tube (6).

Engine Removal

Remove hood by removing hinge bolts after marking their position. Disconnect battery ground cable. Drain radiator and cylinder block by opening drain cocks. Remove radiator cap to speed up draining. Remove air filter with air intake tube, breather tube and air preheater tube.

Remove air preheating regulator (8) with air hose (9).

Disconnect radiator hoses from thermostat and water pump, then remove radiator mounting bolts and radiator. Unscrew temperature sensor (11) from housing (12) and release it from clamps. Disconnect throttle linkage (13), and vacuum line (14) from check valve (15). Pull fuel line (16) from fuel pump (P) and its clamp.

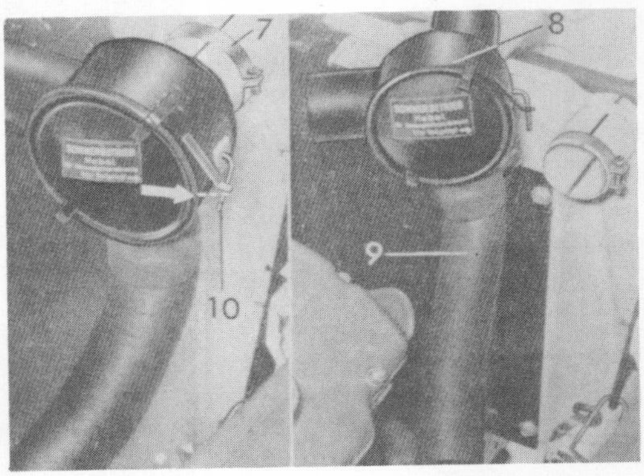

Preheater regulator removal. Preheater regulator (8), clamp (7), air hose (9), summer-winter lever (10).

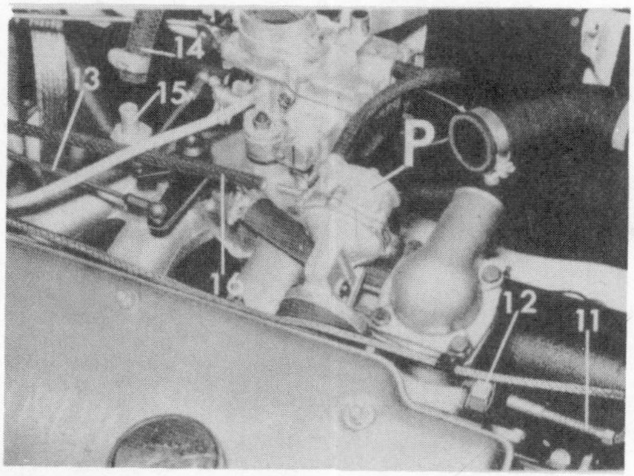

Temperature sensor (11), sensor housing (12), throttle linkage (13), vacuum line (14), check valve (15), fuel line (16), fuel pump (P).

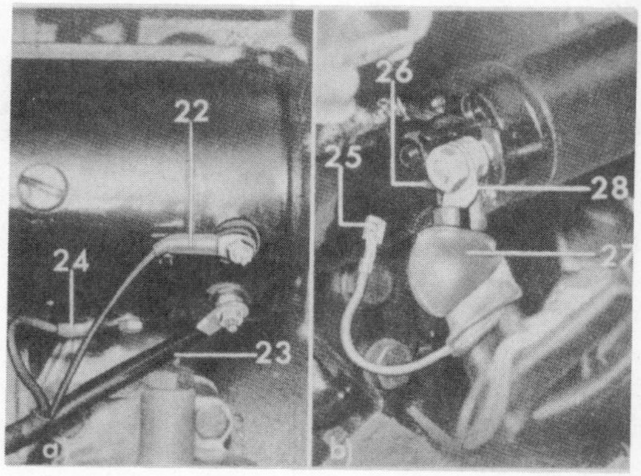

Armature D+, black/red (22), field DF, black (23), ground, brown (24), connector (25), solenoid switch (26), rubber cover (27), cable terminal (28).

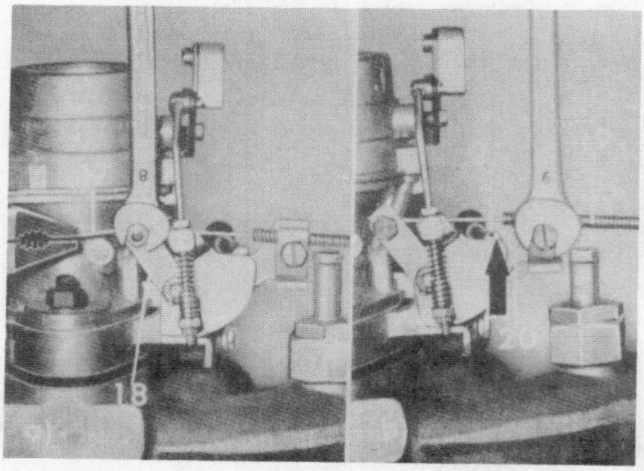

Bowden cable (17), choke lever (18), cable sleeve (19), cable clamp (20). At reassembly, lever (18) must butt against stop (21).

Heater hoses (29, 30), connectors (31, 32), oil pressure switch (34).

Disconnect choke cable (17) from lever (18), and cable sleeve (19) from cable clamp (20) and pull out cable. There is no choke cable on automatic choke models.

Disconnect generator armature wire D+ black/red (22) field wire DF black (23) and brown ground wire (24). Pull plug connector (25) from solenoid switch (26), pull back rubber cover (27) and disconnect starter cable (28). On models with alternator, disconnect red cable at B+ terminal.

Disconnect heater hoses (29 and 30). Disconnect ground band from gearbox flange. Remove socket connection (31) from distributor, and pull connector (32) from oil pressure switch (34).

Disconnect high tension cable from ignition coil and remove distributor cap and rotor.

Remove gearshift lever (D) by first pulling up dust cover (A), rubber housing (B) and dust cover (C), then removing leaf

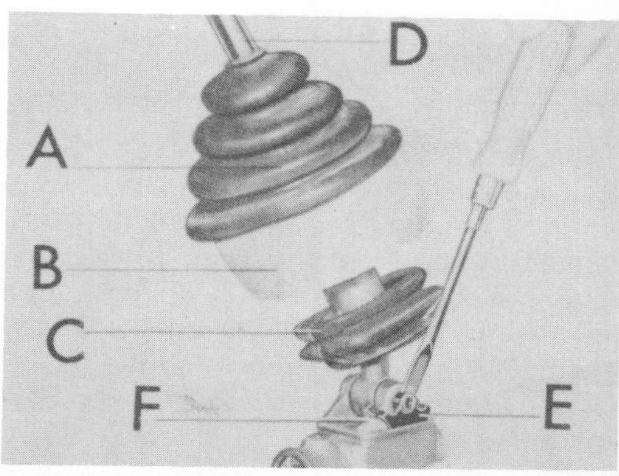

Gearshift lever assembly. Dust covers (A, C), rubber housing (B), lever (D), bolt and leaf spring (E), shift head (F). At reassembly, install bolt (E) in same position.

spring and bolt (E) and bolt from shift head (F). On models with pivot ball on shift lever end, pull up rubber boot and

Engine Specifications

Model	No. of Cyls.	Displacement Cu. In. (cc) (effective)	Bore In. (mm)	Stroke In. (mm)	Compression Ratio	Torque Ft. Lbs./(KGM)/ RPM	Max. Continuous Engine Speed RPM	BHP/RPM SAE
1500	4	91.47 (1499)	3.228(82)	2.795(71)	8.8:1	86.8(12)/3000	5800	90/5900
1600	4	95.99 (1573)	3.307(84)	2.795(71)	8.6:1	91.2(12.6)/3000	5800	94/5700
1600 2 Door	4	95.99 (1573)	3.307(84)	2.795(71)	8.6:1	91.2(12.6)/3000	5800	96/5800
1600TI	4	95.99 (1573)	3.307(84)	2.795(71)	9.5:1	97.3(13.4)/4500	6400	118/6200
1800, 1800A	4	108.2 (1773)	3.307(84)	3.150(80)	8.6:1	105.6(14.6)/3000	5800	102/5800
1800/69	4	107.7 (1766)	3.504(89)	2.795(71)	8.6:1	105.6(14.6)/3000	5800	102/5800
1800TI	4	108.2 (1773)	3.307(84)	3.150(80)	9.5:1	109.2(15.1)/4000	6000	124/5800
2002	4	121.44 (1990)	3.504(89)	3.150(80)	8.5:1	115.7(16)/3000	6000	113/6000
2000, 2000A	4	121.44 (1990)	3.504(89)	3.150(80)	8.5:1	115.7(16)/3000	6000	113/6000
2000TI	4	121.44 (1990)	3.504(89)	3.150(80)	9.3:1	122.9(17)/3600	6000	135/5800
2000CS	4	121.44 (1990)	3.504(89)	3.150(80)	9.3:1	122.9(17)/3600	6000	135/5800
2000CA	4	121.44 (1990)	3.504(89)	3.150(80)	8.5:1	115.7(16)/3000	6000	113/5800
2500	6	152.1 (2494)	3.386(86)	2.82(71.6)	9:1	176(24)/3700	6000	170/6000
2800	6	170.1 (2788)	3.386(85)	3.150(80)	9:1	173.6(24)/3700	6000	192/6000
2800CS	6	170.1 (2788)	3.390(86)	3.150(80)	9:1	173.6(24)/3700	6200	192/6000

Note: Not all these models were imported into the United States.

packing to remove snap-ring and shift lever.

Jack car and place on stands. Disconnect exhaust pipe from manifold, and disconnect exhaust pipe support. Remove muffler mounting screws. Disconnect drive shaft at the gearbox, and tie up the driven shaft so that it does not fall out of gearbox. Disconnect the reverse light switch and speedometer cable from the gearbox housing.

Remove hydraulic line bracket from clutch housing but do not disconnect line from slave cylinder (40). Disconnect return spring from clutch arm. Pull back dust cover (38) and remove snap-ring (39) from slave cylinder. Pull slave cylinder forward and take out pushrod. On models with non-hydraulic clutch linkage, remove intermediate shaft.

Attach hoist to engine and take up slack. Remove the right and left hand engine mounting bolts. Support gearbox with a jack. Remove bolt from cap bearing (41) and bolts (42 and 43) from crossmember.

Slowly lower gearbox and lift out engine. Install engine in reverse sequence.

When refilling radiator, set heater control lever to "HOT". Run engine until water temperature reaches 176°F. (thermostat opening temperature), turn radiator cap back one notch to release pressure, then check coolant level and retighten cap.

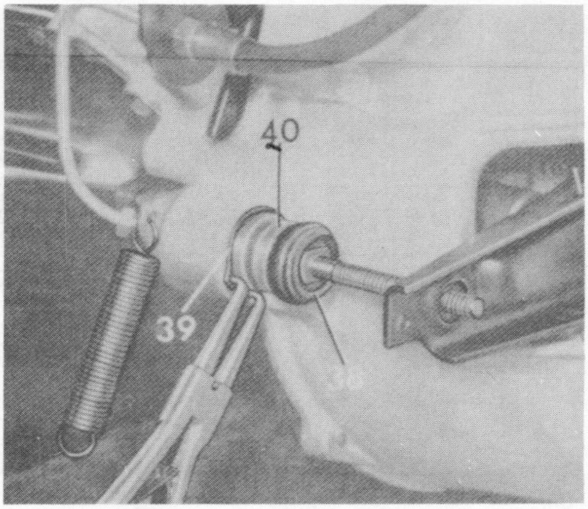

Clutch slave cylinder (40), cylinder dust cover (38), and snap-ring (39).

Intermediate shaft removal for the 1600-2.

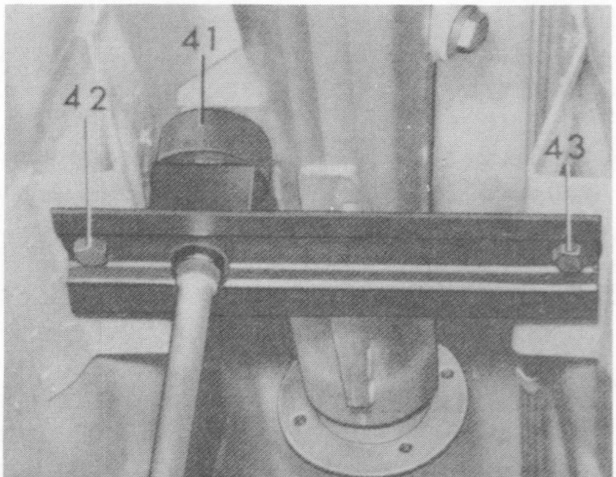

Cap bearing (41) and crossmember mounting bolts (42, 43).

Engine removal and installation.

Engine Installation

When bolting engine of the 1600-2 in place, set right engine support stop as shown in illustration, so that A = .118" (3 mm).

Connect pullrod to intermediate shaft and align shaft bearing support at 90° to the engine before tightening mounting screws.

Adjustment of engine mounting stop.

Installation of intermediate shaft.

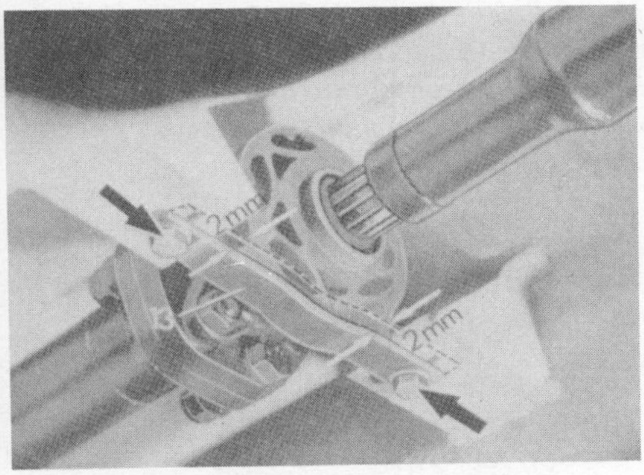

Pre-stress bearing .08″ (2 mm) by means of bearing support (13).

Tighten drive shaft bolts to 21.8 ft. lbs. torque. Pre-stress center bearing .08″ (2 mm).

Install gear shift pin (14) in lever with bolt (15) positioned in centering recess of pin.

Adjust clutch arm play to .1181-.1378″ (3-3.5 mm).

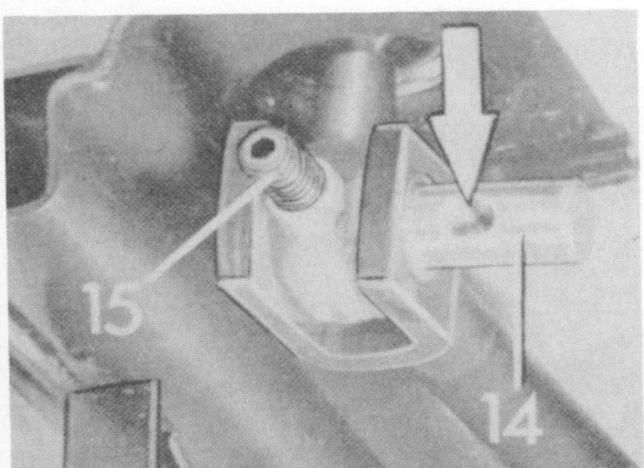

Arrow shows recess in gear shift pin (14) which receives bolt (15).

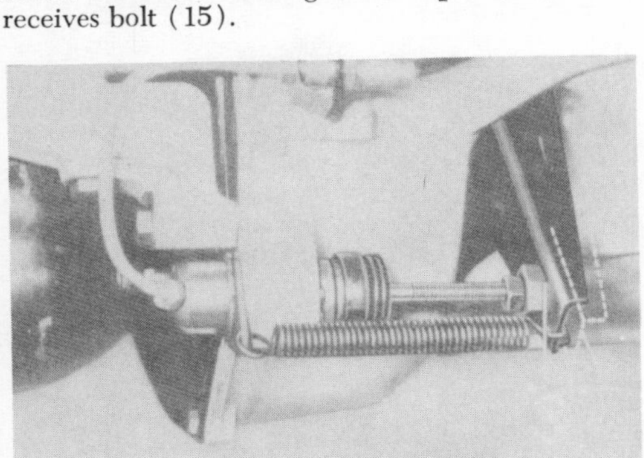

Adjust slave cylinder pushrod for .1181″-.1378″ (3-3.5 mm) correct withdrawal arm clearance.

Engine Disassembly

Cylinder Head Removal

Disconnect the following items: radiator hose from thermostat housing; vacuum hose from check valve; fuel line from fuel pump; temperature sensor from thermostat housing; throttle linkage from carburetor; choke cable from lever and sleeve from clamp; water hose from intake manifold and heater hose from cylinder head; and oil dipstick bracket.

Disconnect wire plug connections on distributor and on oil pressure switch, and remove distributor cap. Disconnect spark plug leads and cable from ignition coil. Detach exhaust pipe from manifold.

Remove nuts and cylinder head cover with its gasket. Note that when No. 1 cylinder is on TDC, the pointer will be opposite the 2nd notch in the drive pulley. The notch in the camshaft flange must coincide with the notch in the cylinder head.

Pointer/drive pulley mark and camshaft/cylinder head marks coincide at TDC of No. 1 cylinder.

Detach timing gear cover at top. Loosen chain tensioner plug (1) and unscrew by hand. WARNING: *spring is under heavy pressure. Depress plug when loosening.*

Remove spring (2) and plunger (K).

Bend down lock plate tabs, remove bolts and camshaft sprocket. Tie up chain with wire to generator housing. Remove cylinder head bolts, cylinder head and gasket.

Cylinder Head Installation

Tighten cylinder head bolts in sequence 1-10. Tighten in three stages; 21.7 ft. lbs., 50.5 ft. lbs., and 49.2-52.0 ft. lbs. After test-running the engine and cooling to 95°F. or less, give cylinder head bolts a final tightening to 49.2-52.0 ft. lbs. Then check and adjust valve clearance. CAUTION: *be sure the gasket water passage holes coincide exactly with those in the block and the head. The TI cylinder head gasket can be used on the 1800 cc engine. But under no circumstances should the cylinder head gasket of an 1800 cc engine be used on the TI engine.*

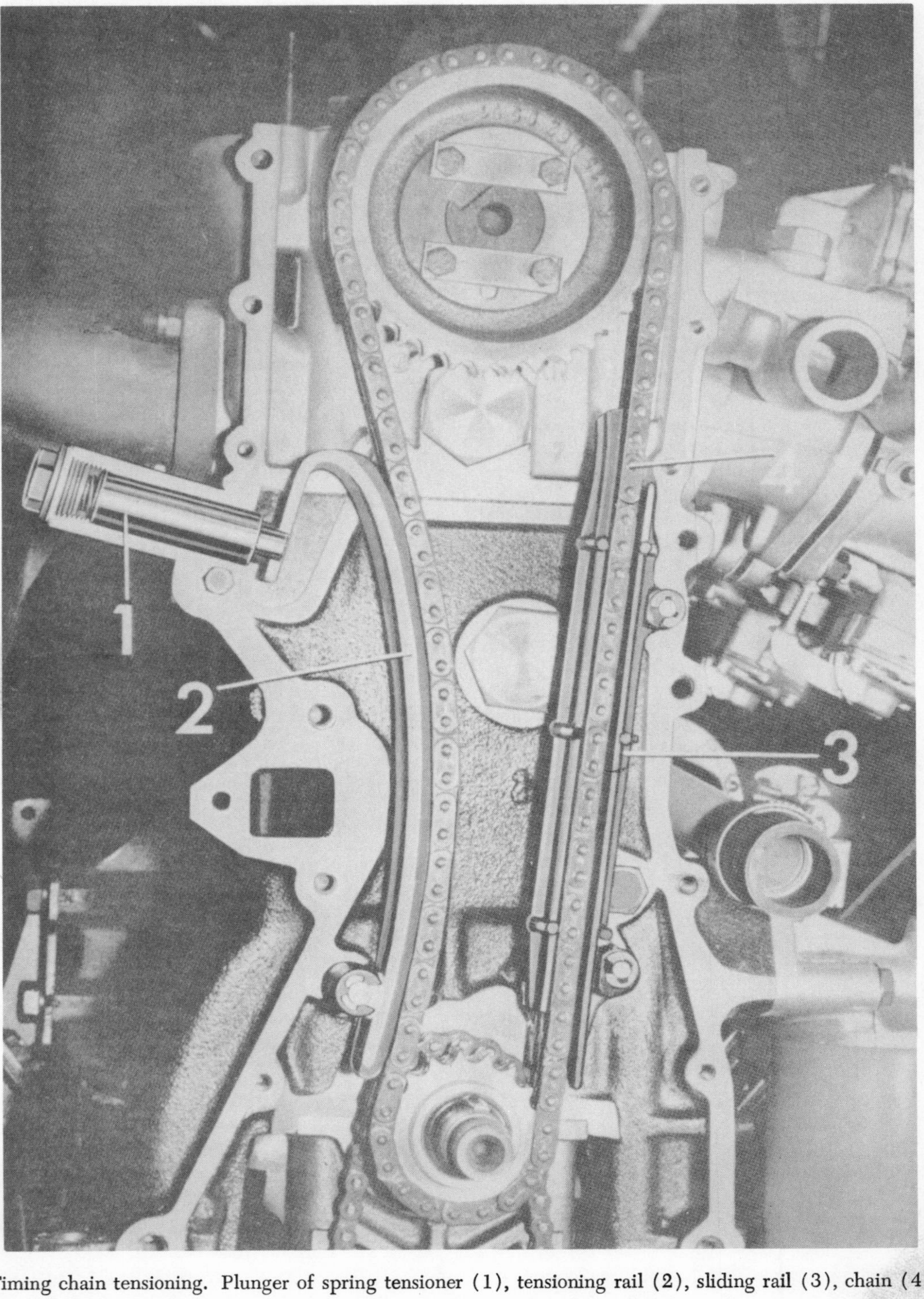

Timing chain tensioning. Plunger of spring tensioner (1), tensioning rail (2), sliding rail (3), chain (4).

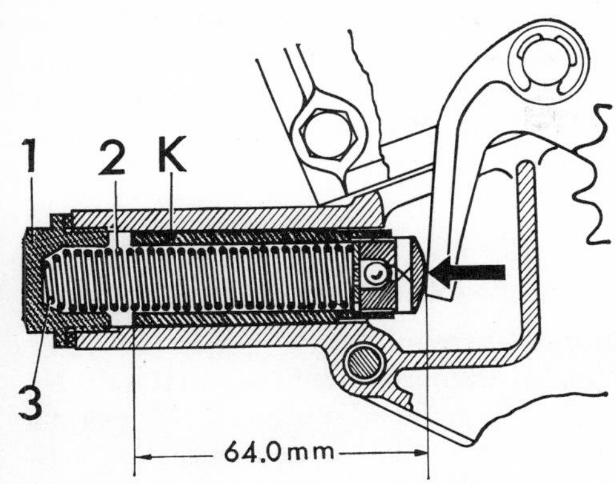

Chain tensioner consists of plug (1), spring (2), and plunger (K). Spring contacts plug at (3). Use only plungers of 2.519" (64 mm) length, or timing chain will slip.

Checking and Adjusting Valve Clearance

Check valve clearance with engine cold, pistons on top dead center and in firing order sequence, that is, 1-3-4-2. Proper cold engine clearance for both intake and exhaust valves is:

.0059 — .0078" (.15 — .20 mm)

To adjust clearance, loosen locknut and turn eccentric adjuster. Measure clearance with feeler gauge. Hold eccentric in proper position and gently tighten locknut. Recheck clearance.

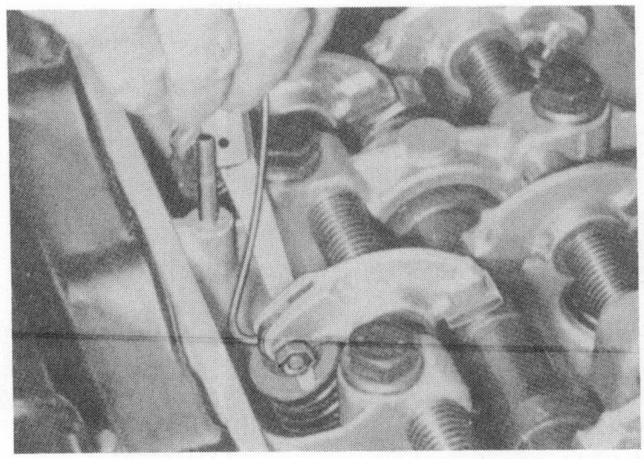

Valve adjustment.

Camshaft Removal

Rocker Clamp BMW 6025 or an equivalent device facilitates camshaft removal. However, before the clamp frame is fitted into position on BMW 2000 engines, the intake and exhaust valves of No. 2 cylinder

Valve Specifications

Model	*Running Clearance In. (mm)*		*Overall Length In. (mm)*		*Head Dia. In. (mm)*		*Stem Dia. In. (mm)*		*Guide Inside Dia. In. (mm)*	*Spring Length Un-Loaded In.*
	Int.	*Exh.*	*Int.*	*Exh.*	*Int.*	*Exh.*	*Int.*	*Exh.*		
1500,1600, 1600-2, 1600TI, 1800,1800A, 1800/69, 1800TI, 2002,2000, 2000A, 2000TI, 2000CS, 2000CA	.00098- .00216 (.025- .055)	.00157- .00275 (.040- .070)	4.087± .00079 103.8± .2)	4.106± .00079 (104.3± .2)			.315, .00157 U/S, .0098 U/S (8, .040 U/S, .025 U/S)	.315, .00157 U/S, .00217 U/S (8, .040 U/S, .055 U/S)	.315, .00059 O/S (8, .015 O/S	1.811 (46)
1500,1600					1.535 (39)	1.378 (35)				
1600-2, 1600TI, 1800, 1800A, 1800/69, 1800TI					1.654 (42)	1.378 (35)				
2002,2000, 2000A, 2000TI, CS,CA					1.732 (44)	1.496 (38)				

U/S—undersize O/S—oversize

must be adjusted to maximum valve operating clearance.

Place compression frame in position, lock it and swing down the two supports (S). NOTE: *swing the supports (S) out to side on BMW 1500, 1600, 1800 and 1800 TI engines.* Tighten bolt (17) until camshaft (19) can be withdrawn after removal of guide plate (18).

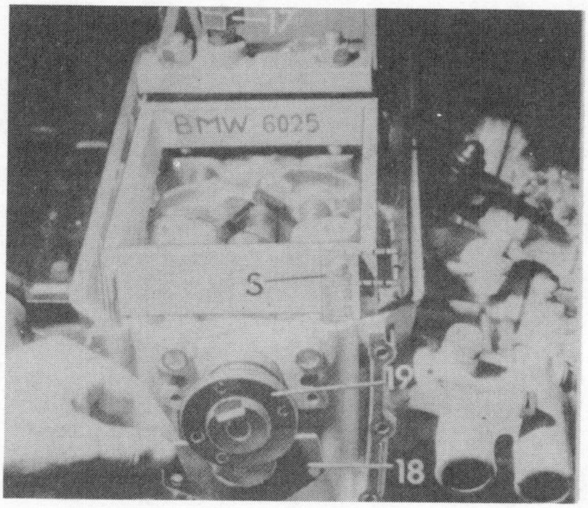

Rocker clamp BMW 6025. Supports (S), tension bolt (17), guide plate (18), camshaft (19).

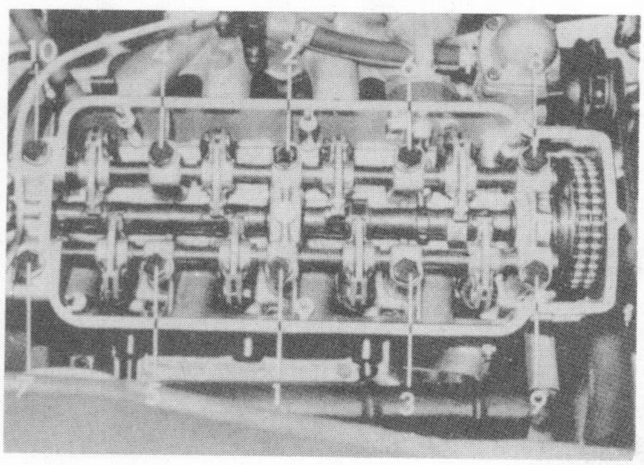

Cylinder head tightening sequence.

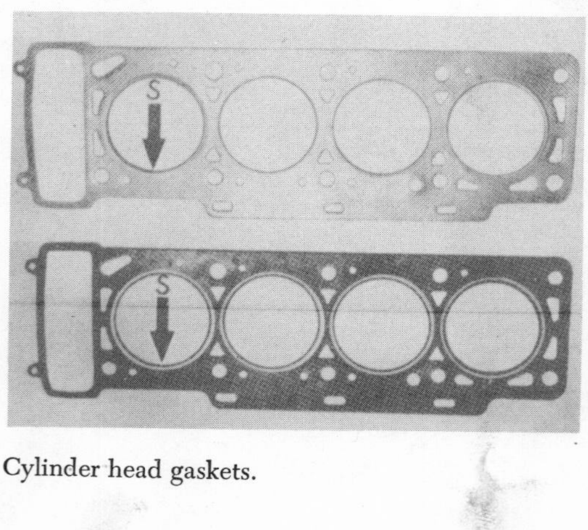

Cylinder head gaskets.

Installation of new camshaft follows reverse sequence of removal. Before placing cylinder head in position, bring No. 1 cylinder to TDC. The notch on the camshaft flange must be aligned with the mark on the housing. Reset valve operating clearances and ignition timing.

Camshaft Installation

Install camshaft with notch on flange aligned with mark on housing and with No. 1 cylinder in TDC position. Mount the sprocket with chain fitted onto the camshaft flange. To relieve tension, insert a screwdriver between the tension arm and the timing case cover. Bleed tensioner by filling oil space, pumping piston until oil comes out at plug, then tightening plug. Reset valve clearances and ignition timing.

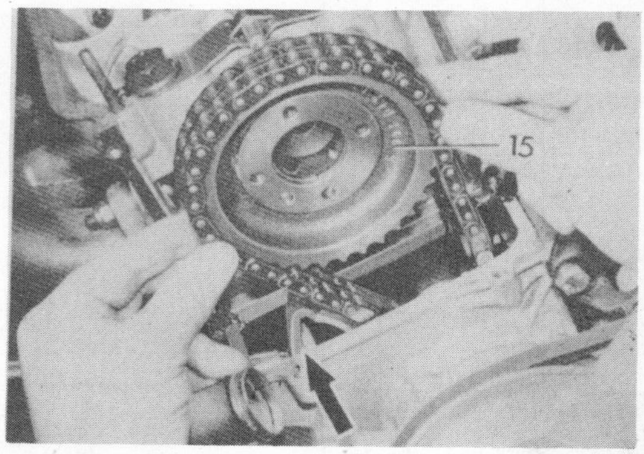

Insert screwdriver (at arrow) to relieve tension when installing sprocket and chain.

Install cylinder head and timing case covers. Hand tighten bolts (1 and 2). Then tighten bolts 3-8, and finally bolts 1 and 2, to specified torque.

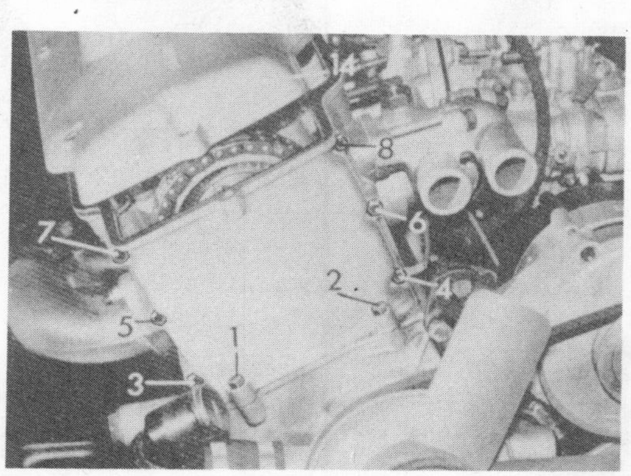

Installing cylinder head and timing case covers. Hand-tighten bolts 1 and 2. Then tighten bolts 3-8, finally bolts 1 and 2.

Crankshaft, Camshaft, and Connecting Rod Specifications 1500, 1600, 1600-2, 1600TI, 1800, 1800A, 1800/69, 1800TI, 2002, 2000, 2000A, 2000TI, 2000CS, 2000CA

	Crankshaft					*Camshaft*		*Connecting Rods*		
No. of Main Bearings	*Main Journal Dia. In. (mm.)*		*Rod Journal Dia. In. (mm.)*	*Main Bearing Clearance (Radial Play) In. (mm.)*	*Crankshaft End Play In. (mm.)*	*Nominal Clearance In. (mm.)*	*End Play In. (mm.)*	*Small End Bore In. (mm.)*	*Big End Bore In. (mm.)*	*Rod Bearing Radial Play In. (mm.)*
	Red	*Blue*								
	Standard Size		*Standard Size*							
5	2.165, .00079 U/S .00114 U/S	2.165, .00079 U/S .00114 U/S	1.8898, .00098 U/S .00114 U/S	.0019– .0027	.0024– .0064	.00134– .0064	.00079– .00512	.945, .000830S	2.047, .000390S	.00114– .00287
	(55, .010 U/S, .020 U/S)	(55, .020 U/S, .029 U/S)	(48, .009 U/S, .025 U/S)	(.03– .068)	(.06– .018)	(.034– .075)	(.02– .13)	(24, .0210S)	(52, .0100S)	(.029– .073)
	First Undersize		*First Undersize*							
	2.155, .00039 U/S .00079 U/S	2.155, .00079 U/S .00114 U/S	1.8799, .0004 U/S .0010 U/S							
	(54.75, .010 U/S .020 U/S)	(54.75, .020 U/S .029 U/S)	(47.75, .009 U/S .025 U/S)							
	Second Undersize		*Second Undersize*							
	2.1457, .00039 U/S .00079 U/S	2.1457, .00079 U/S .00114 U/S	1.8701, .0004 U/S .010 U/S							
	(54.50, .010 U/S .020 U/S)	(54.50, .020 U/S .029 U/S)	(47.5, .009 U/S .025 U/S)							

U/S – Undersize   O/S Oversize

Engine Components

Distributor Removal and Replacement

Remove distributor (Z) mounting bolts and take out distributor. Remove distributor flange (F). When replacing, coat mating surfaces of distributor and cylinder head (K) with a non-hardening sealer. Install distributor with vacuum chamber (U) on right when viewed facing forward. Adjust ignition timing as outlined in Chapter 5.

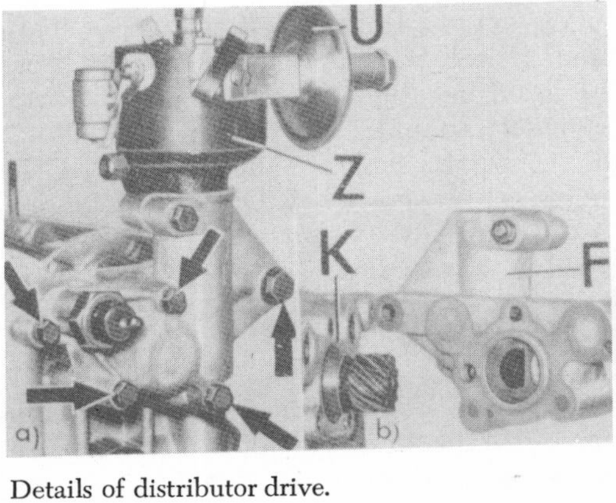

Details of distributor drive.

Rocker Arm Removal and Replacement

Remove guide plate bolts and attach rocker arm holder BMW 601 or equivalent device, tightening nuts down evenly. Take out camshaft and guide plate. Remove rocker arm holder.

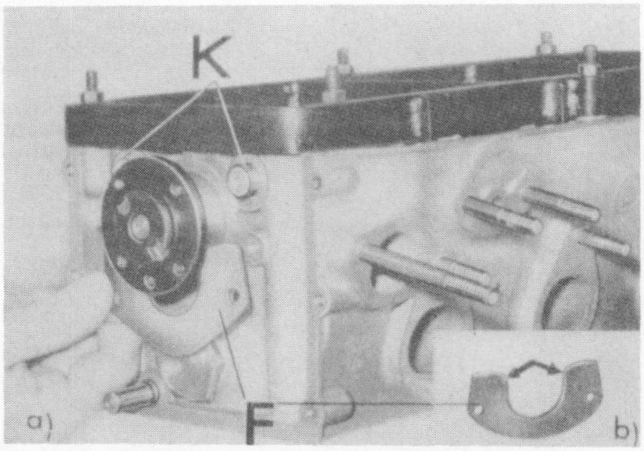

Two bolts hold guide plate (F) and rocker shafts (K).

Push rocker arms (1) and thrust rings (2) far enough to one side on rocker shaft (3) to permit removal of circlips (4). Then drive rocker shafts out the front.

Rocker arms (1), thrust rings (2), rocker shaft (3), circlips (4).

When re-installing, align rocker shafts immediately so that cylinder head bolts can be fitted into their proper recesses. Thrust ring (2) should cover circlip (4). Notch in camshaft flange should be opposite notch in cylinder head. Guide plate should be thoroughly de-burred, and after assembly, camshaft should revolve easily.

Valve, Valve Guide Removal and Replacement

Remove valves with suitable spring compressor. Check spring length. Always replace oil seal rings. A damaged oil seal ring will increase oil consumption. Lay oil seal ring in spring washer. Valve guides can be reamed. To renew valve guides, heat cylinder head to about 356°F. and press guides out into combustion chamber. Press new guides in from rocker shaft side.

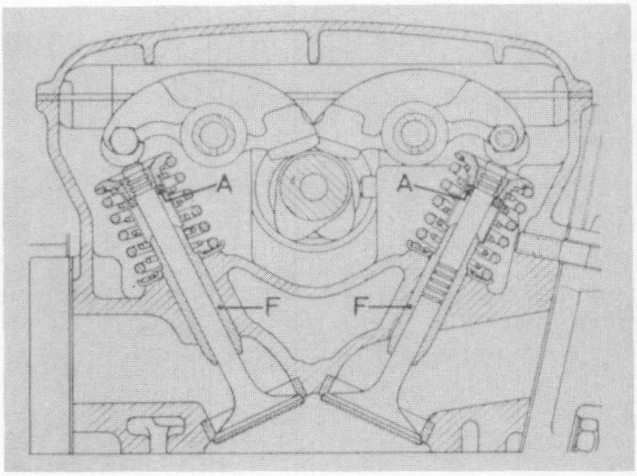

Oil seal rings (A), valve guides (F).

Timing Gear Chain Removal and Replacement

Remove engine, drain oil, remove oil pan and cylinder head cover. Turn crankshaft pulley to set notch opposite pointer, and set notch in camshaft opposite notch in cylinder head. Remove timing gear cover at top. Loosen chain tensioner and remove plunger. WARNING: *tensioner is under heavy spring pressure. Depress plug while removing.*

Remove fan from pulley. WARNING: *do not hold fan blades for leverage; increase fan belt tension by hand and hold onto water pump.* Loosen alternator and remove fan belt. Remove fan pulley with a puller.

Remove alternator and water pump. Remove camshaft sprocket and chain. Lock crankshaft and remove crankshaft pulley nut. Pull off crankshaft pulley. Remove lower timing gear cover and remove chain.

Remove lockring (S) and slide off tensioning wheel (R). Remove sprocket (three bolts) from oil pump housing, and remove housing by pressing gently downward out of the centering sleeves.

With a screwdriver, remove sliding rails (arrow). Remove key (F) and O-ring (R) from crankshaft.

When reassembling, heat sprocket to temperature of 356-392°F. Note correct position for oil hole (B) under oil pump

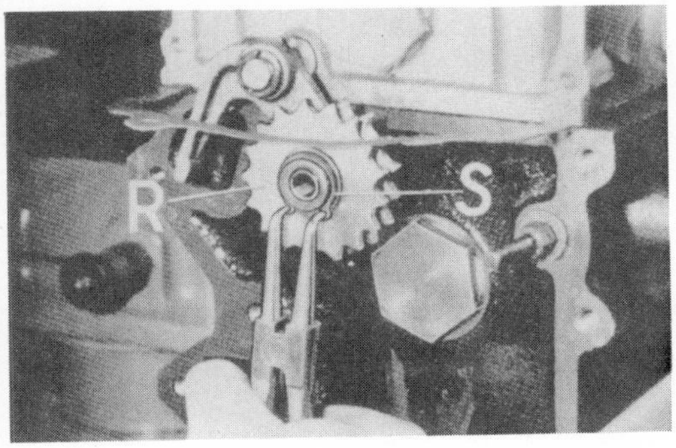

Lockring (S) and timing chain tensioning wheel (R).

Sprocket wheels can be pulled after removing sliding rail (at "a"), key (F) and O-ring (R) at "b."

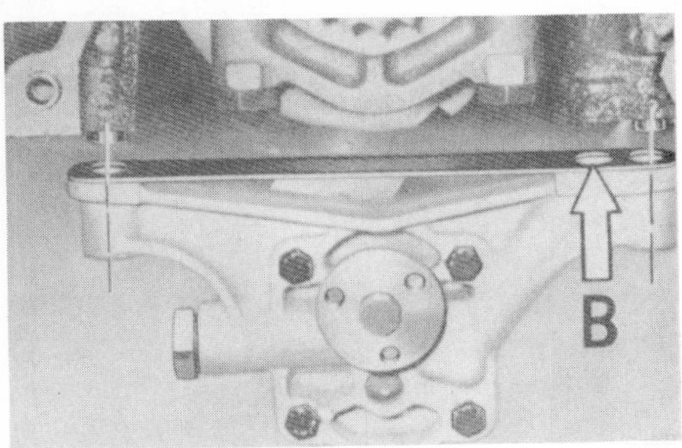

Note position of oil hole (B) in shim.

housing. Install machined faces of sliding rail to face forward toward retainer. Renew O-ring (R).

Chain tension must be set to permit slight depression of the chain (K) with light thumb pressure. Tighten crankshaft pulley to 101.3 ft. lbs. Align notch in camshaft flange with notch in cylinder head. Align pointer with notch in crankshaft pulley. Bend over all lock plates. Renew all copper gaskets and head gasket. Check fan belt for correct tension.

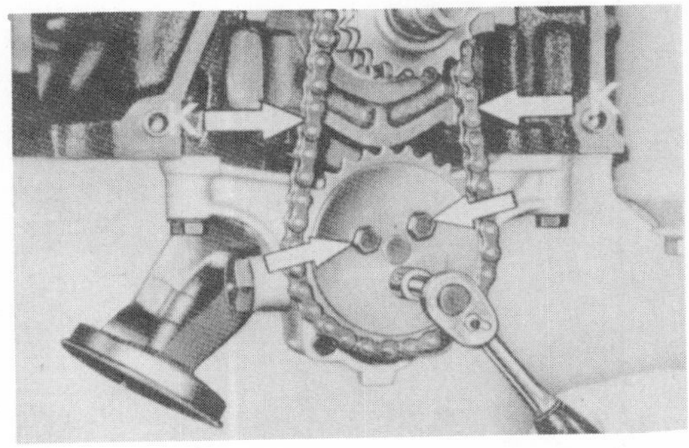

Chain tension should permit slight depression (K) with light finger pressure. Tension is adjusted by shim under oil pump.

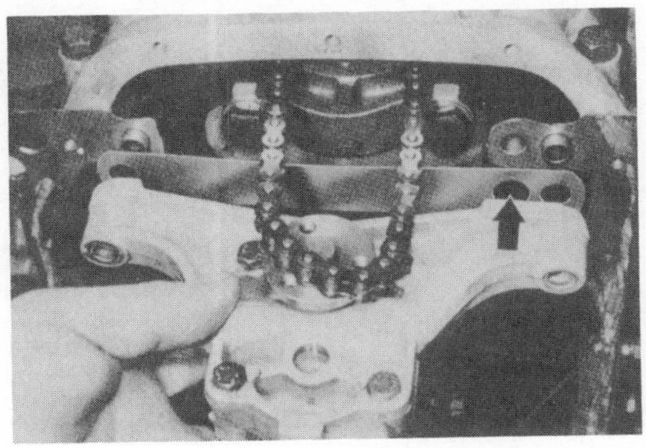

Correct position for shim and oil hole (arrow).

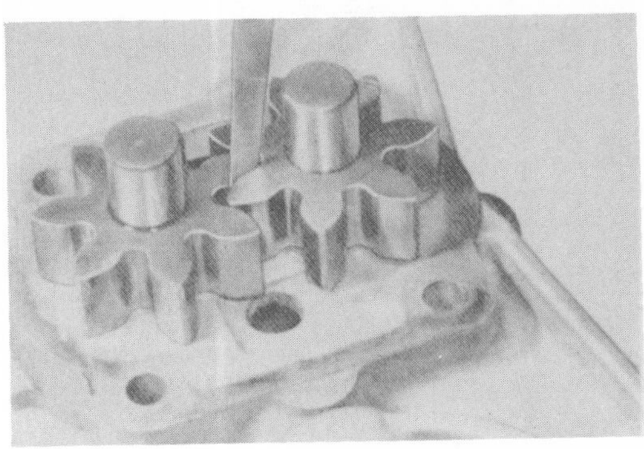

Checking tooth backlash of gear type oil pump.

Oil Pump Servicing

Remove oil pan by removing bolts and pulling forward and turning to the left (facing oil pan). Remove drive chain and sprocket. Remove oil pump mounting bolts from crankcase and supporting plate. When re-installing pump, adjust chain tension with shims until chain can be just depressed with light finger pressure. Be sure to install shims with oil hole in correct position.

Block, Piston, and Ring Specifications

Model	Standard Cyl. Bore In. (mm.)	First Rebore In. (mm.)	Second Rebore In. (mm.)	Standard Piston Dia. In. (mm.)	First Oversize Piston Dia. In. (mm.)	Second Oversize Piston Dia. In. (mm.)	Piston Pin Dia. In. (mm.) White	Piston Pin Dia. In. (mm.) Black	Piston Pin Fit in Piston In. (mm.)	Ring End Gap In. (mm.) First and Second Ring	Ring End Gap In. (mm.) Third Ring	Ring Clearance in Groove In. (mm.) First Ring	Ring Clearance in Groove In. (mm.) Second Ring	Ring Clearance in Groove In. (mm.) Third Ring
1500	3.228, .00087 o/s (82, .022 o/s)	3.2383 (82.25	3.2481 (82.50)	3.2258 (81.935)	3.2356 (82.185)	3.2454 (82.435)	.8662, .00012 u/s (22, .003 u/s)	.8662, .00012 u/s, .00024 u/s (22, .003 u/s, .006 u/s)	.00012–.00032 (.003–.008)	.0118–.0177 (.30–.45)	.0098–.0157 (.25–.40)	.0024–.0034 (.060–.087)	.0014–.0024 (.035–.062)	.00098–.00205 (.025–.052)
1600	3.228, .00087 o/s (82, .022 o/s)	3.2383 (82.25)	3.2481 (82.50)	3.3055 (83.960)	3.3154 (84.210)	3.3252 (84.460)	.8662, .00012 u/s (22, .003 u/s)	.8662, .00012 u/s, .00024 u/s (22, .003 u/s, .006 u/s)	.00012–.00032 (.003–.008)	.0118–.0177 (.30–.45)	.0098–.0157 (.25–.40)	.0024–.0034 (.060–.087)	.0014–.0024 (.035–.062)	.00098–.00205 (.025–.052)
1600–2	3.3071, .00087 o/s (84, .022 o/s)	3.3170 (84.25)	3.3268 (84.50)	3.3055 (83.960)	3.3154 (84.210)	3.3252 (84.460)	.8662, .00012 u/s (22, .003 u/s)	.8662, .00012 u/s, .00024 u/s (22, .003 u/s, .006 u/s)	.00012–.00032 (.003–.008)	.0118–.0177 (.30–.45)	.0098–.0157 (.25–.40)	.0024–.0034 (.060–.087)	.0014–.0024 (.035–.062)	.00098–.00205 (.025–.052)
1600TI	3.3071, .00087 o/s (84, .022 o/s)	3.3170 (84.25	3.3268 (84.50)	3.3055 (83.960)	3.3154 (84.210)	3.3252 (84.460)	.8662, .00012 u/s (22, .003 u/s)	.8662, .00012 u/s, .00024 u/s (22, .003 u/s, .006 u/s)	.00012–.00032 (.003–.008)	.0118–.0177 (.30–.45)	.0098–.0157 (.25–.40)	.0024–.0034 (.060–.087)	.0014–.0024 (.035–.062)	.00098–.00205 (.025–.052)
1800, 1800A	3.3071, .00087 o/s (84, .022 o/s)	3.3170 (84.25)	3.3268 (84.50)	3.3055 (83.960)	3.3154 (84.210)	3.3252 (84.460)	.8662, .00012 u/s (22, .003 u/s)	.8662, .00012 u/s, .00024 u/s (22, .003 u/s, .006 u/s)	.00012–.00032 (.003–.008)	.0118–.0177 (.30–.45)	.0098–.0157 (.25–.40)	.0024–.0034 (.060–.087)	.0024–.0014–(.035–.062)	.00098–.00205 (.025–.052)
1800/69	3.5039, .00087 o/s (89, .022 o/s)	3.5137 (89.25)	3.5236 (89.50)	3.5024 (88.960)	3.5122 (89.210)	3.5220 (89.460)	.8662, .00012 u/s (22, .003 u/s)	.8662, .00012 u/s, .00024 u/s (22, .003 u/s, .006 u/s)	.00012–.00032 (.003–.008)	.0118–.0177 (.30–.45)	.0098–.0157 (.25–.40)	.0024–.0034 (.060–.087)	.0014–.0024 (.035–.062)	.00098–.00205 (.025–.052)
1800TI	3.3071, .00087 o/s (84, .022 o/s	3.3170 (84.25)	3.3268 (84.50)	3.3045 (83.935)	3.3144 (84.185)	3.3242 (84.435)	.8662, .00012 u/s (22, .003 u/s)	.8662, .00012 u/s, .00024 u/s (22, .003 u/s, .006 u/s)	.00012–.00032 (.003–.008)	.0118–.0177 (.30–.45)	.0098–.0157 (.25–.40)	.0024–.0034 (.060–.087)	.0014–.0024 (.035–.062)	.00098–.00205 (.025–.052)
2002	3.5039, .00087 o/s (89, .022 o/s)	3.5137 (89.25)	3.5236 (89.50)	3.5024 (88.960)	3.5122 (89.210)	3.5220 (89.460)	.8662, .00012 u/s (22, .003 u/s)	.8662, .00012 u/s, .00024 u/s (22, .003 u/s, .006 u/s)	.00012–.00032 (.003–.008)	.0118–.0177 (.30–.45)	.0098–.0157 (.25–.40)	.0024–.0034 (.060–.087)	.0014–.0024 (.035–.062)	.00098–.00205 (.025–.052)
2000, 2000A 2000TI, 2000CS, 2000CA	3.5039, .00087 o/s (89, .022 o/s	3.5137 (89.25)	3.5236 (89.50)	3.5024 (88.960)	3.5122 (89.210)	3.5220 (89.460)	.8662, .00012 u/s (22, .003 u/s)	.8662, .00012 u/s, .00024 u/s (22, .003 u/s, .006 u/s)	.00012–.00032 (.003–.008)	.0118–.0177 (.30–.45)	.0098–.0157 (.25–.40)	.0024–.0034 (.060–.087)	.0014–.0024 (.035–.062)	.00098–.00205 (.025–.052)

u/s undersize

Gear as well as rotor type oil pumps are used on BMW cars. In servicing either, unscrew plug to remove spring and plunger. Spring free length is 2.68″ (68 mm) and should not be changed. Check tooth backlash on the gear type. This should be .001-.002″ (.03-.05 mm) and should not exceed .003″ (.07 mm).

For the rotor type, check clearance between outer rotor and housing. This should be .0020-.0079″ (.05-.20 mm). Clearance between inner and outer rotors should be in the range of .0023-.0118″ (.06-.30 mm). Check play between pump housing and rotor sealing face with a straightedge and feeler gauges. Play should be .0013-.0033″ (.034-.084 mm). If components are not within these specifications they should be replaced.

Servicing Piston and Rod Assemblies

Pistons and rods can be serviced without removing engine from car. To remove pistons, remove cylinder head and oil pan, position piston to BDC, remove bearing cap and push piston and connecting rod upward.

Wrist pins can be replaced cold. They are color coded: W on piston crown — wrist pin marked white; S on piston crown — wrist pin marked black. Oil holes in the connecting rod for wrist pin lubrication should face forward in direction of travel.

Connecting rod bolts are expansion bolts and must be discarded after removal. Do not reuse bolts that have been in service. Rods and bearing caps are marked in pairs for each cylinder and should not be interchanged. Number 4 is at the flywheel end.

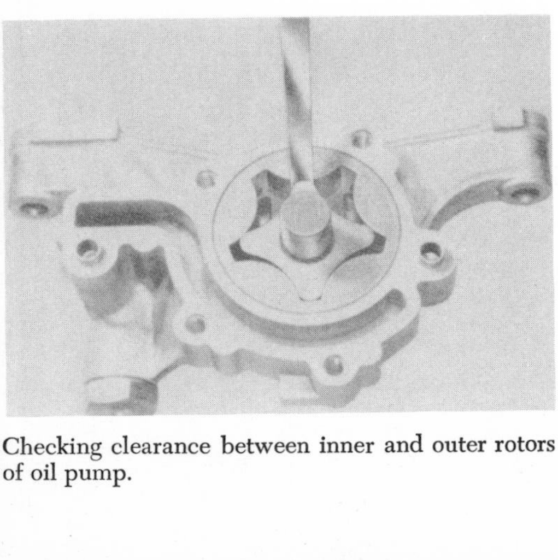

Checking clearance between inner and outer rotors of oil pump.

Check ring clearance in piston groove and ring end gap with ring inserted in cylinder bore and compare with specifications. Piston clearance in cylinder should be no more than .0016″ (.040 mm) as measured .433″ (11 mm) down from edge of piston skirt. For the 1500 engine, piston clearance should not exceed .00256″ (.065 mm).

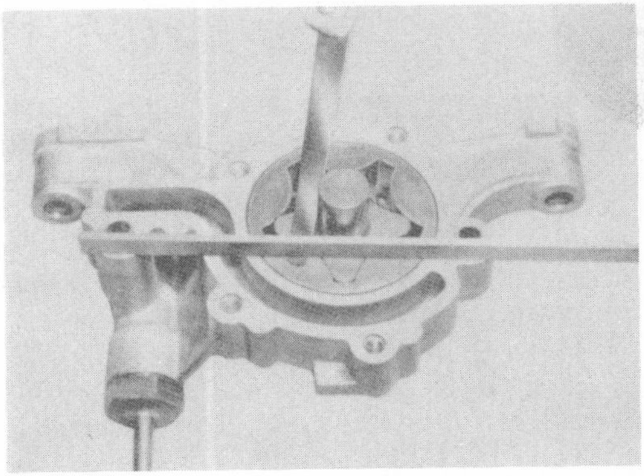

Checking play between pump housing and rotor sealing face.

Wrist pins and pistons are color coded. W on piston for white marked wrist pin; S on piston for black marked wrist pin.

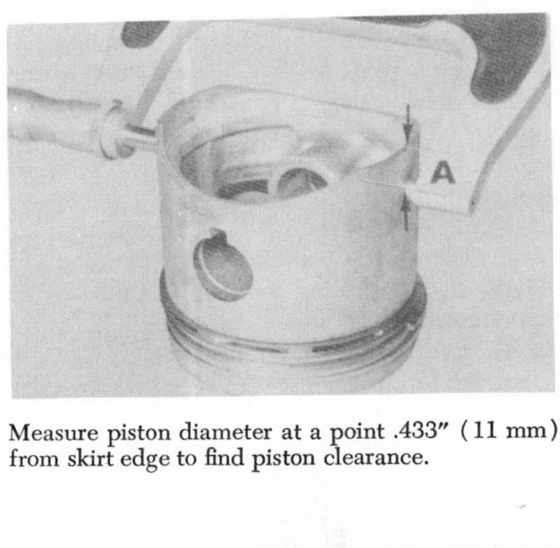

Measure piston diameter at a point .433″ (11 mm) from skirt edge to find piston clearance.

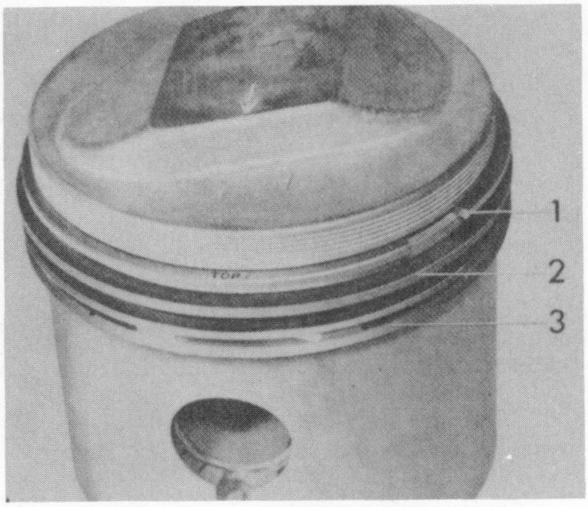

Install rings with "top" marking up as follows: 1. Rectangular ring 2. stepped ring 3. equal chamfer scraper ring. Set ring gaps 180° apart.

Each ring is marked for top and bottom. Install in following grooves in piston:

(top) Rectangular ring
(middle) Stepped ring
(bottom) Equal chamfer scraper ring

Only pistons and rods of the same weight classifications should be used. Weight class of piston is stamped on crown with a + or —. Arrow stamped on the crown points forward in direction of travel. Rod class is coded by means of colors.

Flywheel Removal and Replacement

Remove gearbox and clutch assemblies. Maximum permissible out of true at diameter of 7.874" (200 mm) is .0003" (.10 mm). Lock flywheel in position. Pry off lock plate and discard plate. Remove bolts and flywheel. At reassembly, use new lock plate and torque bolts to specifications.

Crankshaft Removal and Replacement

Remove bottom section of timing cover, drive chain and oil pump. Check crankshaft end play which should not exceed .0024-.0064" (.06-.18 mm). Remove flywheel. Remove connecting rod and main bearing caps, noting markings. Lift out crankshaft.

Main bearing number 3, the thrust bearing, determines the end play of the crankshaft. Color coding indicates main bearing diameter. The standard diameter crankshaft has a single red or blue dot on the counterweight. Reground crankshafts carry one color stripe (at B) to indicate the 1st undersize main bearing journal, and two

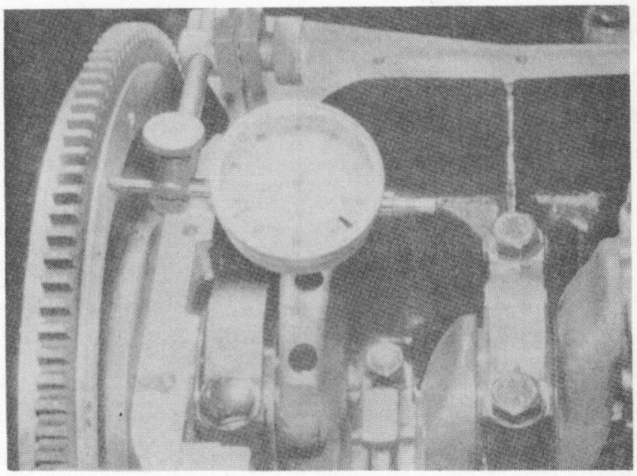

Checking crankshaft end play with a micrometer.

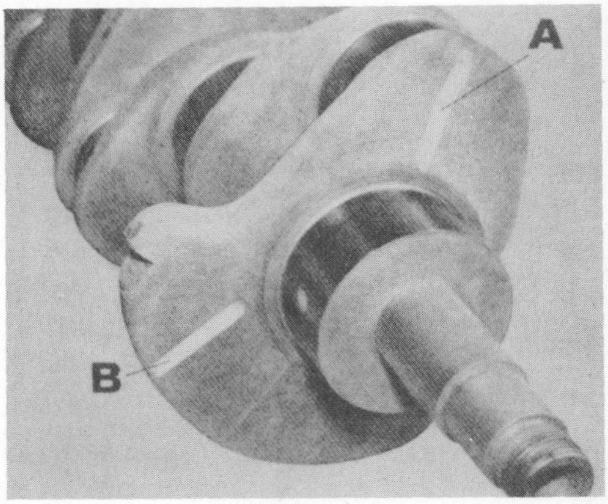

Rod bearing journal diameter marker (A) and main bearing journal diameter marker (B) for reground crankshaft. Single stripe indicates 1st undersize and two stripes indicate 2nd undersize.

stripes to indicate the 2nd undersize. One color stripe (at A) indicates the 1st undersize rod journal, and two stripes, the 2nd undersize. See Crankshaft, Camshaft, and Connecting Rod Specifications chart for sizes.

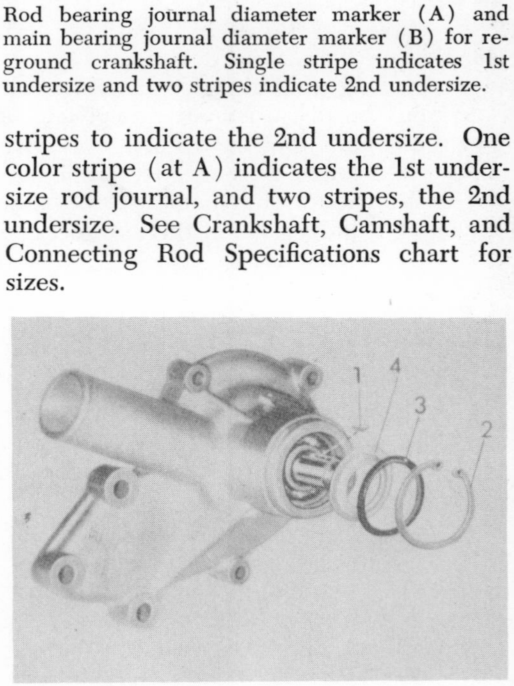

Water pump key (1), snap-ring (2), spacer (3), seal (4).

Check bearing clearance with Plastigage, type PG1. For undersize crankshafts, use corresponding oversize bearing shells. Measure each bearing separately with crankshaft motionless and at TDC. Tighten bearing caps to recommended torque.

Use of sleeve (608) to press water pump shaft from impeller (F).

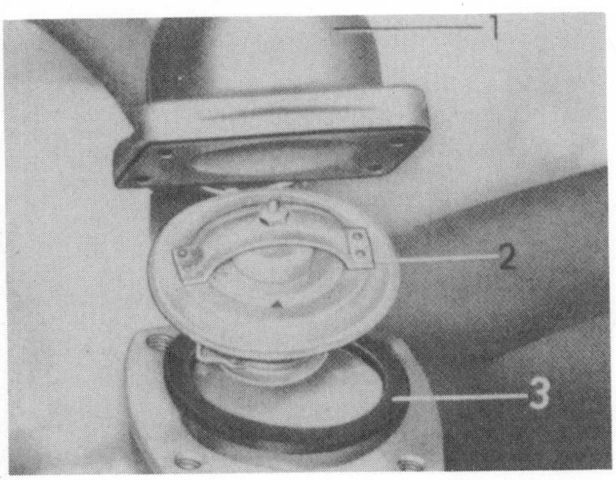

Thermostat components: housing (1), thermostat (2), gasket (3). Opening temperature: 163°-171°F or 181°F.

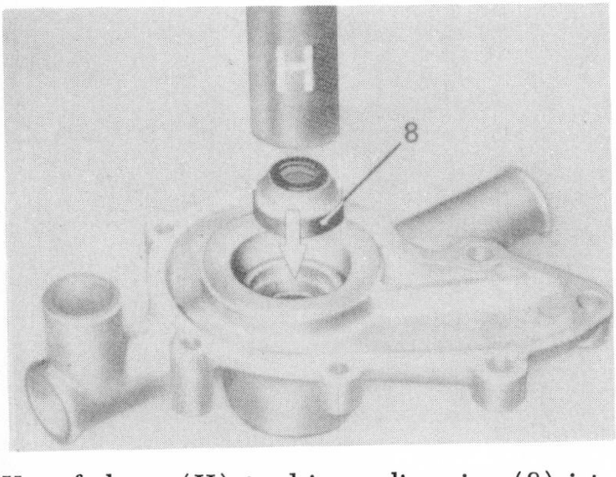

Use of sleeve (H) to drive sealing ring (8) into water pump housing.

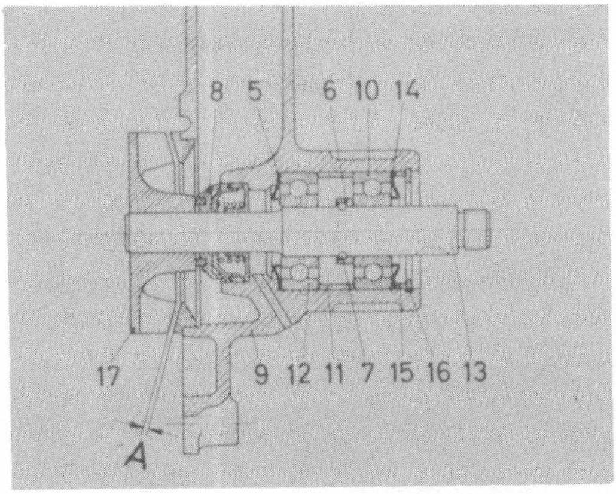

Water pump components: seal (5), lockrings (6, 7), seal ring (8), housing (9), ball bearing (10), spacer (11), ball bearing (12), shaft (13), seal ring (14), spacer (15), circlip (15, 16), impeller (17).
Dimension A = .038"-.047" (.8-1.2 mm).

Exhaust emission control system valve.

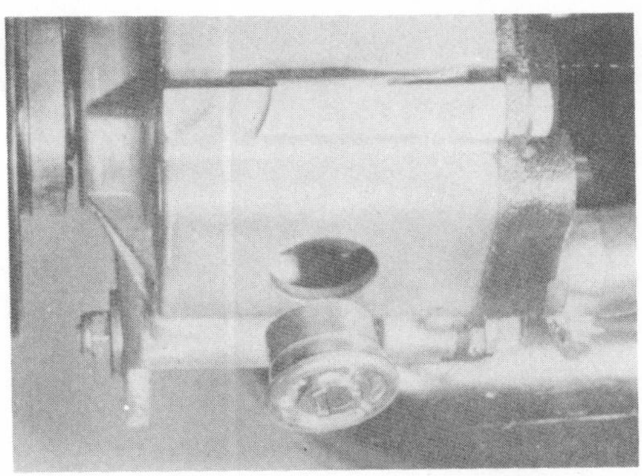

Pressure regulator unit.

Water Pump Servicing

Remove air filter, radiator, and fan, and pull fan pulley from water pump shaft. Remove mounting screws and water pump. Disassemble by removing flange (on one type), snap-ring, spacer and seal. Remove key from shaft and press shaft with bearing off the impeller. Drive sealing ring (8) out of housing.

When water pump is reassembled, there should be a clearance (A) of .038-.047" (.8-1.2 mm) between housing and impeller.

Exhaust Emission Control System Adjustments

It is important that all components be kept in precise adjustment for control of exhaust emissions. Properly adjusted dwell angle is essential to ignition timing, and the procedure for checking this is described in Chapter 5. Ignition timing and carburetor adjustment procedures for emission controlled engines are given in Chapter 1.

If carburetor cannot be adjusted properly, or backfiring occurs when the throttle is closed, change control valve.

Check operation of air pump by disconnecting blow-off line, and while accelerating engine, pressing hand lightly on pressure release valve to determine if it is operating. Valve should open at 1700-2000 rpm. If it opens sooner, replace the pressure regulator. Remove regulator with two screwdrivers. Press in new regulator carefully. If valve opens at higher engine speed, then the air pump must be changed. Check and renew pivot bushings if necessary. Adjust V-belt tension so that it can be depressed by finger pressure .2-.4" (5-10 mm).

Remove check valve for inspection and cleaning by loosening hose from air pump and hose clamp, and unscrewing valve from pipe. Injection pipes may be unscrewed after removing exhaust manifold. When replacing, allow injection pipes to extend .04" (1 mm) beyond flange.

Air pump mounting bolts (1).

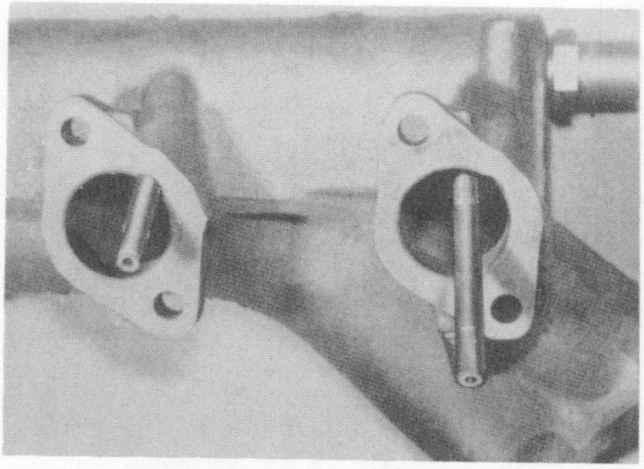

Injection pipes should extend .04" (1 mm) outside manifold flanges.

Exhaust gas system check valve hose (1) and pipe manifold clamp (arrow).

Chapter 4
Fuel System

Fuel Pump

BMW 1500, 1600, 1800 and 2000 Series cars are equipped with Solex carburetors, all of which are downdraft except for the side-draft types used on the 1600 TI, 1800 TI, 2000 TI and 2000 CS. Models 2500, 2800 and 2800 CS use dual Zenith downdraft carburetors. BMW's use Solex mechanical fuel pumps.

Fuel Pump Cleaning and Assembly

Sludge deposited in the fuel chamber or on the filter may be removed after removing the pump cover. Inlet and outlet valves should be inspected and replaced (by replacing the housing) if damaged. Check springs for good condition. Do not stretch springs for greater pressure; if weak or distorted, replace. Wash control mechanism for inlet chamber in fuel oil and lightly lubricate with thin oil. Fuel pump seals, even if only slightly damaged should be replaced. Lightly coat new seals with grease before assembly. If a new diaphragm is to be installed, soak it in kerosene for a few minutes before assembly.

Remove fuel pump. Remove insulating flange and plunger. Disassemble pump by removing screw (1), then screws (6). Remove screws and cover plate (9). Lift lockplate (10) from shaft (11), and tap shaft out with punch and hammer. Remove rocker arm (13) and its spring (12), and lift up diaphragm (14). Be careful not to change the length of the diaphragm spring which governs pump pressure. The valves in the upper section of the pump are part of the housing and cannot be replaced separately.

Fuel pump lines (1, 2), mounting bolts (3, 4) and serial number location (KN).

Since pump pressure is influenced by plunger length and insulating flange thickness, use replacement parts of the same length and thickness. For vehicles up to chassis No. 917583, combined thickness of flange and gaskets should be .19685″ (5 mm); plunger length should be 3.59456″ (91.3 mm). For vehicles from chassis No.

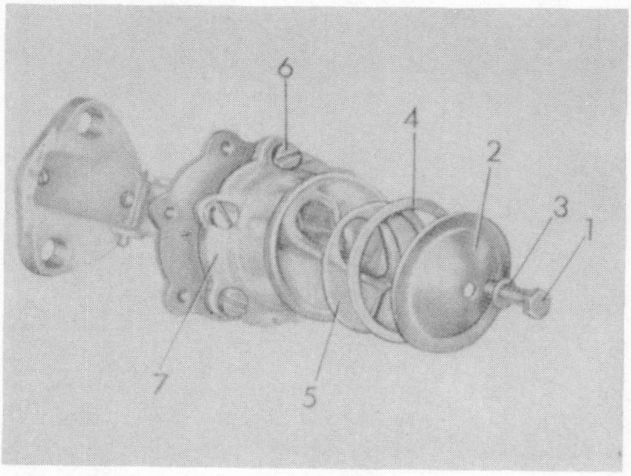

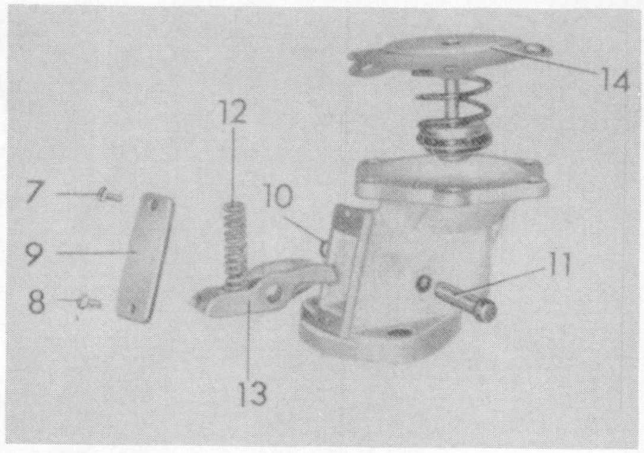

Fuel pump components: assembly screw and washer (1, 3), cap (2), gasket (4), filter (5), upper housing and screws (6, 7), cover plate and screws (8, 9), lockplate (10), shaft (11), rocker arm spring (12), rocker arm (13), diaphragm and spring (14).

Carburetor Specifications

Model	*Carburetor Type*	*Venturi Size*	*Main Jet Size*	*Idle (Pilot) Jet Size*	*Idle Air Port Size*	*Air Correct. Jet Size*	*Injection Pump Tube Size*	*Float Weight Oz./Gr.*	*Fuel Depth In Chamber In. (mm) Below Joint*
1500	Solex 36 PDSI	26	135	47.5	.50	110	.8	1.15/.85	.67-.75 (17-19)
1600	Solex 36 PDSI	26	140	47.5	.50	100	.8	1.15/.85	.67-.75 (17-19)
1600-2	Solex 38 PDSI	26	130	47.5	.50	110	.8	1.15/.85	.67-.75 (17-19)
1600TI	2 Solex 40 PHH	30	0120	50		155	.4	.4/10	***
1800, 1800A	Solex 38 PDSI	30	165, 160**	45,** 47.5	.50	155,** 90	.8	.3/8.5	.67-.75 (17-19)
1800/69	Solex 38 PDSI	30	165, 160**	45,** 47.5	.50	155,** 90	.8	.3/8.5	.67-.75 (17-19)
1800TI	2 Solex 40 PHH	32	0145	57.5		240	.5	.4/10	***
2000, 2000A	Solex 40 PDSIT,* 40 PDSI	30	155	45	.50	130	100	.3/8.5	.67-.75 (17-19)
2002	Solex 40 PDSIT* 40 PDSI	30	155	45	.50	130	100	.3/8.5	.67-.75 (17-19)
2000TI	2 Solex 40 PHH	34	0130	52.5		155	.5	.4/10	***
2000CS	2 Solex 40 PHH	34	0130	52.5		155	.5	.4/10	***
2000CA	Solex 40 PDSIT* 40 PDSI	30	155	45	.50	130	100	.3/8.5	.67-.75 (17-19)

***With automatic choke.** ****With air filter on carburetor.** *****Fuel line marked on exterior of float chamber housing.**

917584, thickness of flange and gaskets should be .78742″ (20 mm); plunger length should be 4.19299″ (106.5 mm). Carefully position diaphragm when reassembling. Pack lower part of pump with grease.

Carburetors

Carburetor Servicing

Carburetor repair kits are recommended for each overhaul. Kits contain a complete set of gaskets and new parts to replace those that generally deteriorate most rapidly. Not substituting *all* of the new parts supplied in the kits can result in poor performance later.

Air cleaner removal — all models with single downdraft carburetor.

Zenith/Solex carburetor repair kits are of three basic types — repair, Vit, and gasket. The following summarizes the parts in each type:

Vit kits
- all gaskets
- float needle valve
- volume control screw
- all diaphragms
- spring

Repair kits
- all jets and gaskets
- all diaphragms
- float needle valve
- volume control screw
- spring for pump diaphragm
- pump ball valve
- main jet carrier
- float
- complete intermediate rod
- intermediate pump lever
- complete injector tube
- some cover hold down screws and washers

Gasket kits
- all needed gaskets

Carburetor Overhaul

Carburetor overhaul should be performed only in a clean, dust-free area. Disassemble carburetor carefully, keeping look-alike parts separated to prevent accidental interchange at assembly. Note all jet sizes. When reassembling, make sure all screws and jets are tight in their seats. Tighten all screws gradually, in rotation. Do not tighten needle valves into seats. Uneven jetting will result. Use a new flange gasket.

Carburetor Cleaning

Wash carburetor parts — except diaphragm and electric choke units — in a carburetor cleaner, rinse in solvent, and blow dry with compressed air. Carburetors have numerous small passages that can be fouled by carbon and gummy deposits. Soak metal parts in carburetor solvent until thoroughly clean. The solvent will weaken or destroy cork, plastic, and leather components. These parts should be wiped with a clean, lint-free cloth. Clean all fuel channels in float bowl and cover. Clean jets and valves separately to avoid accidental interchange. Never use wire or sharp objects to clean jets and passages as this will seriously alter their calibration.

Check throttle valve shafts for wear or scoring that may allow air leakage affecting starting and idling. Inspect float spindle and other moving parts for wear. Replace if worn. Replace float if fuel has leaked into it. Accelerator pump check-valves should pass air one way but not the other. Test for proper seating by blowing and sucking on valve and replace if necessary. Wash valve again to remove breath moisture. Check bowl cover with a straight edge for warped surfaces. Closely inspect valves and seats for wear and damage.

Downdraft Carburetor Disassembly — 1500, 1600, 1600-2, 1800, 1800 A, 1800/69, 2000, 2000 A, 2002, 2000 CA

To remove carburetor, disconnect air filter (2) at (1 and 3) and remove filter. Remove fuel line (6) and vacuum line (7). Disconnect linkage (8), choke cable (17), if installed, from lever (18), and cable sleeve (19) from carburetor. Remove two mounting nuts and carburetor.

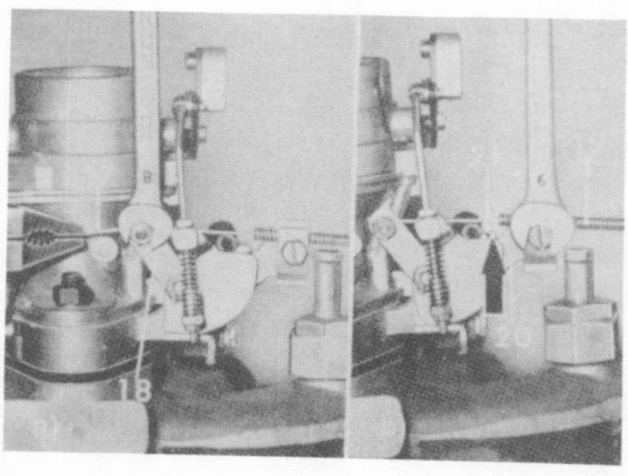

Disconnecting choke cable — single downdraft carburetor.

Remove carburetor cover (11) with gasket (12). Remove float spindle keeper (13) and lift out float (14) with its shaft. Remove main jet plug (15), washer (18) and main jet (H). Unscrew float needle valve (16) and lift out with its gasket (17). Unscrew air correction jet (19). Unscrew idle mixture adjusting screw (G) and remove with spring. Unscrew idling jet (20). Unscrew enrichment valve (A) and remove with washer. Disconnect pump linkage and remove with washer. Disconnect pump linkage and remove pump cover (21) with linkage. Remove diaphragm (22) and spring (23).

After cleaning and checking components, reassemble carburetor, install on engine, and make the following inspections and adjustments.

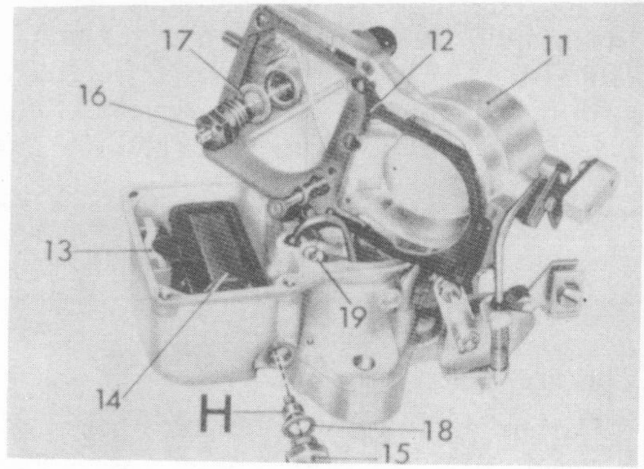

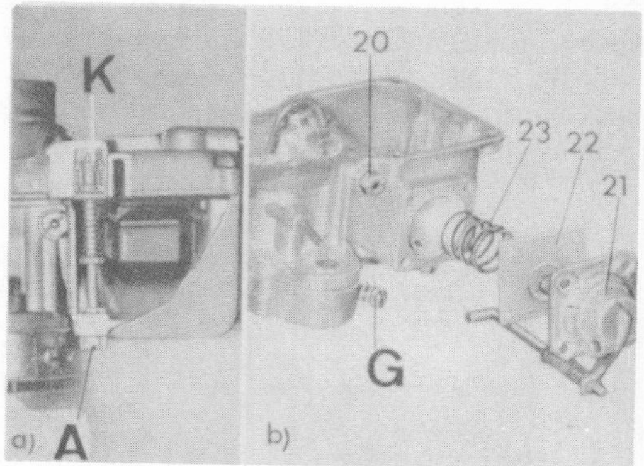

Downdraft carburetor components: cover (11), gasket (12), float spindle keeper (13), float (14), main jet plug (15), float needle valve (16), float needle valve gasket (17), washer (18), main jet (H), air correction jet (19), idling jet (20), pump cover (21), diaphragm (22), spring (23), enrichment valve (A), piston (K), idle mixture adjustment screw (G).

Warm engine to normal operating temperature. Set idling speed with stop-screw (24). Adjust idling mixture with screw (25) until engine reaches maximum idling speed, then correct idling speed with screw (24). Allow engine to run briefly at idling speed. Shut down engine to check fuel level in carburetor bowl. Remove fuel line (26) and seal off supply line. Remove carburetor cover (27). Fuel level (N) should be .67-.75″ (17-19 mm) in depth. Fuel level varies with the thickness of the float needle valve gasket (29). The original thickness of this gasket is .04″ (1 mm). If fuel level is not within specifications, replace this gasket. Use a thinner gasket to raise the level and a thicker one to lower the level.

Carburetor adjusting procedures for models with emission controls are given in Chapter 1.

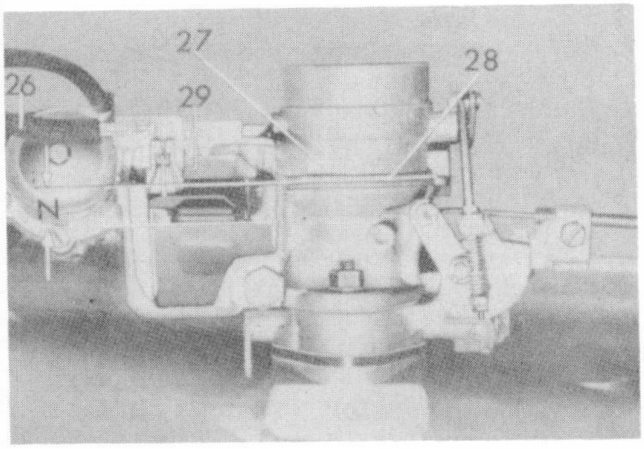

Downdraft carburetor adjustment and fuel level measurement. Idling stop-screw (24), idling mixture adjustment (25), fuel line (26), cover and gasket (27, 28), fuel depth (N).

Pump injection volume is adjusted by loosening locknut (15) and turning nut (17) of linkage (16). Screw in to increase volume; screw out to decrease. Correct injection volume is .7-.9 cc.

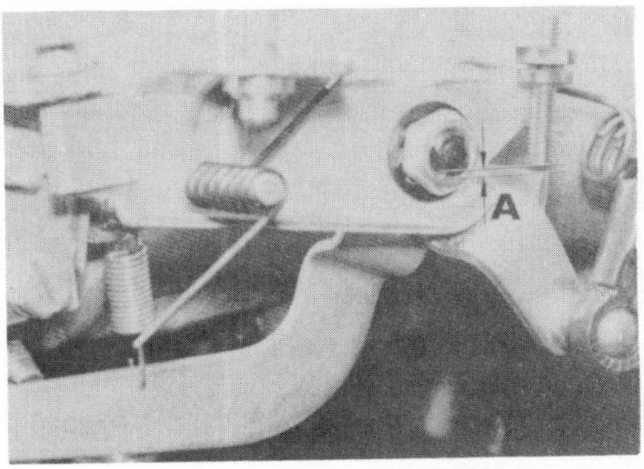

Choke butterflies are correctly adjusted when clearance at (A) is .008" (.2 mm).

Dual Twin-Choke Carburetor Servicing — 1600 TI, 1800 TI, 2000 TI, 2000 CS

To remove carburetors, disconnect and remove air filter. Remove screws (3 and 4) from support (1). Disconnect choke rod (5) and springs (6). Disconnect fuel lines. Remove mounting nuts and carburetors. Install carburetors in reverse order from above.

Twin carburetor removal. Fuel lines (1, 2), support (L), support screws (3, 4), rod (5), springs (6), Arrows show carburetor mounting screws.

Adjust rod length (B) to 1.614", (41 mm).

— Carburetor compl.
— Throttle body with throttle spindle, throttle butterfly, fixing screws
1 Throttle body
2 Throttle spindle with intermediate lever
3 Throttle butterfly
4 Fixing screw
5 Return spring
6 Intermediate lever compl.
7 Distance washer (between throttle lever and intermediate lever)
8 Throttle lever compl.
9 Tab washer
10 Throttle spindle end nut
11 Slow running adjustment screw (on throttle lever)
12 Slow running adjustment screw spring
13 Volume control screw
14 Volume control screw spring
15 Bowden cable bracket
16 Cable clamp
17 Clamping screw
18 Hexagon screw (for bowden cable bracket)
19 Spring washer (for hexagon screw)
20 Bearing pin
21 Bearing pin spring washer
— Starter lever with clamping screw and roller bracket
22 Starter lever
— Clamping screw compl.
23 Clamping screw
24 Bushing
25 Washer
26 Hexagon nut
27 Grip roller
28 Spring washer
29 Washer
30 Split pin
31 Starter control rod
32 Clamping ring (for starter control rod)
33 Spring (for starter control rod)
34 Shoulder nut (for starter control rod)
35 Hexagon nut (for starter control rod)
36 Throttle body fixing screw
37 Insulating gasket
38 Float chamber with pressed-in emulsion tube and injector tube
39 Float 8.5 gr.
40 Float toggle spindle
41 Holder for float toggle spindle
42 Choke tube
43 Enrichment valve
44 Enrichment valve washer
45 Pilot jet
46 Main jet
47 Main jet screw plug
48 Screw plug washer
49 Air correction jet
50 Diaphragm compl.
51 Diaphragm spring
— Pump cover compl.
52 Pump cover
53 Pump lever
54 Pump lever spindle
55 Fixing screw
— Pump control rod compl.
56 Pump control rod
57 Pump control rod washer
58 Pump control rod spring
59 Pump control rod split pin
60 Pump control rod clip
61 Float chamber cover gasket
62 Float chamber cover compl. with depression actuated piston
— Depression actuated piston compl.
63 Spring (for depression actuated piston)
— Cover plate
64 Washer
65 Spring washer
66 Float needle valve 2 mm with ball
67 Float needle valve washer
68 Strangler spindle compl. (with lever, grip roller)
69 Grip roller
70 Grip roller washer
71 Strangler
72 Strangler fixing screw
73 Assembly screw with spring washer
— Enrichment tube
— Collet

Adjusting Dual Twin-Choke Carburetors

Make the following basic adjustments before starting engine:

Disconnect and remove air filter.

Carefully tighten idling mixture adjusting screws (1-4) until they are fully in, then release one-half turn.

Loosen synchronizing screw (5) until it no longer touches throttle lever (7).

Unscrew idling stop screw (6) as far as it will go.

Screw in synchronizing screw (5) until it just contacts throttle lever (7).

Screw in idling stop screw (6) until it just contacts the throttle plate lever.

Turn idling stop screw (6) in an additional two turns.

All four carburetor throats must be ad-

NOTE: *correct ignition timing and valve adjustment are necessary for proper carburetor tuning.*

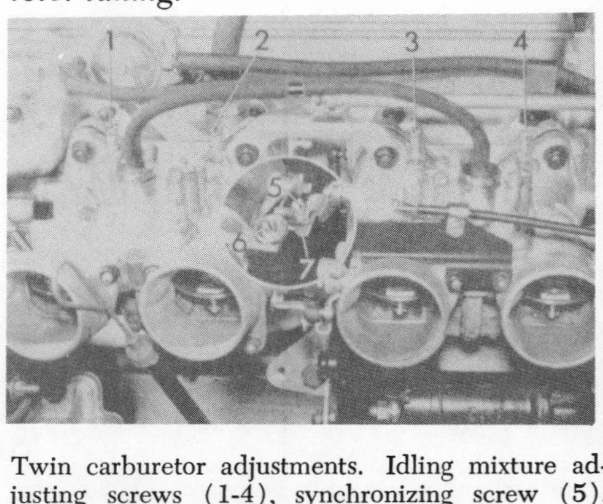

Twin carburetor adjustments. Idling mixture adjusting screws (1-4), synchronizing screw (5), idling stop screw (6), throttle lever (7).

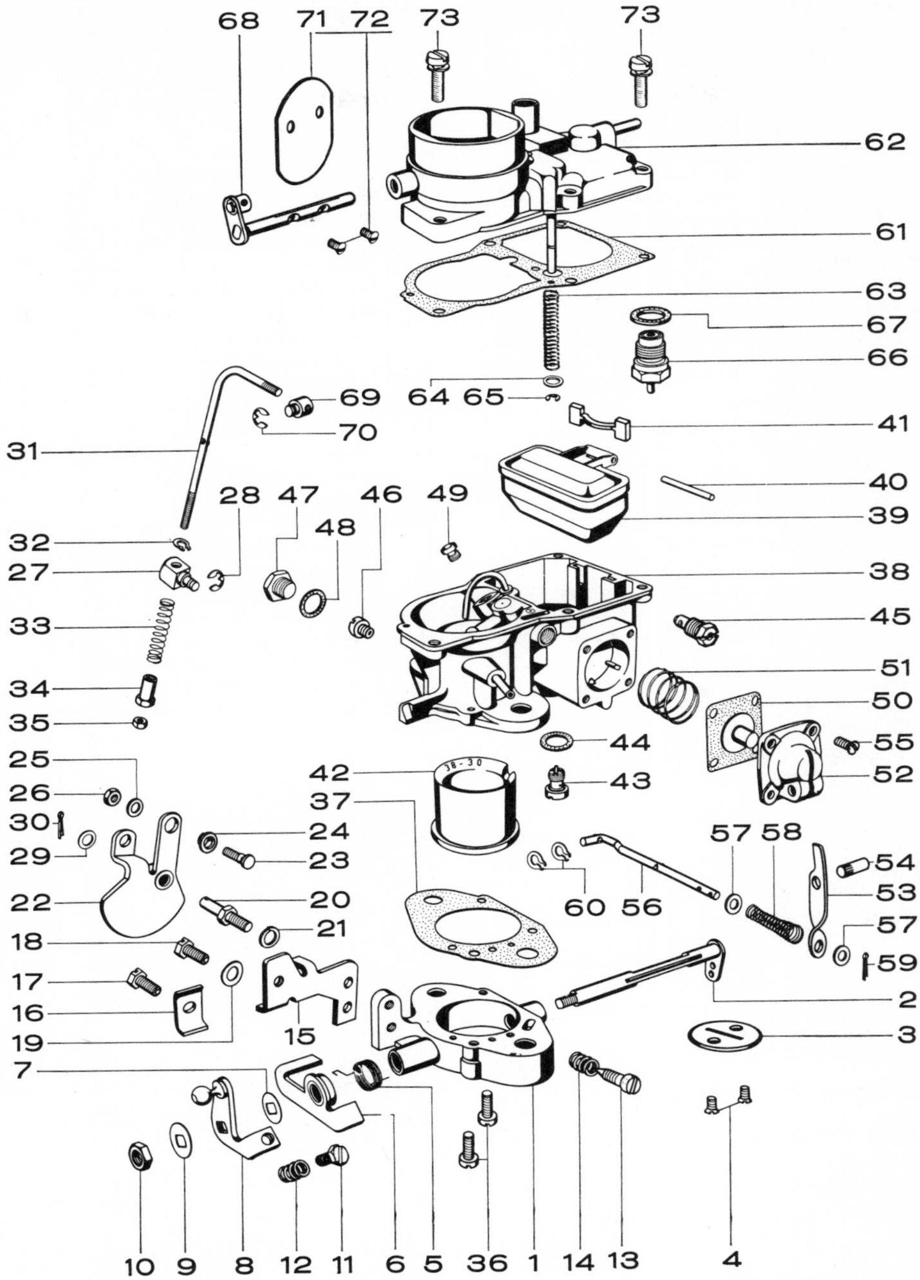

Components of Solex 36 PDSI carburetor used on 1500 and 1600 models.

justed to pass an equal volume of air. This can be done by using a carburetor synchronizing gauge, or by listening through a short section of water hose to the pitch of the hiss made by the entering air. The gauge is adjusted on the throat of one carburetor for a piston height near the middle of the scale. The unit is then switched to the other carburetor and, if necessary, the carburetor is re-set so that the position of the piston matches that for the first carburetor. The idle stop screws may then be adjusted for equal idling with the help of the synchronizing gauge.

With the engine running at 1200 rpm:

Synchronize carburetor (2) of second cylinder with carburetor (3) of third cylinder by means of adjusting screw (5).

— Carburetor compl.
1 Body compl.
2 Enrichment valve compl.
3 Enrichment valve washer
4 Idle jet compl.
5 Main jet
6 Main jet screw plug
7 Screw plug washer
8 Air correction jet
9 Diaphragm compl.
10 Diaphragm spring
11 Pump cover compl.
12 Pump cover fixing screw
13 Choke tube
14 Choke tube fixing screw
15 Hexagon nut
16 Insulating gasket
17 Throttle body compl.
18 Throttle level compl.
19 Toothed washer (on throttle spindle)
20 Throttle spindle end nut
21 Slow running adjustment screw
22 Slow running adjustment screw spring
23 Control rod (between starter and throttle lever)
24 Control rod clip
25 Control rod nut
26 Control rod compl. (between intermediate lever and pump lever)
27   Control rod
28   Spring
29   Split pin
30   Clip
31   Washer
32   Washer
33 Volume control screw
34 Volume control screw spring
35 Throttle body fixing screw
36 Float compl.
37 Float toggle spindle
38 Float toggle spindle holder
39 Float chamber cover gasket
40 Float chamber cover compl.
41   Spring (for starter diaphragm)
42   Valve cover (for starter diaphragm)
43   Valve cover fixing screw
44   Spindle with abutment lever compl.
45   Strangler lever compl.
46   Strangler lever
47   Clamp roller
48   Clip
49   Hexagon nut
50   Clip
51 Insulating washer
52 Starter cover compl.
53 Starter cover compl.
54   Water connection
55   O-ring
56   Cylindrical screw (with internal hexagon)
57   Washer
58 Retaining ring
59 Fixing screw (for retaining ring)
60 Float needle valve compl.
61 Float needle valve washer
62 Assembly screw

Synchronize carburetor (1) of first cylinder with carburetor (2) of second cylinder by means of adjusting screw (8).

Synchronize carburetor (4) of fourth cylinder with carburetor (3) of third cylinder by means of adjusting screw (9).

Adjust idling mixture screws for maximum engine idling speed.

Set engine idling speed to 800 rpm by means of idling stop screws.

Tuning twin carburetors. Synchronizing adjustments (5, 8, 9), carburetor throats (1-4).

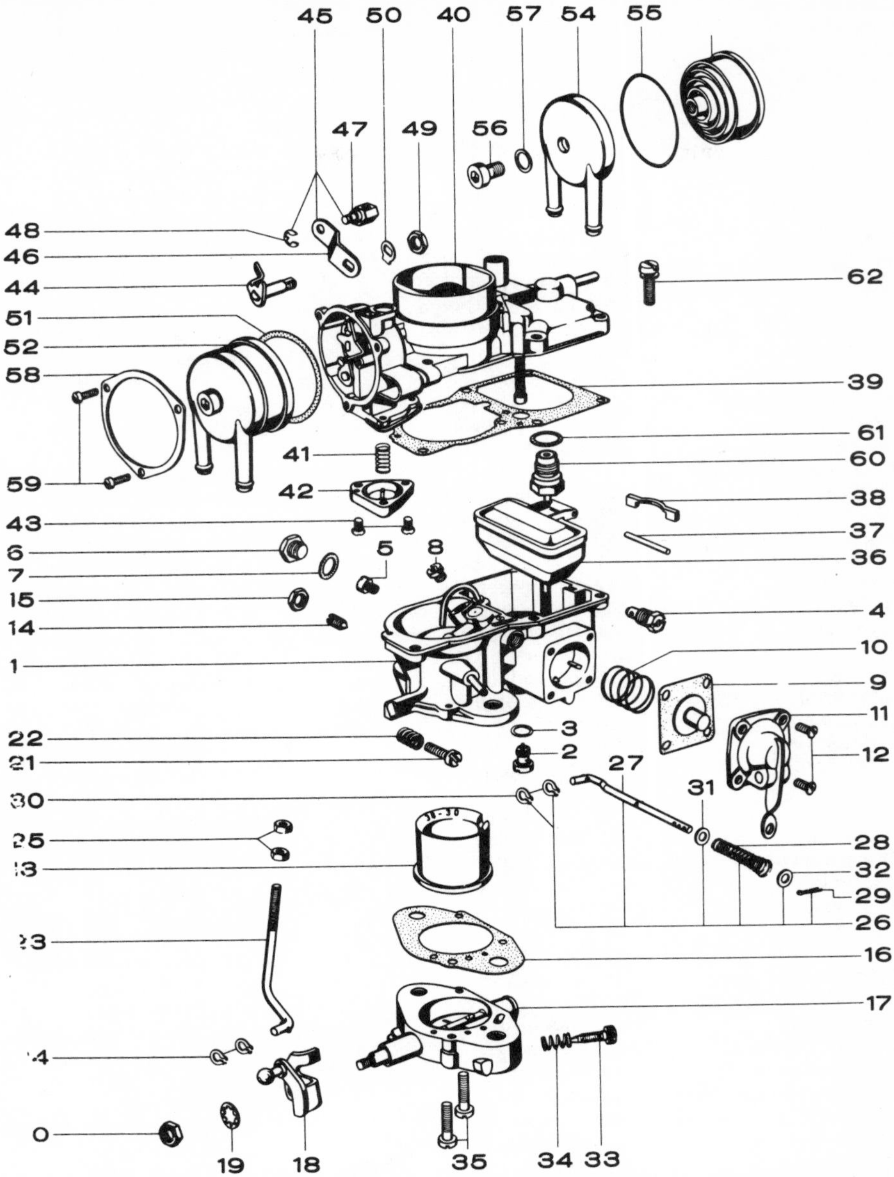

Components of Solex 40 PDSIT carburetor used on 2002, 2000, and 2000 CA models.

1, 1a Throttle valve
2 Pin screw
3 Screw
4 Screw
5 Joint lever
6 Return spring
7 Safety washer
8 Roller
9 Safety washer
10 Flat washer
11 Safety washer
12 Idle mixture screw
13 Pressure spring
14 Adjustment screw
15 Spring washer
16 Hex head nut
17 Flat washer
18 Throttle lever
19 Safety washer
20 Spacer
21 Choke body
22 Return spring
23 Diaphragm spring
24 Pressure spring
25 Valve cover
26 Screw
27 Seal ring
28 Hex head nut
29 Countersunk screw
30 Operating lever
31 Transfer lever
32 Spring washer
33 Hex head nut
34 Gasket
35 Gasket
36 Star washer
37 Countersunk screw
38 Spring washer
39 Screw
40 Safety washer
41 Stop lever
42 Pressure spring
43 Stop screw
44 Hex head nut
45 Choke cover
46 Stop ring
47 Hex head nut
48 Hex head nut
49 Clamp
50 Isolation flange
51 Spring washer
52 Screw
53 Float bowl
54 Spring washer
55 Bearing bolt
56 Safety washer
57 Cheesehead screw
58 Spring washer
59 Vacuum chamber
60 Lockwasher
61 Bearing bolt
62 Operating lever
63 Cheesehead screw
64 Hex head nut
65 Expansion ring
66 Threaded pin
67 Cable holder
68 Seal ring
69 Spring washer
70 Cheesehead screw
71 Connecting rod
72 Return spring
73 Connecting rod
74 Flat washer
75 Pressure spring
76 Washer
77 Tension ring
78 Seal ring
79 Air valve
80 Bushing
81 Needle valve
82 Seal ring
83 Float
84 Shaft
85 Bracket
86 Cheesehead screw
87 Spring washer
88 Main jet
89 Mixture tube
90 Air correction jet
91 Main jet
92 Mixture tube
93 Air correction jet
94 Idle jet
95 Jet
96 Pump suction valve
97 Seal ring
98 Pump pressure valve
99 Seal ring
100 Jet
101 Seal ring
102 Sprayer
103 Pressure screw
104 Seal ring
105 Pump piston
106 Pump lever
107 Inner pump lever
108 Countersunk screw
109 Cheesehead screw
110 Lockwasher
111 Spring washer
112 Complete operating lever
113 Platin block
114 Carburetor body gasket
115 Carburetor top
116 Seal ring
117 Cover
118 Lockwasher
119 Cheesehead screw
120 Lockwasher
121 Cheesehead screw
122 Cheesehead screw
123 Cheesehead screw
124 Joint piece
125 Safety washer
126 Cheesehead screw
127 Fuel return valve
128 Ring hose piece
129 Seal ring
130 Threaded fitting
131 Seal ring
132 Operating lever
133 Vacuum regulator
134 Rubber hose
135 Lockwasher
136 Cheesehead screw

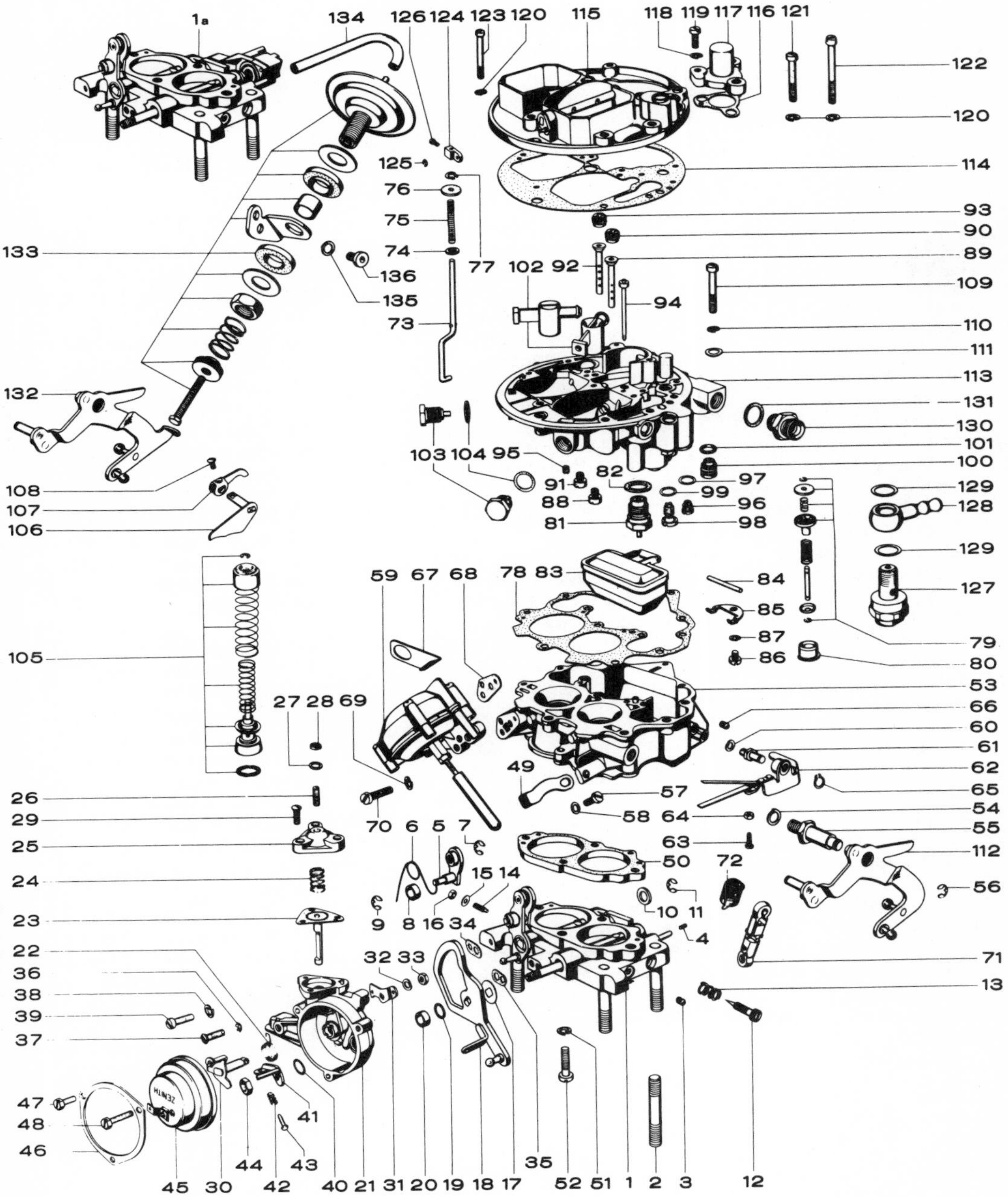

Components of typical Zenith 35/40 INAT downdraft carburetor, used in dual installations on 2500, 2800, 2800 CS.

1 Jets inspection cover
2 Screw securing carburetor cover
2A Securing screw for well-bottom cover
3 Gasket for jets inspection cover
4 Normal washer
4A Normal washer
5 Carburetor cover
6 Gasket for carburetor cover
7 Emulsioning tube holder
8 Air corrector jet
9 Idling jet-holder
10 Emulsioning tube
11 Idling jet
12 Main jet
13 Plate for carburetor bowl
14 Choke
15 Auxiliary venturi
16 Dust cover
17 Spring
18 Spring retaining cover
19 Shim washer—DCOE 15
19A Shim washer—DCOE 16
20 Air intake horn
21 Retaining plate
22 Auxiliary venturi fixing screw
22A Choke fixing screw
23 Spring washer
23A Spring washer
24 Carburetor anchoring nut
24A Nut for air intake
25 Stud bolt
26 Throttle control lever—DCOE 16
27 Lockwasher
28 Hexagonal nut
29 Gasket for cap
30 Cap for bottom of bowl
31 Carburetor body
34 Lever fixing pin
35 Pump control lever
36 Stud bolt
37 Stud bolt
38 Ball bearing
39 Throttle securing screw
40 Throttle valve
41 Throttle spindle
42 Starter control securing screw
43 Normal washer
44 Cap securing screw
45 Cap for pump opening
46 Gasket for cap
47 Starter control, including:
48 Starter control lever, complete with:
49 Starter lever
50 Nut for screw
51 Cable securing screw
52 Lever securing nut
53 Lever return spring
54 Sheath securing screw
55 Cover for sheath support
56 Strainer
57 Starter shaft
58 Spring washer
59 Starter valve
60 Spring for starter valve
61 Spring retainer and guide
62 Spring washer
63 Spring retaining plate
64 Pump control rod
65 Spring for plunger
66 Pump plunger
67 Spring for idling adjustment screw
67A Throttle adjusting spring—DCOE 15
68 Idling adjustment screw
69 Throttle adjusting screw—DCOE 15
70 Screw for progression holes inspection
71 Gasket for pump jet
72 Pump jet
73 Seal
74 Screw plug
75 Intake and discharge valve
76 Starter jet
77 Float
78 Fulcrum pin
79 Ball for valve
80 Stuffing for ball
81 Retaining screw for stuffing ball
82 Gasket for needle valve
83 Needle valve
84 Gasket for union
85 Spherical union
86 Gasket for union
87 Screw plug for union
88 Strainer
89 Gasket for filter plug
90 Filter inspection plug
91 Plug for protecting strainer
92 Throttle control lever—DCOE 15, including:
93 Spring
94 Throttle adjusting screw
95 Spring
96 Throttle control lever

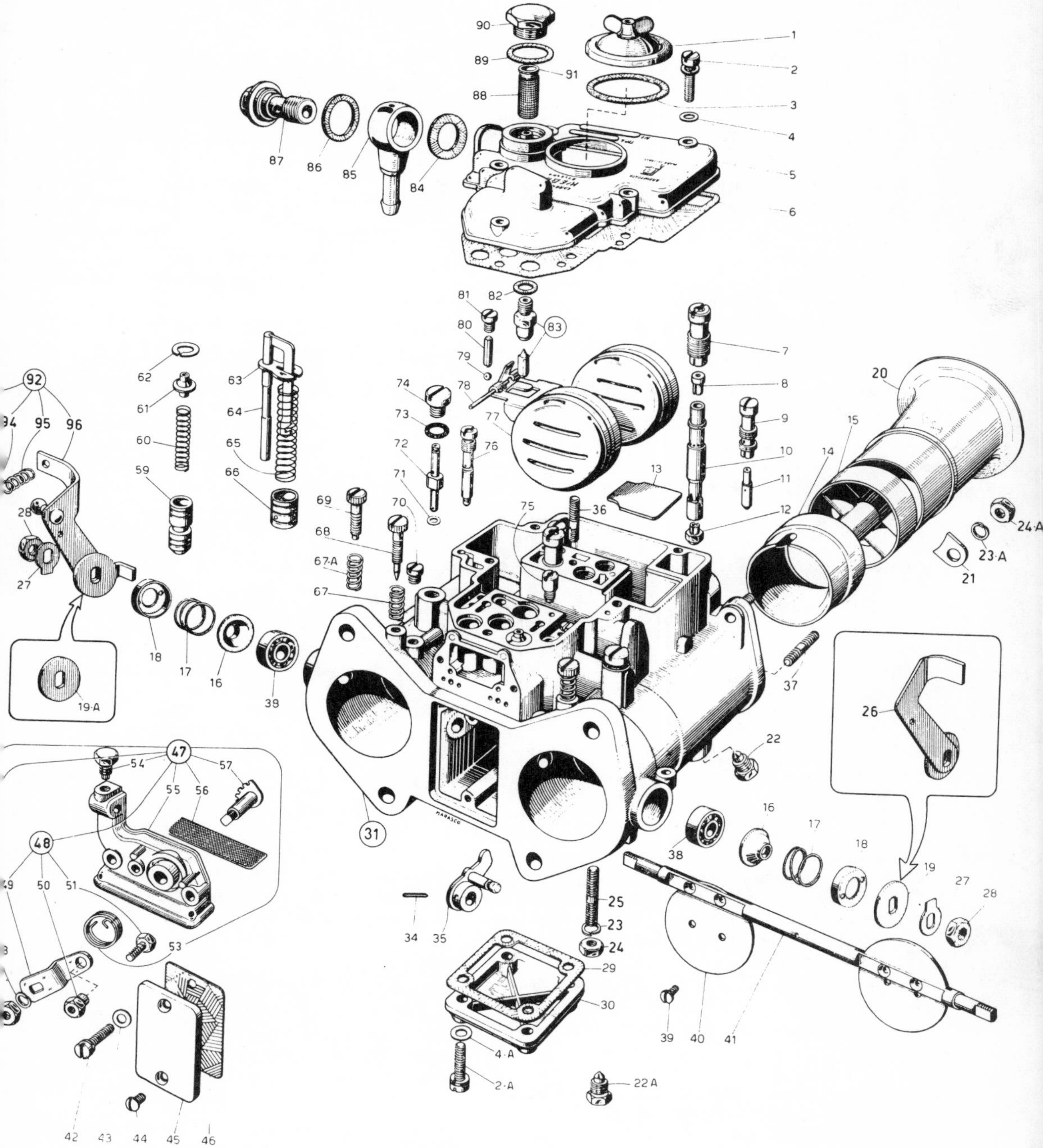

Components of Weber 45 DCOE 15/16 sidedraft carburetors, used in a dual installation on the 1800 TISA.

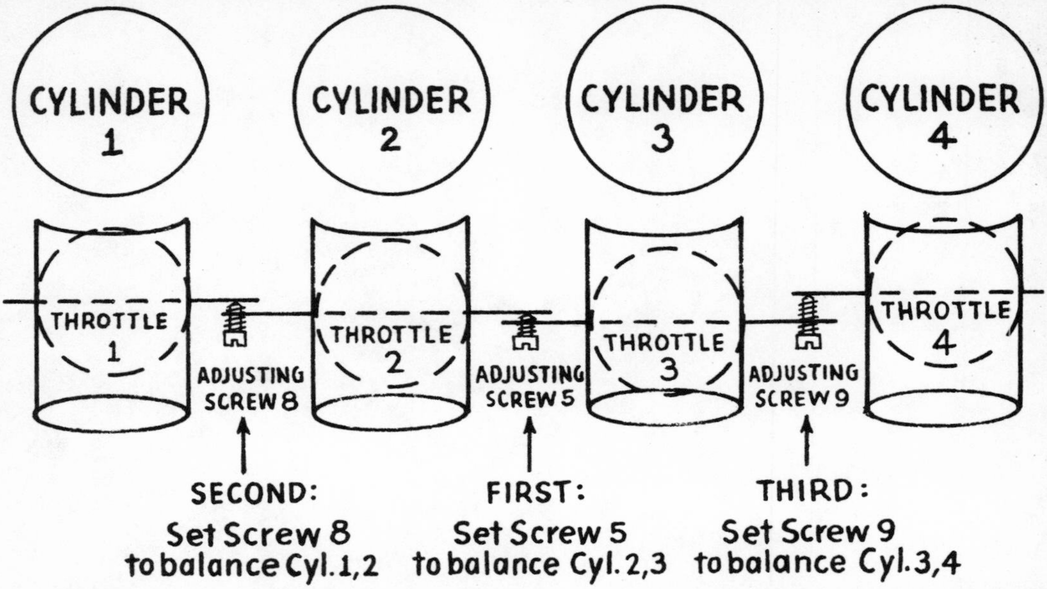

Throttle balancing sequence for dual twin-choke sidedraft carburetors — 1600 TI, 1800 TI, 2000 TI, 2000 CS.

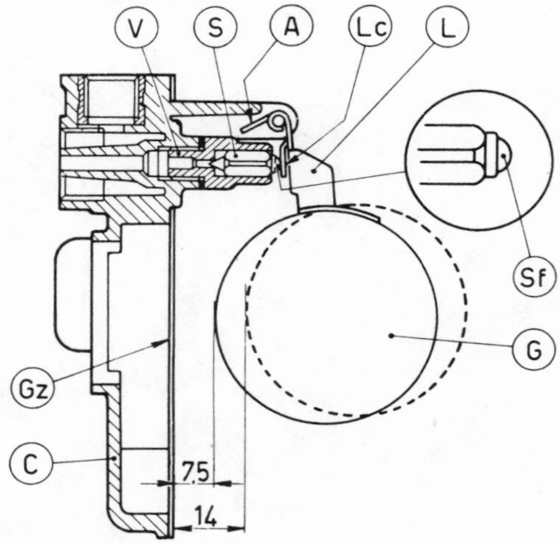

Procedure for adjusting float level on Weber 45 DCOE 15/16 carburetors: Make sure that the weight of the float (G) is correct (26 gr.), that float can pivot freely, and is not pitted.

Make sure that needle valve (V) is tightly screwed in its housing and that pin ball (Sf) of the damping device, incorporated in the needle (S), is not jammed.

Keep the carburetor cover (C) in vertical position as indicated, since the weight of the float (G) could lower the pin ball (Sf) fitted on the needle (S).

With carburetor cover (C) in vertical position and float clip (Lc) in light contact with the pin ball (Sf) of the needle (S), the distance of both half-floats (G) from upper surface of carburetor cover (C), without gasket, must measure 7.5 mm.

After the levelling has been done, check that the stroke of float (G) is 6.5 mm. If necessary adjust the position of the lug (A).

Should the float (G) not be correctly placed, bend the tabs (L) of the float, taking care that the tab (Lc) is perpendicular to the needle axis (S) and that it doesn't have any indentations on the contact surface which might affect the free movement of the needle itself.

Fit the carburetor cover making sure that the float can move without any hindrance or friction.

NOTE — The float level must be checked whenever it is necessary to replace float or needle valve: in the latter case it is advisable to replace the sealing gasket, making sure that the new needle valve is tightly screwed into its housing.

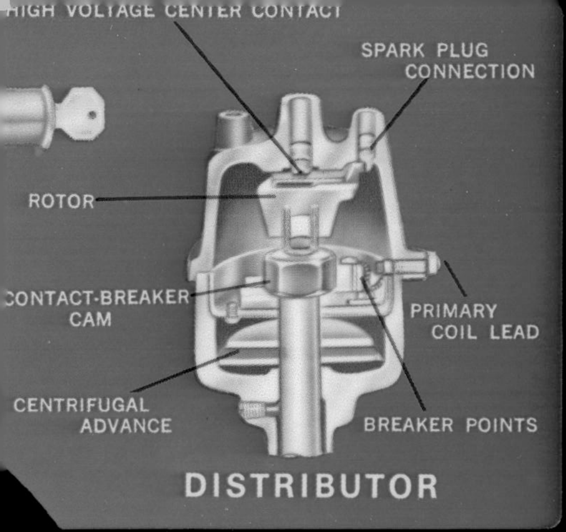

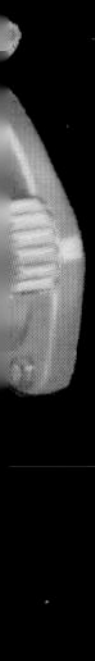

Internal-combustion gasoline engines run only if air, fuel, compression and spark are brought together in the cylinders at the same instant. This illustration shows a typical electrical system, the nerve center of any engine, with its major parts interconnected. The system includes the starting circuit (battery, solenoid and starter), the spark circuit (coil, condenser, breaker points, rotor and spark plugs), and the charging circuit (generator and regulator-cutout). Keeping the electrical system in good order eliminates most sources of engine trouble.

THE ELECTRICAL SYSTEM

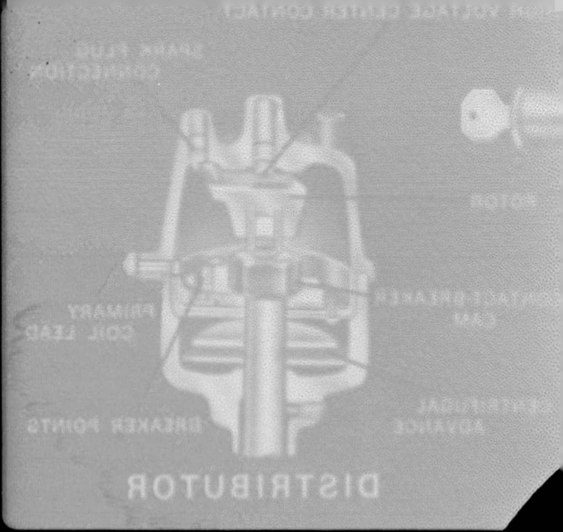

Internal-combustion gasoline engines run only if air, fuel, compression and spark are brought together in the cylinders at the same instant. This illustration shows a typical electrical system, the nerve center of any engine, with its major parts interconnected. The system includes the starting circuit (battery, solenoid and starter), the spark circuit (coil, condenser, breaker points, rotor and spark plugs), and the charging circuit (generator and regulator-cutout). Keeping the electrical system in good order eliminates most sources of engine trouble.

THE ELECTRICAL SYSTEM

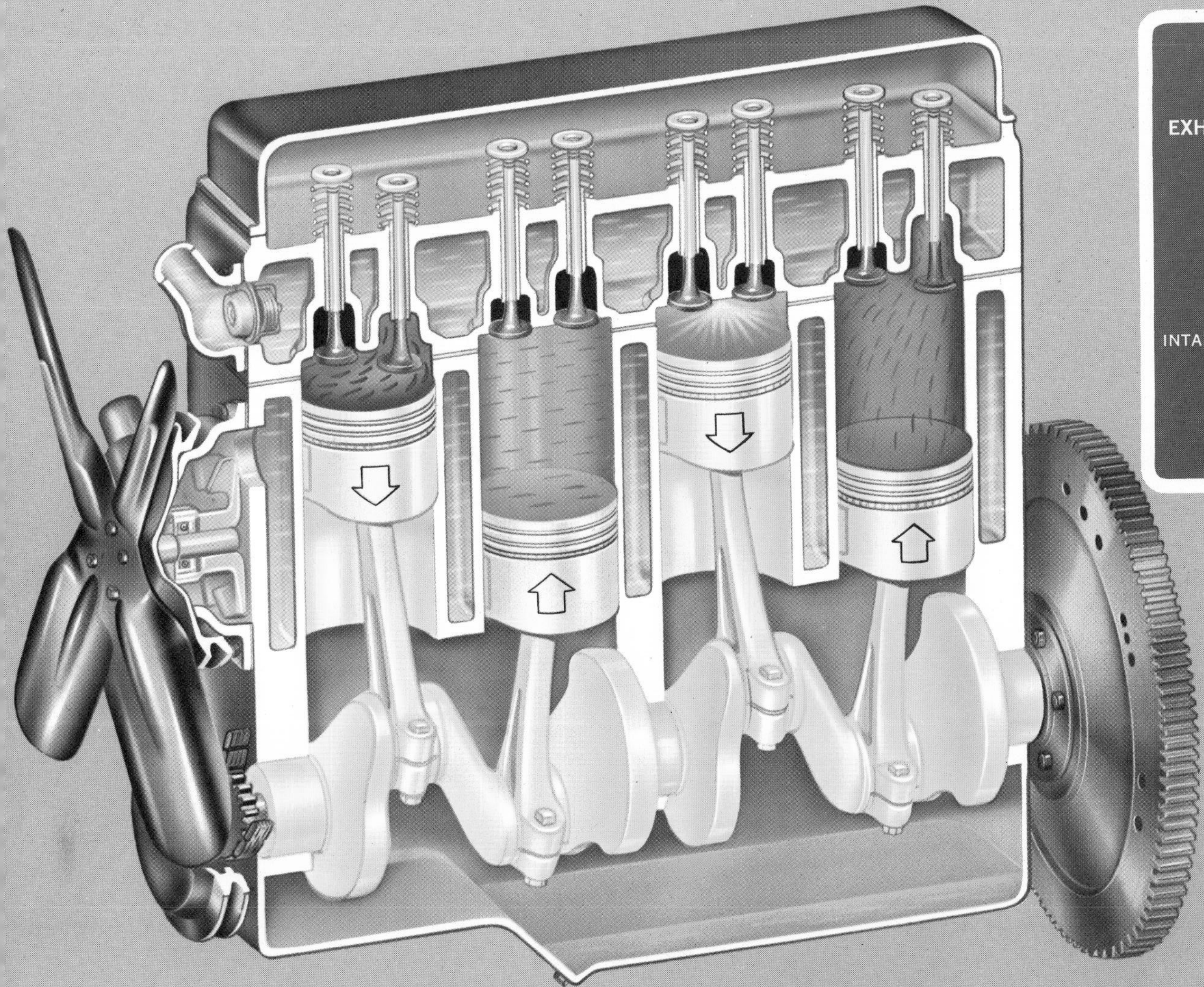

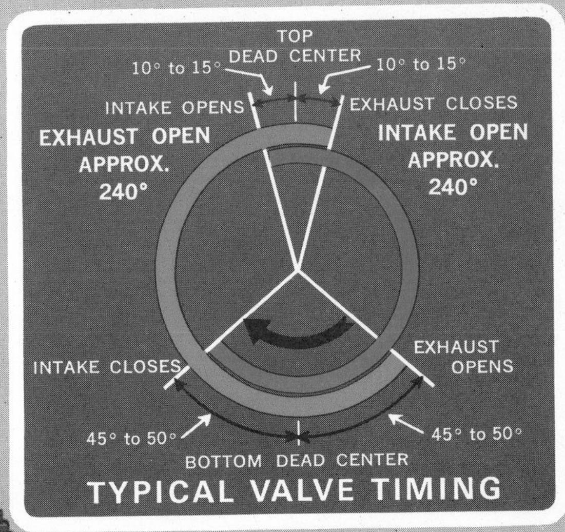

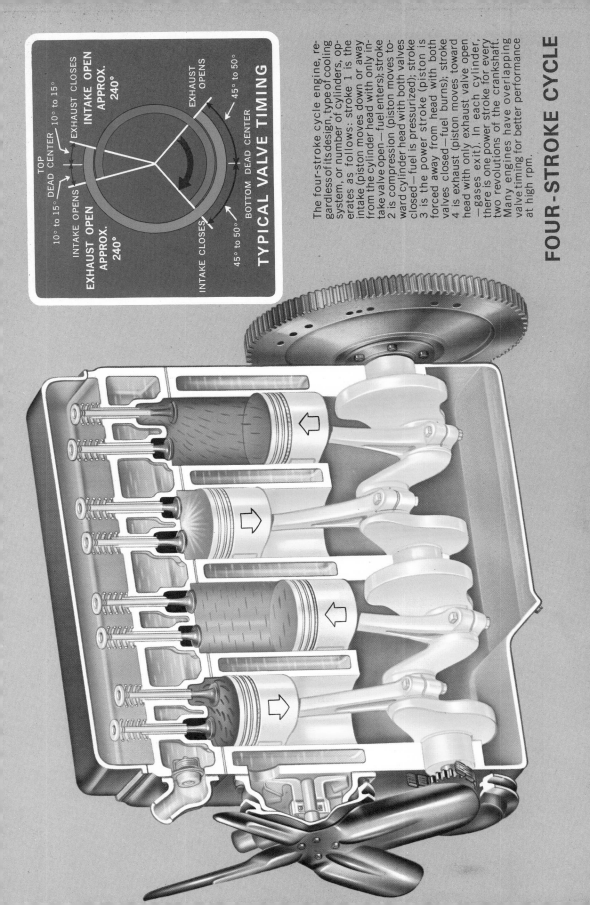

The four-stroke cycle engine, regardless of its design, type of cooling system, or number of cylinders, operates as follows: stroke 1 is the intake (piston moves down or away from the cylinder head with only intake valve open—fuel enters); stroke 2 is compression (piston moves toward cylinder head with both valves closed—fuel is pressurized); stroke 3 is the power stroke (piston is forced away from head with both valves closed—fuel burns); stroke 4 is exhaust (piston moves toward head with only exhaust valve open—gases exit). In each cylinder, there is one power stroke for every two revolutions of the crankshaft. Many engines have overlapping valve timing for better performance at high rpm.

FOUR-STROKE CYCLE

Chapter 5
Electrical Systems

BMW 1500, 1600, 1800, 1800 A, 1800 TI and some 1600-2 models are equipped with 6-volt systems. These use 200 watt DC generators except for the 1800 TI which has a 350 watt alternator. All 12-volt systems employ 450 watt alternators. Starters, generators, alternators, regulators, and coils are all manufactured by Bosch.

Alternator and Regulator

The alternator is a continuous output (even at idle) diode-rectified AC generator. It has three-phase stator (housing) windings assembled on the inside of a laminated core that is the middle section of the housing. Rectifier diodes which change AC to DC are connected to the windings (3 diodes to each phase). If the alternator does not meet output specifications, the alternator and regulator are usually replaced. The alternator requires no lubrication. The diodes in the alternator are one-way devices, allowing current to flow only from the alternator to the battery; battery current cannot discharge through the alternator. As a result, a current breaker, or cutout relay, is not needed in the regulator. The regulator used with the alternator needs only a voltage regulator which requires no adjustment.

DC Generator and Regulator

The DC generator has a rotating armature with copper windings that intersect lines of magnetic force between magnetic field poles. At the start, the magnetic field is weak because it is only residual. However, as current flows from the armature windings, part of the flow is fed into and excites the magnetic field. Increasing speed intensifies the magnetic field and thereby increases the voltage from the windings. The magnetic field becomes saturated with energy and no further increase in armature speed will add to the output.

Since voltage produced by the generator is in direct proportion to the product of armature speed and exciting current in the magnetic field, a constant voltage output can be maintained by making compensating adjustments to the exciting current. Armature speed is based on engine rpm and is therefore not independently controllable. The regulator maintains a constant voltage output by interrupting the exciting current.

Testing DC Generator and Regulator

After checking condition and tension of the fan belt, connect a 60-0-60 range ammeter in series with the regulator and battery by disconnecting the red lead from the

Electrical Equipment Specifications

Model	Battery		Starter	Generator		Alternator		Regulator			Coil	
	Amp-Hrs.	Volts/Ground	Bosch Type	Bosch Type	Max. Amp. Output	Bosch Type	Max. Amp. Output	Bosch Type	Cut-In V.	Reg. V.	Bosch Type	Mean Watts
1500, 1600, 1600-2	77	6/N	GF(R) 6V	LJ/GEG200/ 6/2400R	50			RS/VA200/ 6A/(1/1)	5.9-6.5	6.3-7.6	TE6B4	12-15
1600-2 (Later Models)	36	12/N	EF(R) 12V			KI/14V/ 35A20	35	AD1/14V			K12V	19
1600TI	44	12/N	EF(R) 12V			KI/14V/ 35A20	35	AD1/14V		13.5-14.2	K12V	19
1800, 1800A	77	6/N	GF(R) 6V	LJ/GEG200/ 6/2400R	50			RS/VA200/ 6A/(1/1)	5.9-6.5	6.3-7.6	TE6B4	12-15
1800/69	77	12/N	EF(R) 12V			KI/14V/ 35A20	35	AD 1/14V		13.5-14.2	TE6B4	12-15
1800TI	66	6/N	GF(R) 6V			KI/7V/ 50A17	50	ADN 1/7V		6.3-7.6	TK6A3	13-16
2002, 2000, 2000A, 2000TI, 2000CS, 2000CA	44	12/N	GF(R) 12V			KI/14V/ 35A20	35	ADN 1/14V		12.6-14.6	K12V	19
2500, 2800	55	12/N	GF(R) 12V			KI/14V/ 35A20	35	ADN1/14V		12.6-14.6	K12V	19

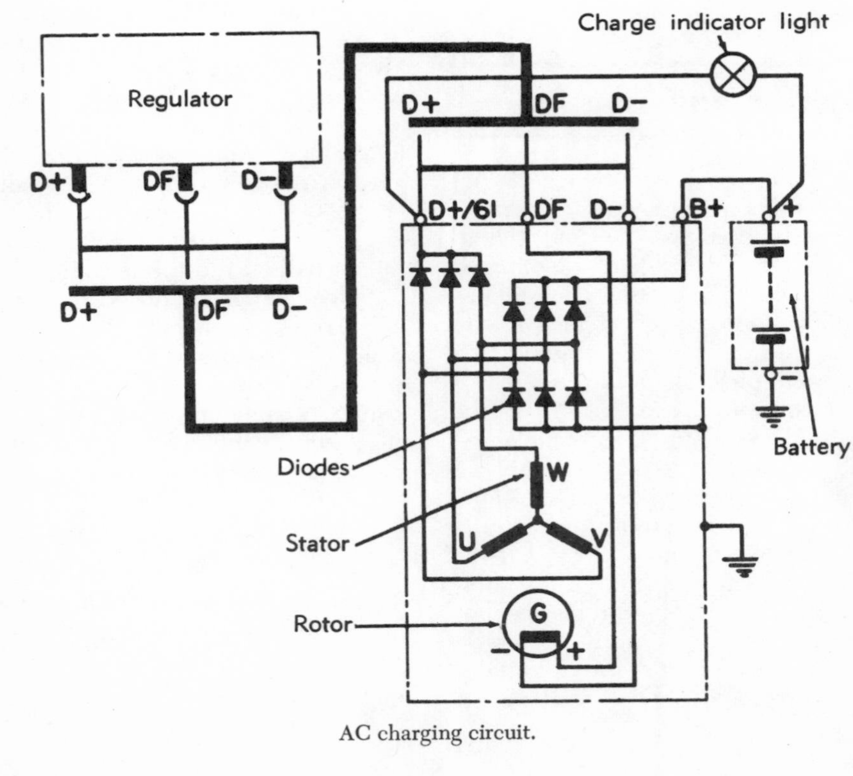

AC charging circuit.

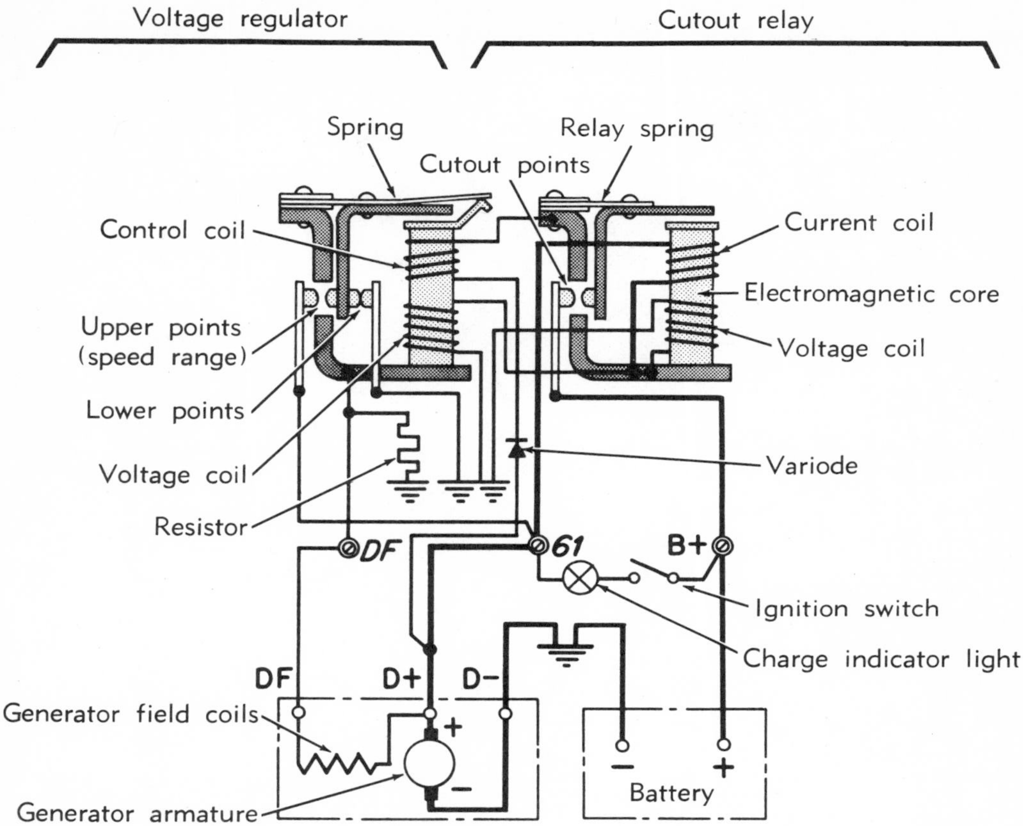

DC charging circuit.

"B+" regulator terminal and adding an ammeter between the terminal and the red wire. Set engine speed to around 2500 rpm. Output should be at least 20 amperes on a 12-volt DC generator and 50 amperes on a 6-volt unit. A lower output indicates trouble in the generator or regulator. Find the cause by disconnecting the generator field lead (DF) from the regulator and connecting it to the battery side of the ammeter. If output is still low, the generator is faulty.

To test for a faulty regulator, remove the red battery lead from the ammeter and connect a voltmeter positive lead to this terminal. Connect the voltmeter negative lead to ground. Increase engine speed until voltage peaks within 13.5-14.2 range (6.3-7.6 for 6-volt units). If voltage is not in this range, remove cover and adjust spring tension of voltage regulator armature to obtain a middle reading of about 14 volts. If voltage reading fluctuates, clean voltage regulator contacts with fine sandpaper or an ignition file. Do not use emery paper. If voltage continues to fluctuate, or cannot be adjusted to obtain the required reading, the regulator is faulty.

Cutout Relay Adjustment

Connect the positive lead of a voltmeter to the generator armature terminal (D+) at top of regulator. Attach voltmeter negative lead to ground. Connect an ammeter in series with the battery lead and the regulator terminal (red lead B+). Increase engine speed and observe voltage increase (until relay points close) and then slightly drop as circuit is completed to the battery. The highest voltmeter reading before the drop is the closing or "cut-in" voltage. This should be 5.9-6.5 volts. If closing voltage is not within limits, adjust by bending the cutout relay armature spring support. Increase tension to increase voltage — decrease tension to decrease voltage.

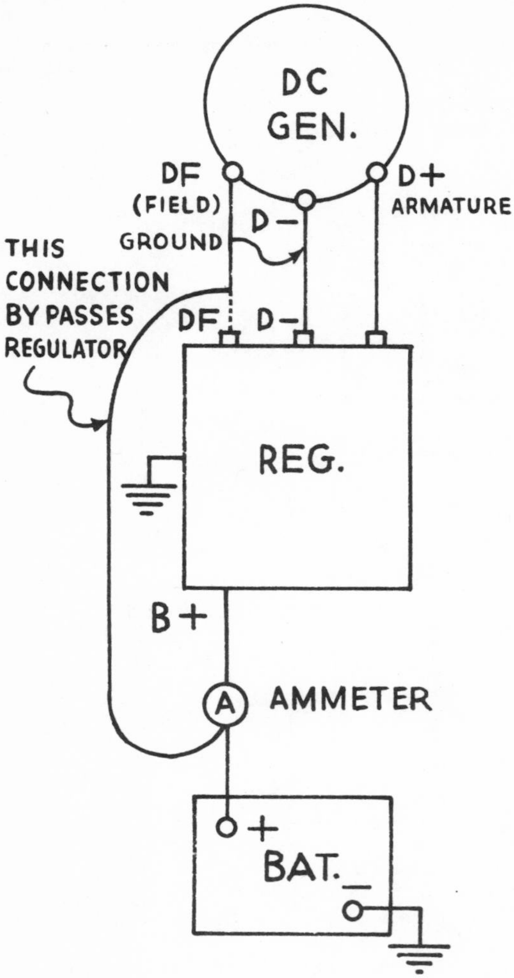

Ammeter connections for testing generator and regulator.

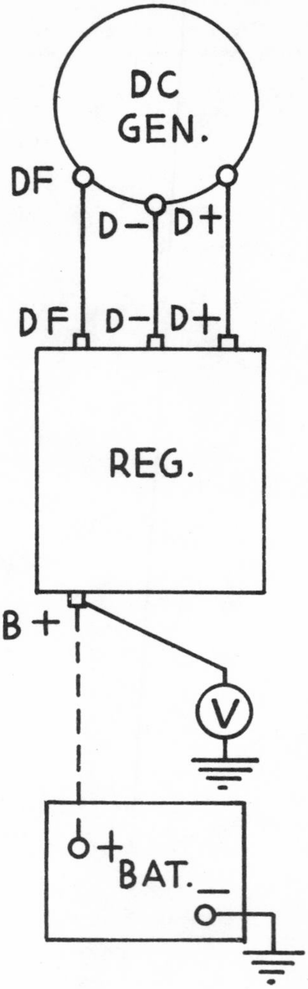

Voltmeter connections for adjusting voltage regulator.

DC Generator Overhaul

Remove nut and pulley. Pulley may be pulled off shaft by hand after tapping end of shaft lightly with a plastic covered hammer. Remove lock washer from shaft with side cutting pliers. Remove cover band, disconnect and lift out brushes. Remove through-bolts and pull housing apart. Take out armature and inspect housing, commutator, and windings for thrown solder.

Check armature for short circuit to ground by use of test prods (commutator bars to shaft) and test lamp. Check around all segments of commutator. Lamp should not light.

Scan commutator bars. Lamp should light by contact between all adjacent bars.

Check field coil for short circuit to ground (housing to DF). Lamp must not light.

Checking for grounded armature of generator.

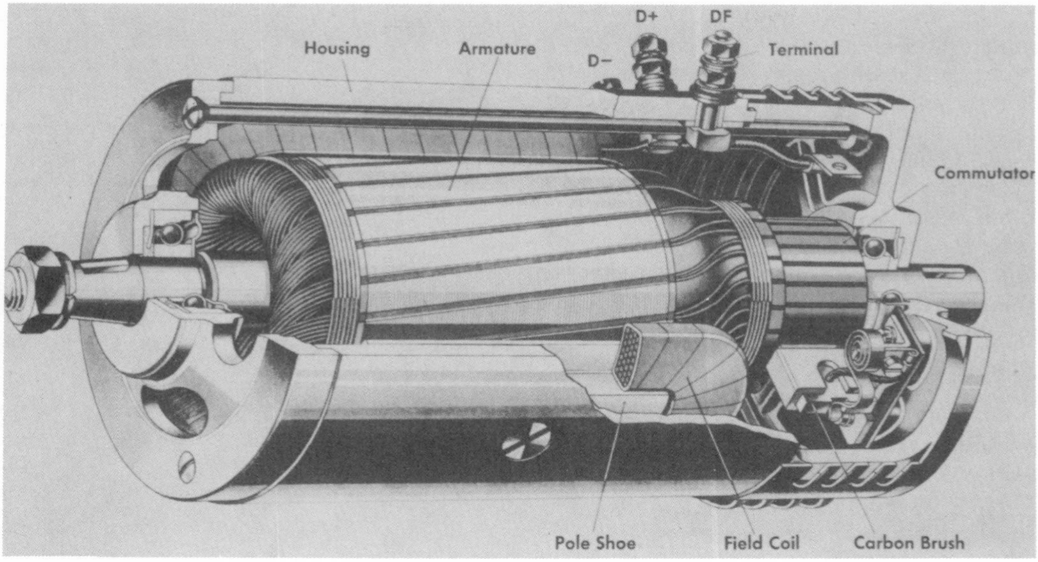

Cutaway view of Bosch DC generator.

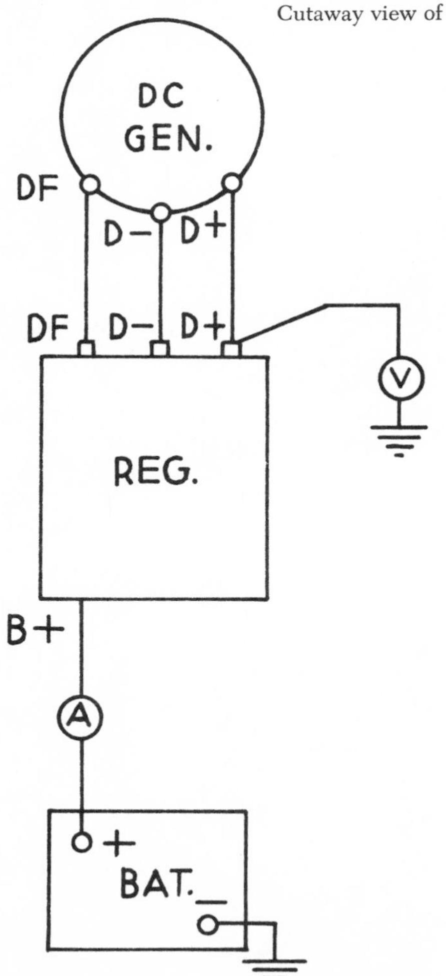

Voltmeter and ammeter connections for adjusting cutout relay.

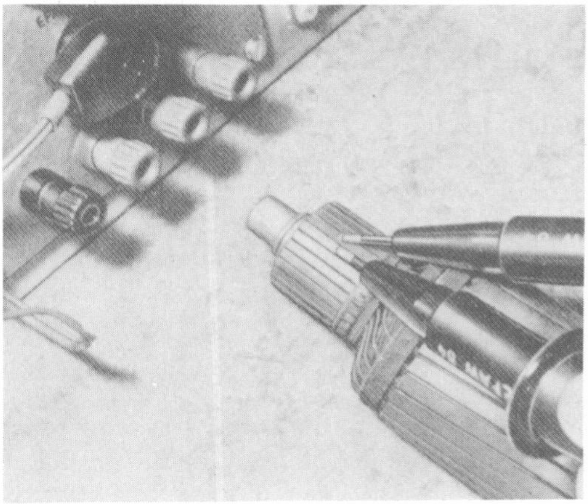

Checking for armature continuity.

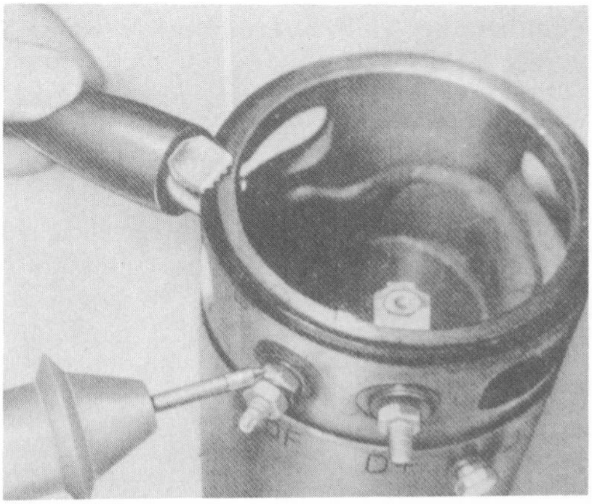

Checking for grounded field of generator.

Check field coil continuity (D+ to DF). Lamp should light.

Check brush holders in same way for short circuits to ground, and check brush tension which should be approximately 2 ft. lbs. (.9 kg).

Remove bearing parts from drive end frame. Clean and inspect ball bearings, replace worn parts and pack assemblies with high temperature grease. Wipe generator parts with clean cloth. Grease-cutting compounds might damage armature and coil insulation. Inspect all parts for wear or damage. Soldering must be done with rosin flux: *never use acid flux on electrical connections.* Reassemble using reverse procedure.

Testing Alternator and Regulator

WARNING: *the alternator contains diodes which can be damaged by voltage peaks. Therefore, do not disconnect cables between battery, generator and regulator when the engine is running. Also, if battery charger is to be used with the battery in place, disconnect both the positive and negative leads of the battery before connecting the charger to the battery.* The charge warning light serves to excite the field of the alternator. If it does not light with the ignition switch on and engine stopped, it should be checked and replaced if necessary. Also check plug of cable D+ /61 for continuity.

Usually on alternator systems, the warning light will go out while the engine is idling. If it continues to glow brightly, the regulator, generator and cable D+ /61 should be checked for shorts to ground. If the warning lamp glows at half intensity whether the engine is running or stopped, check cable DF and terminal, soldered bridge joints in regulator, carbon brushes, and sliprings, for good conductivity. If warning lamp burns brightly with engine stopped, but glows faintly even when engine is run at moderate to high speeds, the alternator or charge circuit may be faulty. To check this, connect a 4-watt test lamp directly to D+ and B+ on the alternator. If lamp does not glow when engine is run at moderate speed, then the fault is in the charging circuit. If lamp burns brightly, then goes out, the fault is in the alternator.

If warning lamp glows with the ignition switch off, but goes out when it is switched on, the battery is being discharged by a defective positive diode in the alternator. In this case, disconnect the red cable B+ from the alternator to eliminate further battery discharge. The vehicle may be driven as far as the battery charge allows. The alternator will have to be repaired or replaced.

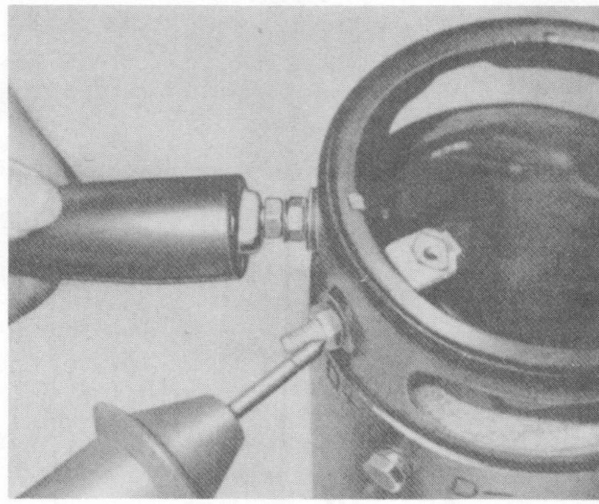

Checking for generator field continuity.

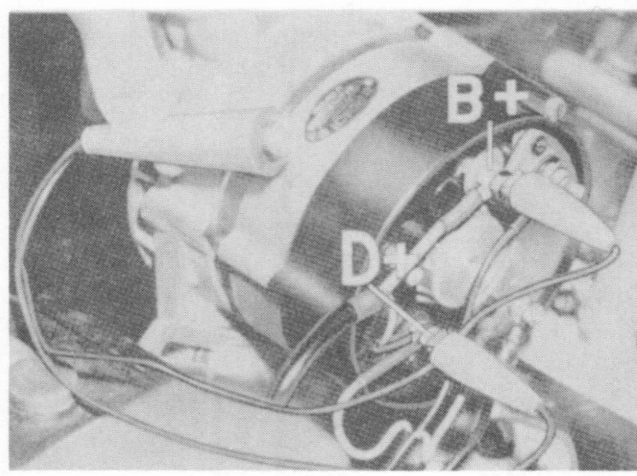

Connections of 4-watt test lamp to alternator.

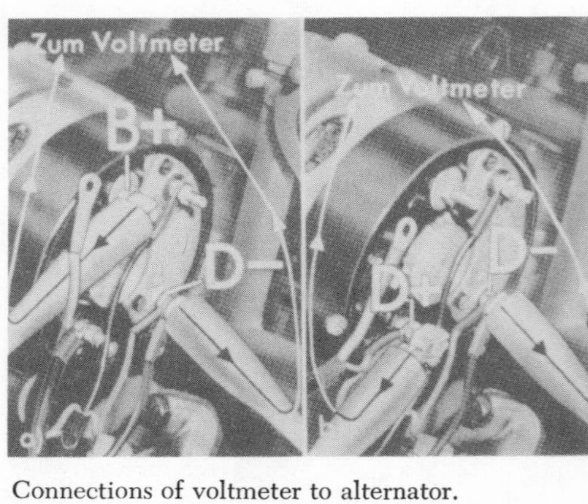

Connections of voltmeter to alternator.

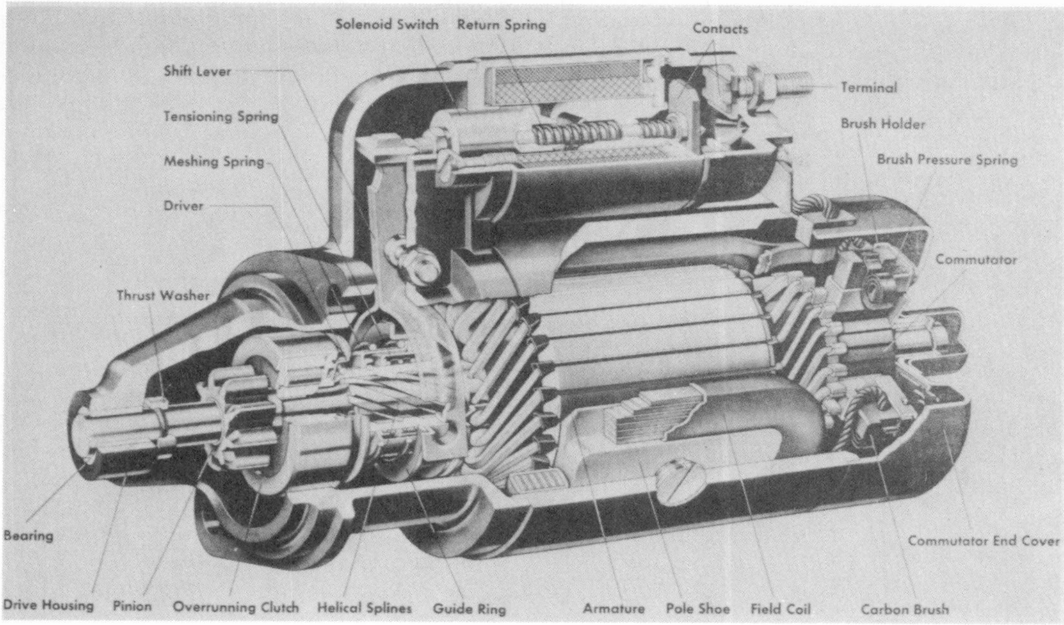

Cutaway view of starter.

Further checks for faulty alternator or regulator are made with a voltmeter. Disconnect the red cable (B+) from the alternator. WARNING: *do not disconnect this cable if the alternator is an SEV type with an electronic regulator.* Connect a voltmeter to B+ and D—. Accelerate engine. The 6-volt systems should produce a reading of 6.7-7.2 volts, and 12-volt systems a reading of 13.5-14.2 volts. If these values are not obtained, measure the voltage between D+ and D—. If the voltage difference between terminals D+ and B+ is less than 0.5 volt, the regulator must be replaced. If the voltage is between 1.5 and 4 volts, the alternator is faulty.

Starter brush holder plate removed. At reassembly, install washers (1, 2) on armature shaft.

Starter System

Starter Servicing

Disconnect battery ground cable from negative terminal. Remove starter cables and starter. Remove solenoid from motor housing, saving the gasket. Remove support bracket and dust cap. Remove brush holder plate and take out brushes. Remove through-bolts and separate commutator end-frame and field frame assemblies.

Remove bolt, nut and lockwasher from solenoid shift lever fulcrum. Remove armature and drive assembly from shift (yoke) lever. To remove drive assembly from armature, place a cylinder such as a 2″ pipe coupling over the end of the shaft to bear against the pinion stop retainer. Tap the retainer toward the armature to uncover the snap ring. (Models with castle nut, remove cotter pin and left-hand thread castle nut). Remove snap ring from groove in shaft, and slide retainer and pinion drive assembly from shaft. Remove spring.

Carefully inspect all mechanical parts for wear and damage, wash in kerosene, and blow dry with compressed air. Do not submerge armature or roller clutches in solvent. Check condition and tension of brushes. Check field coil and armature commutator with an AC test lamp for short

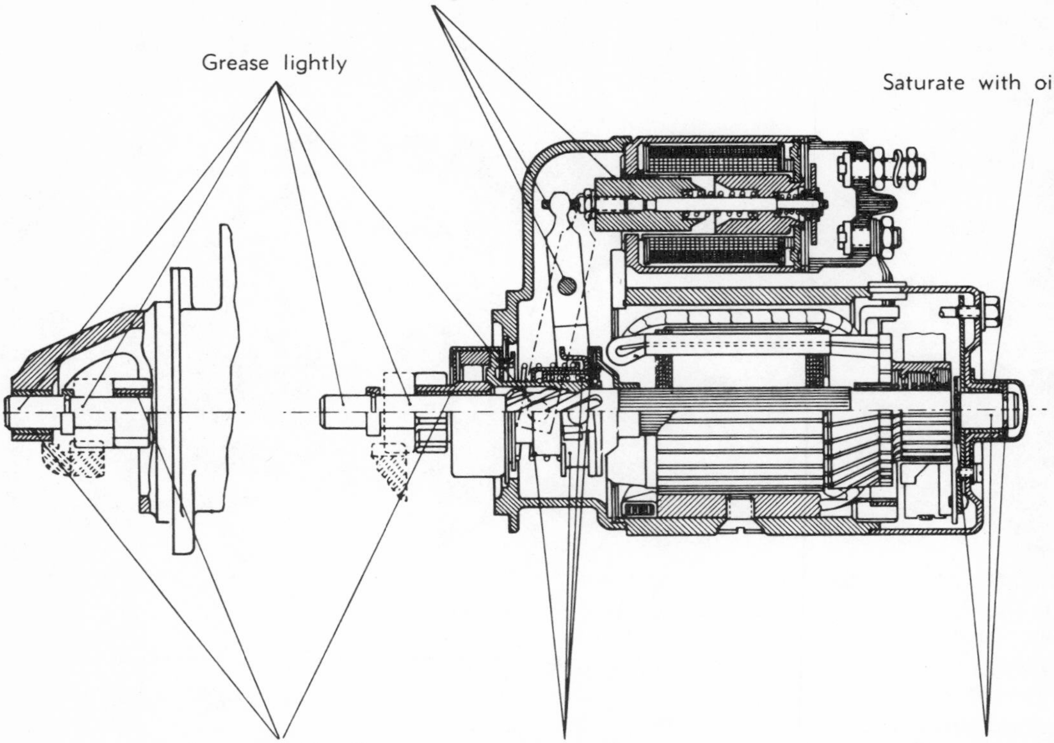

Points to be lubricated when reassembling starter.

circuits to the shaft and pole pieces. The test lamp should not light.

Check brush holder for shorts, inspect armature commutator for burnt or flat spots. Coat polished metal surfaces, other than the commutator, with engine oil. Lubricate points illustrated. When reassembling starter, lubricate armature shaft with silicone grease. Install assist spring and then the drive assembly with the pinion outward. Slide the pinion stop retainer down over the shaft with the recessed side out. Place a new snap ring on the drive end of the shaft and hold it in place with a block of wood. Tap the block with a hammer to force the snap ring over the end of the shaft, then slide the ring down into the groove in the shaft. Pry stop retainer into position over snap ring.

Lubricate drive housing bushings with silicone grease and set the armature drive assembly with the shift lever in the housing. Lubricate shift lever linkage at solenoid end. Position shift lever and attach bolt, nut and lockwasher. Use care in tightening the pole shoe screws to prevent dis-

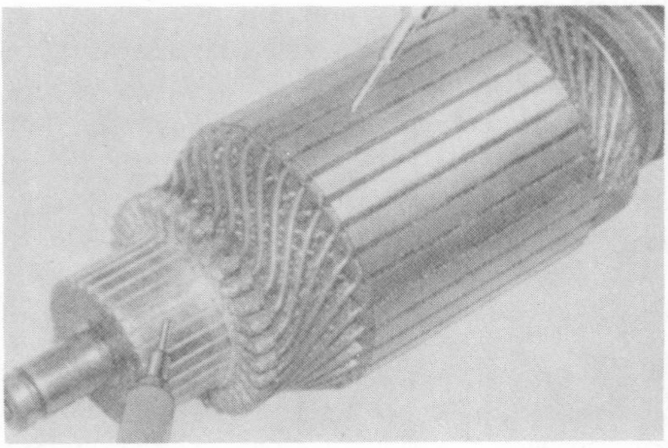

Checking starter armature for shorted commutator.

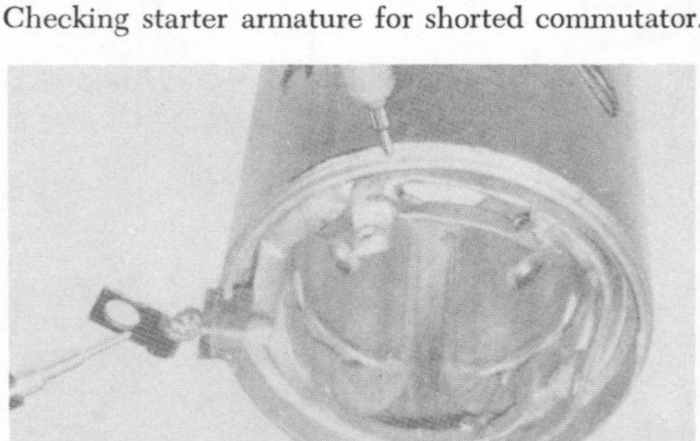

Checking starter for grounded field coil.

tortion of parts. Position the field frame over the armature and place washer on commutator end of armature assembly. Install commutator end-frame after lubricating bushing. Install through-bolts and tighten. Connect field leads to motor terminal of solenoid with connecting nut and washer. Attach solenoid with its gasket to drive housing. Connect the four brushes and install cover band.

Ignition System

The BMW ignition system employs distributor, ignition coil and spark plug components manufactured by Bosch. See the General Tune-up Specifications Chart for other suitable spark plugs. Circuitry and operation is conventional. Current flows from the battery through the ignition switch to the ignition coil. Through primary and secondary windings in the coil, high voltage is developed to fire the spark plugs. The distributor has two functions within the circuit. The first is to time the collapse of the magnetic field in the coil so that a pulse of high voltage (secondary circuit) is sent to the spark plugs. This is done by the breaker points. The second function is the distribution of spark to the correct plug. The rotor and cap provide this distribution. The condenser, connected in parallel with the breaker point circuit, prevents arcing between the points as they separate, permitting an instantaneous magnetic field collapse in the coil.

Distributor Replacement

To remove the distributor for overhaul or replacement, remove cap and rotate crankshaft to place No. 1 cylinder in firing position with timing marks properly aligned. The distributor rotor should point to the notch on the distributor housing. Disconnect vacuum line and primary ignition wire, and remove fastening bolts and distributor.

Install distributor with vacuum advance unit on right when viewed facing forward. Rotor should be just about aligned with mark on distributor housing. Set point gap and dwell angle and adjust ignition timing.

Contact Point Assembly

When installing points, lightly lubricate distributor cam with high temperature grease. Do not lubricate excessively or lubricant will be thrown onto contact points. Position stationary breaker plate and install lock screw loosely for later adjustment. Install breaker arm on pivot pin. Place spring insulating washer in spring support. Attach breaker arm lead. Install washer and hairpin clip on pivot pin. Adjust point spacing gap and tighten lock-screw.

Distributor components: primary wire terminal (1), breaker arm lead (2), clip (3), breaker arm pivot pin (4), breaker arm spring support (5), stationary contact (6). Adjustment screw can be seen beneath contact points.

Point gap can be set by using a feeler gauge; point dwell by using a dwell meter. Accurate measurements with a feeler gauge require careful, precise use of the feeler. The dwell meter, which measures the distance in degrees traveled by the rotating cam while the points are closed, should be first calibrated, switched to the four (or six) cylinder position, and connected between the distributor primary terminal and ground. Remove the distributor cap and rotor. Loosen the breaker set screw approximately ⅛th turn. Observing the dwell meter, reset screw of stationary contact to obtain specified dwell angle of 59-61°. Tighten set screw and recheck dwell. Install rotor and cap, start engine and make a final dwell angle check.

Ignition Timing

Timing marks on the crankshaft pulley should be aligned with a pointer on the housing. (Some models have a steel ball

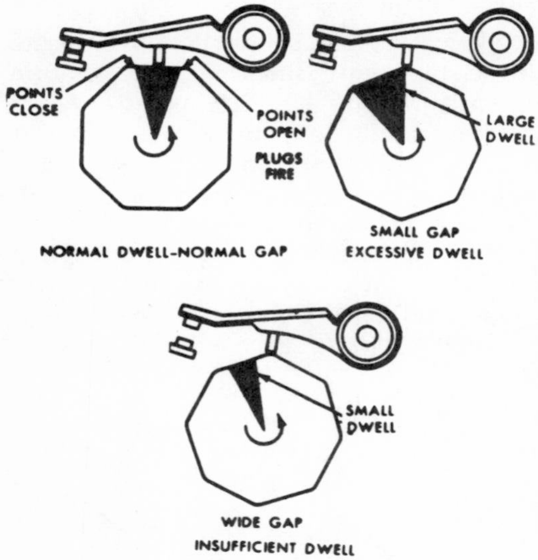

Distributor dwell angle (or cam angle) is determined by contact point gap setting. Dwell is increased by decreasing point gap.

in flywheel or inspection opening. Timing is correct when center of steel ball is visible at reference edge). With point gap correctly set and timing marks aligned, distributor housing is rotated counterclockwise slightly until contact points just start to open. The precise instant the points open can be accurately indicated by connecting a (6 or 12 volt) test lamp between the distributor primary terminal and ground. With the ignition switch on, the test lamp will light the moment the contact points open. This method of static timing is only to be used for a rough initial setting.

In using a timing light, connect timing light to No. 1 spark plug. Disconnect all vacuum hoses from the distributor and plug the hoses. Start engine and set idle speed to rpm shown in General Tune-up Specifications Chart. Idle performance must be smooth. Rotate distributor as necessary to align timing marks with timing light pulses. If timing light is not available, timing can be adjusted by marking advance and retard points on the distributor with chalk. With vacuum lines disconnected and engine idling, rotate distributor to point where engine reaches its highest rpm. Mark this point. Next, retard spark by slowly reversing the distributor to the point of lowest rpm. Mark this point. Center distributor between the two marks and tighten it.

It must be emphasized that the only really accurate way to set ignition timing is by use of a stroboscopic timing light. Ignition timing procedures for engines with emission controls are given in Chapter 1.

Timing is correct when steel ball is centered.

Timing marks on crankshaft pulley:
OT = TDC notch
Z = static timing notch
Z = 2000 rpm timing notch

Instruments

Removal of Instrument Panel — 1600-2, 2002

Remove two screws and hood over instrument panel. From behind panel, disconnect speedometer cable and remove two large plastic knurled nuts. Push panel forward. Unplug large wiring harness plug from rear of combined instrument at left side of panel. Individual instruments may now be readily removed. Reverse procedure to install panel.

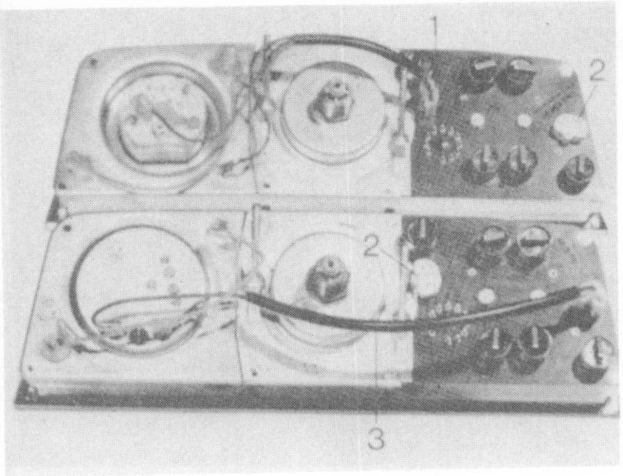

Replacing clock with tachometer, 1600-2, 2002.

Installing Tachometer — 1600-2, 2002

Some 2002 models have installed, as an option, a VDO electrical tachometer. This instrument replaces the standard clock. The necessary wiring to permit easy installation of the tachometer is part of the standard wiring harness in the 1600-2 and 2002.

To replace the clock with the tachometer:

1. Disconnect wire from clock. Remove clock unit from instrument panel.
2. Switch locations of clock/tachometer wire plug (1) and blank plug (2).
3. Install tachometer head in instrument panel. Connect wire.
4. Wiring color coding is as follows:

green	+
brown	—
grey	bulbs
1	to coil

Light and Indicator Bulb Wattages

	1500	*1600*	*1600-2*	*1600 TI*	*1800, 800A*	*1800 69*	*1800 TI*	*2002*	*2000, 2000A*	*2000 TI*	*2000 CS*	*2000 CA*
Headlights, Low/High	45/40	45/40	45/40	45/40	45/40	45/40	45/40	45/40	45/40	45/40	45/40	45/40
Side and Parking	4	4	4	4	4	4	4	4	4	4	4	4
Front Flashing	18	18	21	21	18	18	18	21	21	21	21	21
Stop	18	18	21	21	18	18	18	21	21	21	21	21
Reverse	15	15	15	15	15	15	15	15	15	15	15	15
Rear Flashing	18	18	21	21	21	21	21	21	21	21	21	21
Tail and Parking	5	5	5	5	5	5	5	5	5	5	5	5
License Plate	5	5	5	5	5	5	5	5	4	4	5	5
Interior	5	5	10	10	10	10	10	10	5	5	5	5
Instrument	2	2	3	3	2	2	2	3			2	2
Battery Charge Indicator	2	2	4	4	2	4	4	4	4	4	4	4
High Beam Indicator	2	2	3	3	2	2	2	3	2	2	2	2
Flashing Indicator	2	2	3	3	2	2	2	3	2	2	2	2
Oil Pressure Indicator	2	2	3	3	2	2	2	3	2	2	2	2
Choke & Fuel Level Indicator	2	2			2	2	2		2	2	2	2
Selector Gate (Automatic Only)					2				2			2
Luggage Compartment											5	5
Engine Compartment											5	5

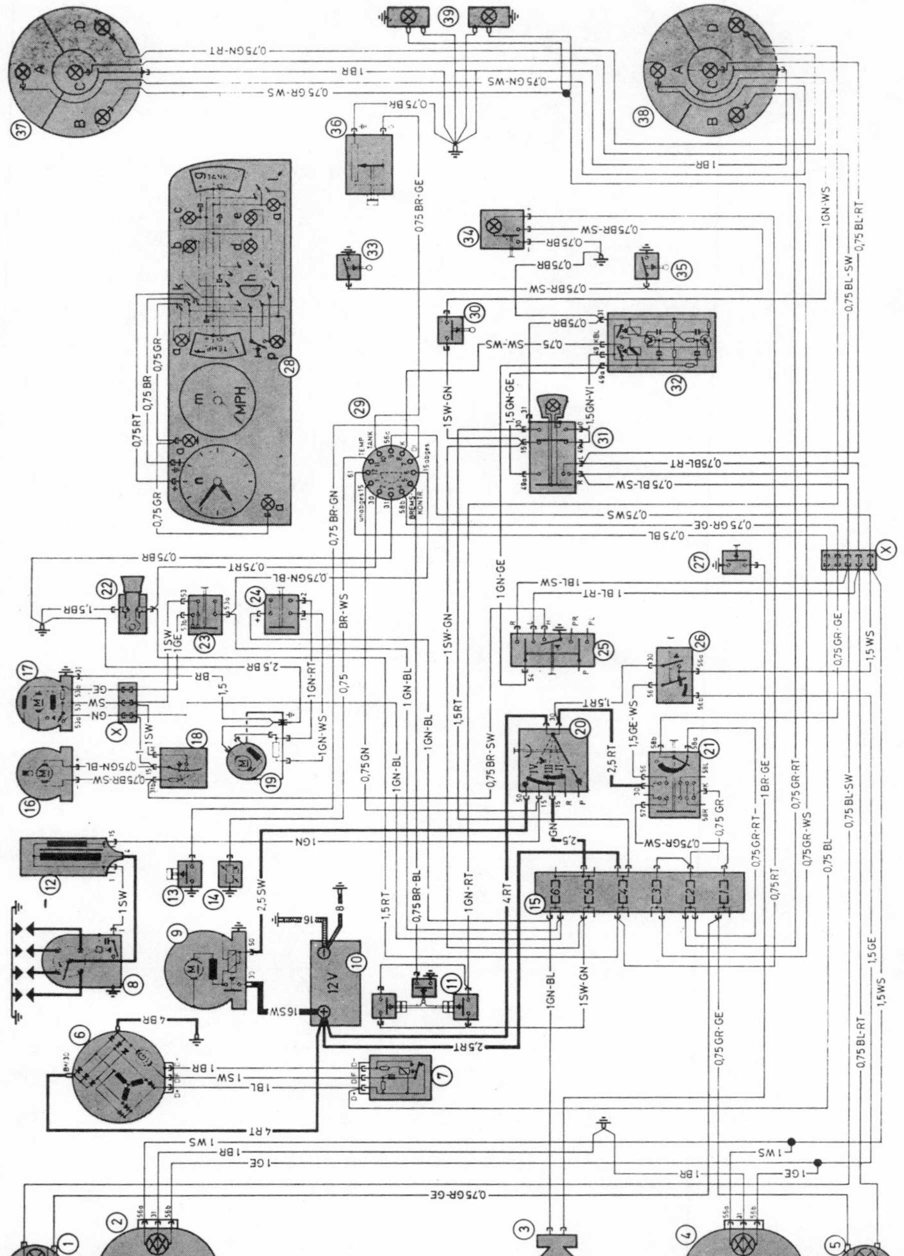

Wiring diagram, BMW 1600-2, US model.

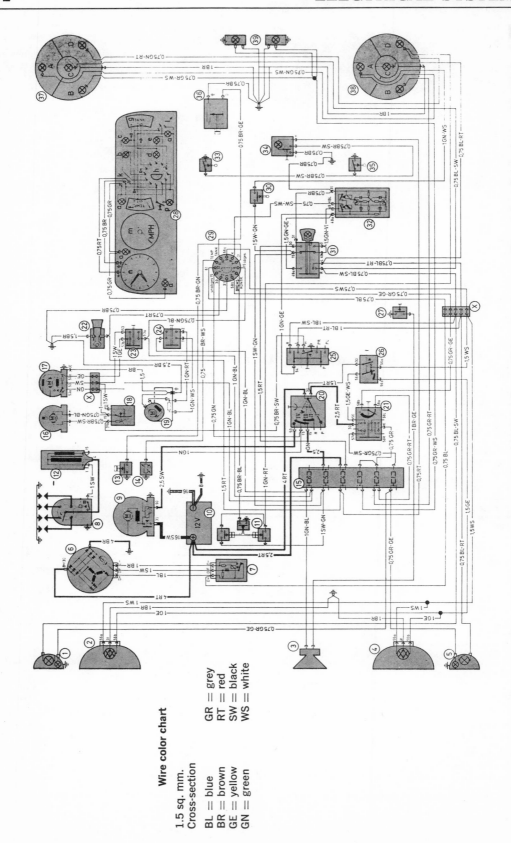

Wire color chart

1.5 sq. mm.
Cross-section

BL = blue	GR = grey
BR = brown	RT = red
GE = yellow	SW = black
GN = green	WS = white

Key to wiring diagram, p. 72.

1 Turn signal light (front right) with parking light
2 Headlight (right)
3 Horn
4 Headlight (left)
5 Turn signal light (front left) with parking light
6 Alternator
7 Voltage regulator
8 Distributor
9 Starter
10 Battery
11 Stop light switch
12 Ignition coil
13 Oil pressure
14 Water temperature
15 Fuse box
16 Windshield washer pump
17 Windshield wiper motor
18 Washer delay relay
19 Blower motor
20 Ignition switch
Positions:
I Halt (lock)
II Garage (off)
III Fahrt (on)
IV Start (start)
21 Headlight switch
22 Cigar lighter and socket
23 Windshield wiper switch
24 Blower switch
25 Turn signal light and windshield washer
26 Dimmer switch and headlight flasher
27 Horn button
28 Instrument panel
a) instrument illumination
b) battery charge warning light (red)
c) oil pressure (orange)
d) high beam warning light (blue)
e) turn signal indicator light (green)
f) water temperature gauge
g) fuel gauge
h) 12 pole connector
k) 3 pole connector (clock)
l) 3 pole connector
m) speedometer
n) clock
p) dual brake system and check switch
29 Instrument panel terminals
30 Back-up light
31 Hazard warning signal switch
32 Hazard warning signal relay
33 Courtesy light switch (right)
34 Interior light
35 Courtesy light switch (left)
36 Fuel gauge float contact
37 Rear lamp cluster (right)
A) Back-up light
B) Rear light
C) Turn signal light
D) Stop light
38 Rear cluster (left)
A) Back-up light
B) Rear light
C) Turn signal light
D) Stop light
39 License plate lights
X Flat pin connector

Key to wiring diagram, p. 74.

1 Turn signal lamp (front right) with parking lamp
2 Headlamp (right)
4 Headlamp (left)
5 Turn signal lamp (front left) with parking lamp
6 Alternator
7 Voltage regulator
8 Distributor
9 Starter
10 Battery
11 Stop lamp switch
12 Ignition coil
13 Oil pressure warning sending unit
14 Water temperature sending unit
15 Fuse box
16 Windshield washer pump
17 Windshield wiper motor
18 Washer delay relay
19 Blower motor
20 Ignition switch
Positions:
I Halt (lock)
II Garage (off)
III Fahrt (on)
IV Start (start)
21 Headlamp switch
22 Cigar lighter and socket
23 Windshield wiper switch
24 Blower switch
25 Turn indicator and windshield washer switch
26 Dimmer switch and headlamp flasher
27 Horn button
28 Instrument panel
a) dial illumination
b) battery charge lamp (red)
c) Oil pressure lamp (orange)
d) high beam indicating lamp (blue)
e) turn indicating lamp (green)
f) water temperature gauge
g) fuel gauge
h) 12-pole connector
k) 3-pole connector (clock)
l) 3-pole connector (tachometer)
m) speedometer
n) clock
p) dual brake system warning lamp and check switch
29 Instrument panel connecting socket
30 Back-up lamp switch
31 Hazard warning lamp switch
32 Hazard warning lamp relay
33 Courtesy light switch (right)
34 Interior light
35 Courtesy light switch (left)
36 Fuel level sending unit
37 Rear combination lamp, right
A back-up lamp
B rear lamp
C turn signal lamp
D stop lamp
38 Rear combination lamp, left
A back-up lamp
B rear lamp
C turn signal lamp
D stop lamp
39 License plate lamps
X Terminal
40 Horn right
41 Horn left
42 Horn relay

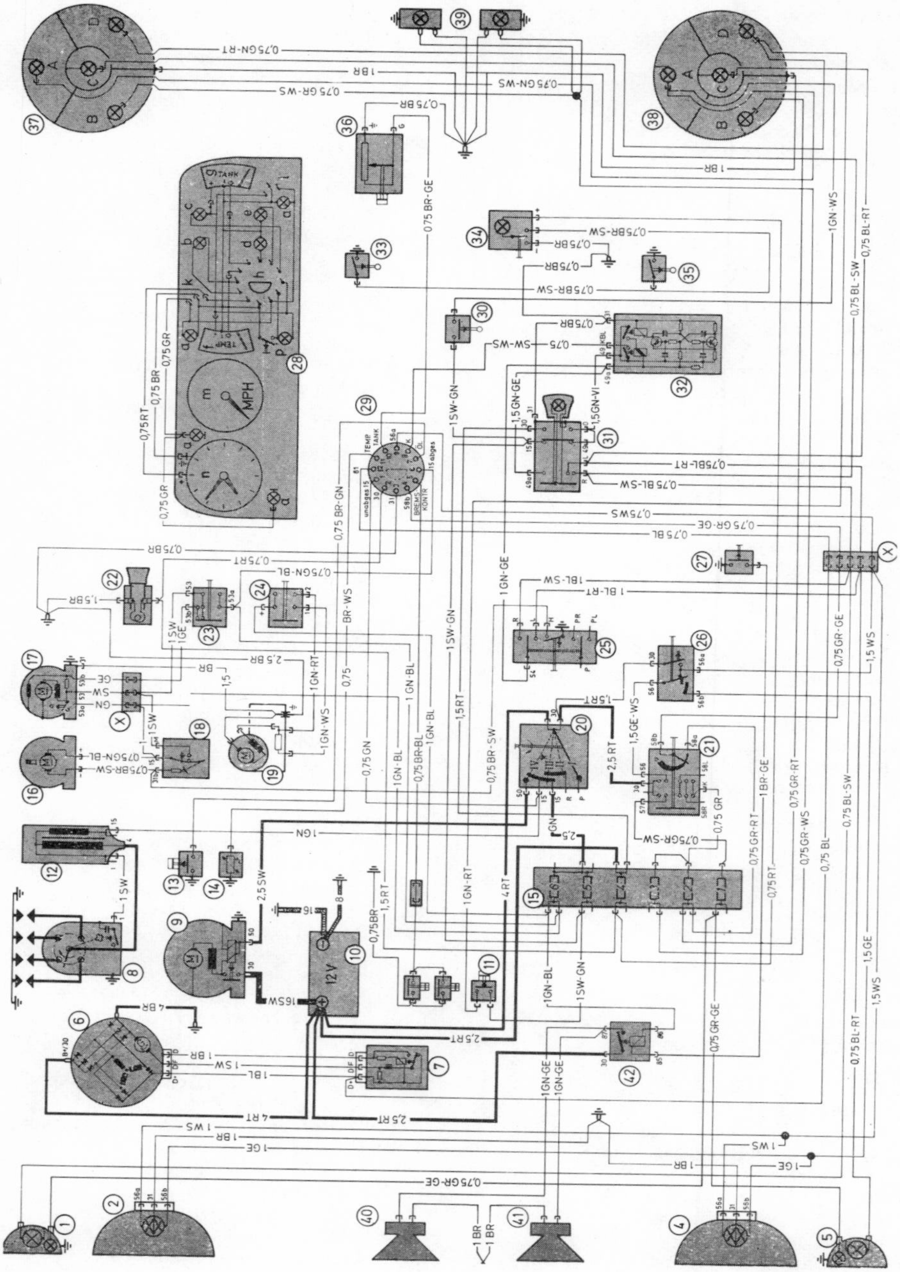

Wiring diagram, BMW 2002, US model.

Wire color chart

1.5 sq. mm.
Cross-section

BL = blue
BR = brown
GE = yellow
GN = green

GR = grey
RT = red
SW = black
WS = white

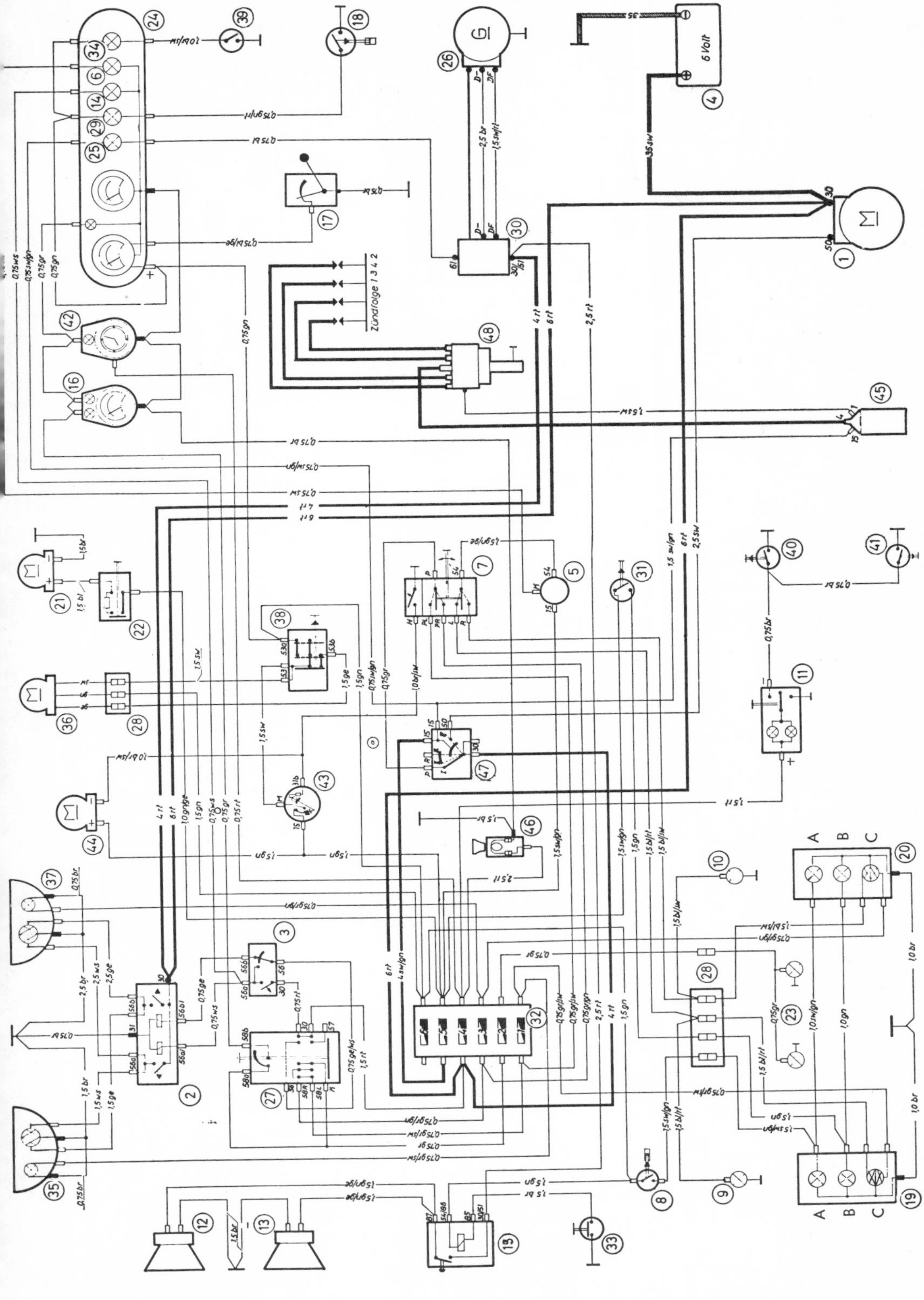

Wiring diagram, BMW 1500, 1600.

Key to wiring diagram, p. 75.

1 Starter
2 Dip relay
3 Dip switch
4 Battery
5 Flasher unit
6 Flasher telltale
7 Flasher/parking light switch with washer contact
8 Stop light switch
9 Turn indicator front LH
10 Turn indicator front RH
11 Roof light
12 Two-tone horn 1
13 Two-tone horn 2
14 Main beam telltale
15 Horn relay
16 Speedometer
17 Fuel gauge mechanism
18 Oil pressure contact
19 Rear light LH
A Stop light
B Reversing light
C Turn indicator/parking light rear
21 Heater blower motor
22 Heater switch
23 Number plate light
24 Combined instrument
25 Battery charge telltale
26 Generator
27 Light switch
28 Cable connector
29 Oil pressure telltale
30 Regulator
31 Reversing light switch
32 Fuse box
33 Horn button
34 Choke telltale
35 Headlight LH
36 Screenwiper motor
37 Headlight RH
38 Screenwiper switch
39 Choke cable contact
40 Door switch LH
41 Door switch RH
42 Clock
43 Delay relay
44 Screenwasher pump
45 Coil
46 Cigar lighter
47 Ignition/starter switch
48 Distributor

Cable coding:
0.75 sq. mm cross-section
Colour:
BL = blue
BR = brown
GE = yellow
GN = green
GR = grey
RT = red
SW = black
WS = white

Fuses:
1–2–3–5 = 8 Amp
4–6 = 25 Amp

Ignition / starter switch:
Positions:
I Halt
II Garage
III Fahrt (Drive)
IV Start

Key to wiring diagram, p. 77.

1 Turn indicator RH
2 Headlight RH with parking light
3 Foglamp RH
4 Horn
5 Foglamp LH
6 Headlight LH with parking light
7 Turn indicator LH
8 Dip relay
9 Generator
10 Regulator/switch unit
11 Distributor
12 Starter
13 Battery (6 Volt)
14 Stop light switch
15 Foglamp relay
16 Foglamp switch
17 Coil
18 Oil pressure contact
19 Water temperature sensor
20 Reversing light switch
21 Fuse box
22 Screenwasher pump
23 Screenwiper motor
24 Delay relay
25 Heater blower motor
26 Ignition/starter switch
27 Light switch
28 Cigar lighter
29 Screenwiper switch
30 Heater switch
31 Flasher unit
32 Turn indicator/parking light/screenwasher switch
33 Horn ring
34 Inline fuse for radio
35 Dip switch
36 Instrument panel
37 12-pole plug for "k" on instrument panel (view from cable side)
38 Radio aerial
39 Radio
40 Door switch RH
41 Interior light
42 Door switch LH
43 Fuel gauge mechanism
44 Rear light RH
45 Number plate light RH
46 Number plate light LH
47 Rear light LH
X Flat pin connector

Cable coding:
1.5 sq. mm cross-section
Colour:
BL = blue
BR = brown
GE = yellow
GN = green
GR = grey
RT = red
SW = black
WS = white

Instrument panel:
a Instrument lighting
b Clock
c Speedometer
d Thermometer
e Fuel gauge
f Charge telltale (red)
g Oil pressure telltale (orange)
h Main beam telltale (blue)
i Turn indicator telltale (green)
k 12-pole plug for Posn. 37 (seen from connection side)
m 3-pole plug for clock cable
n 3-pole plug for revolution counter cable
p Revolution counter (special equipment, replaces clock)

Special equipment:
Posn. Nos. 3–5–15–16 = Foglamps
34–38–39 = Radio and aerial
36 p = Revolution counter

Fuses:
Nos. 1–2–3–4–5 = 8 Amp.
Nos. 6 = 25 Amp.
Radio = 5 Amp.

Firing order: 1–3–4–2

Ignition / starter switch:
I Halt
II Garage
III Fahrt (Drive)
IV Start

Rear lights:
A = Reversing light
B = Rear light
C = Turn indicator
D = Stop light

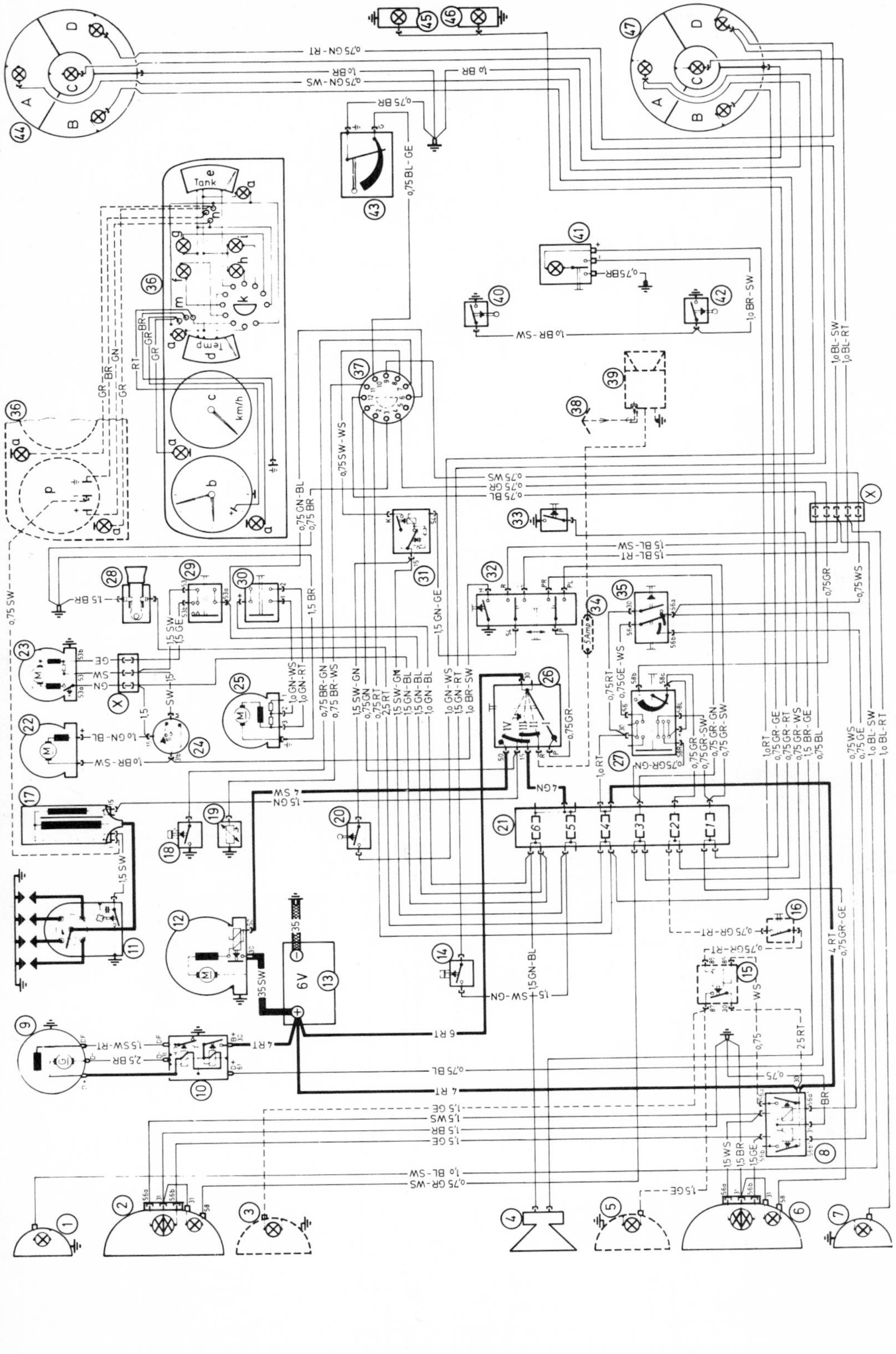

Wiring diagram, BMW 1600-2, 6-volt.

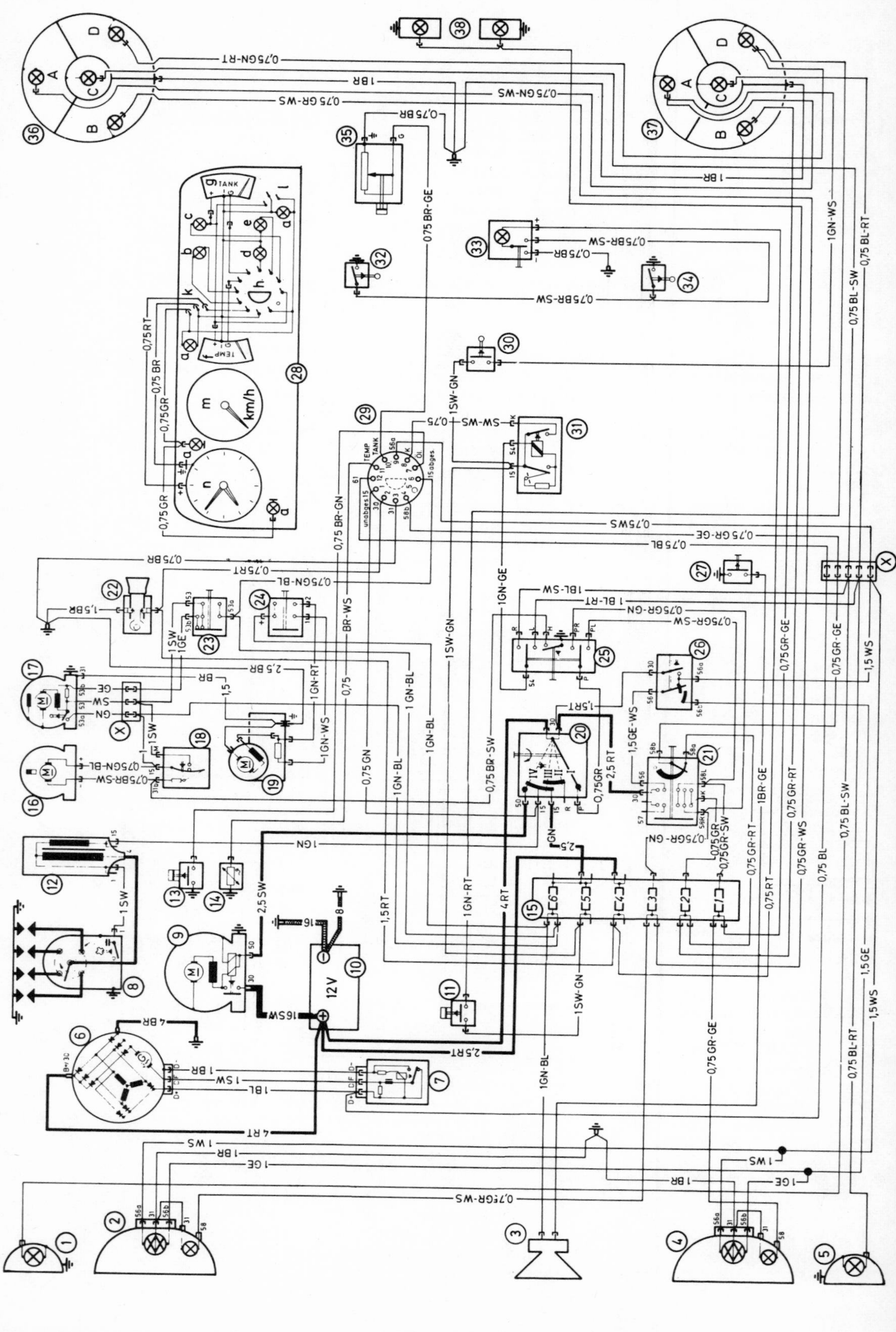
1
2
3
4
5
6
7
8
9
10
11
12
13
14
15
16
17
18
19
20
21
22
23
24
25
26
27
28
29
30
31
32
33
34
35
36
37
38
12V
TANK
TEMP
km/h
0,75 GN-RT
1 BR
0,75 GN-WS
0,75 GR-WS
0,75 BR
0,75 BR-SW
0,75 BR-GE
1 GN-WS
0,75 BL-RT
0,75 BL-SW
1 BL-SW
1 BL-RT
0,75 GR-GN
0,75 GR-SW
0,75 WS
0,75 GR-GE
0,75 BL
0,75 RT
0,75 GN-BL
1,5 BR
2,5 BR
1 GN
2,5 SW
16 SW
4 BR
1 SW
1 BL
4 RT
2,5 RT
1 WS
1 GE
0,75 GR-WS

Key to wiring diagram, p. 78.

1 Turn indicator front RH
2 Headlight RH with parking light
3 Horn
4 Headlamp LH with parking light
5 Turn indicator front LH
6 Alternator
7 Voltage regulator
8 Distributor
9 Starter
10 Battery
11 Stop light switch
12 Coil
13 Oil pressure contact
14 Remote thermometer contact
15 Fuse box
16 Screenwasher pump
17 Screen wiper motor
18 Delay relay
19 Heater blower
20 Ignition/starter switch
21 Light switch
22 Cigar lighter
23 Screenwiper switch
24 Blower switch
25 Turn indicator/parking light/ screenwasher switch
26 Dip switch/headlight flasher
27 Horn ring
28 Instrument panel
29 12-pole plug for instrument panel (seen from cable side)
30 Reversing light switch
31 Flasher unit
32 Door switch RH
33 Interior light
34 Door switch LH
35 Fuel gauge tank mechanism
36 Rear light RH
37 Rear light LH
38 Number plate light
X Flat pin connector

Instrument panel:
a Instrument lighting
b Charge telltale (red)
c Oil pressure telltale (orange)
d Main beam telltale (blue)
e Turn indicator telltale (green)
f Water temperature gauge
g Fuel gauge
h 12-pole plug
k 3-pole plug for clock
l 3-pole plug for revolution counter
m Speedometer
n Clock

Ignition / starter switch:
I Halt
II Garage
III Fahrt (Drive)
IV Start

Rear lights:
A = Reversing light
B = Rear light
C = Turn indicator
D = Stop light

Firing order: 1–3–4–2

Cable coding:
1.5 sq. mm cross-section

Basic colour:
BL = blue
BR = brown
GE = yellow
GN = green
GR = grey
RT = red
SW = black
VI = violet
WS = white

Key to wiring diagram, p. 80.

1 Turn indicator front RH
2 Headlight RH with parking light
3 Horn RH
4 Horn LH
5 Headlight LH with parking light
6 Turn indicator front LH
7 Alternator
8 Voltage regulator
9 Horn relay
10 Distributor
11 Starter
12 Battery
13 Stop light switch
14 Coil
15 Oil pressure contact
16 Remote thermometer contact
17 Fuse box
18 Screenwasher pump
19 Screen wiper motor
20 Delay relay
21 Heater blower
22 Ignition/starter switch
23 Light switch
24 Cigar lighter
25 Screenwiper switch
26 Blower switch
27 Turn indicator/parking light/ screenwasher switch
28 Dip switch/headlight flasher
29 Horn ring
30 Instrument panel
31 12-pole plug for instrument panel (seen from cable side)
32 Reversing light switch
33 Flasher unit
34 Cable for heated rear window (Special Equipment)
35 Door switch RH
36 Interior light
37 Door switch LH
38 Fuel gauge tank mechanism
39 Rear light RH
40 Rear light LH
41 Number plate light
X Flat pin connector

Instrument panel:
a Instrument lighting
b Charge telltale (red)
c Oil pressure telltale (orange)
d Main beam telltale (blue)
e Turn indicator telltale (green)
f Water temperature gauge
g Fuel gauge
h 12-pole plug
k 3-pole plug for clock
l 3-pole plug for revoluton counter
m Speedometer
n Clock
p Revolution counter

Ignition / starter switch:
I Halt
II Garage
III Fahrt (Drive)
IV Start

Rear lights:
A = Reversing light
B = Rear light
C = Turn indicator
D = Stop light

Firing order: 1–3–4–2

Cable coding:
1.5 sq. mm cross-section

Basic colour:
BL = blue
BR = brown
GE = yellow
GN = green
GR = grey
RT = red
SW = black
VI = violet
WS = white

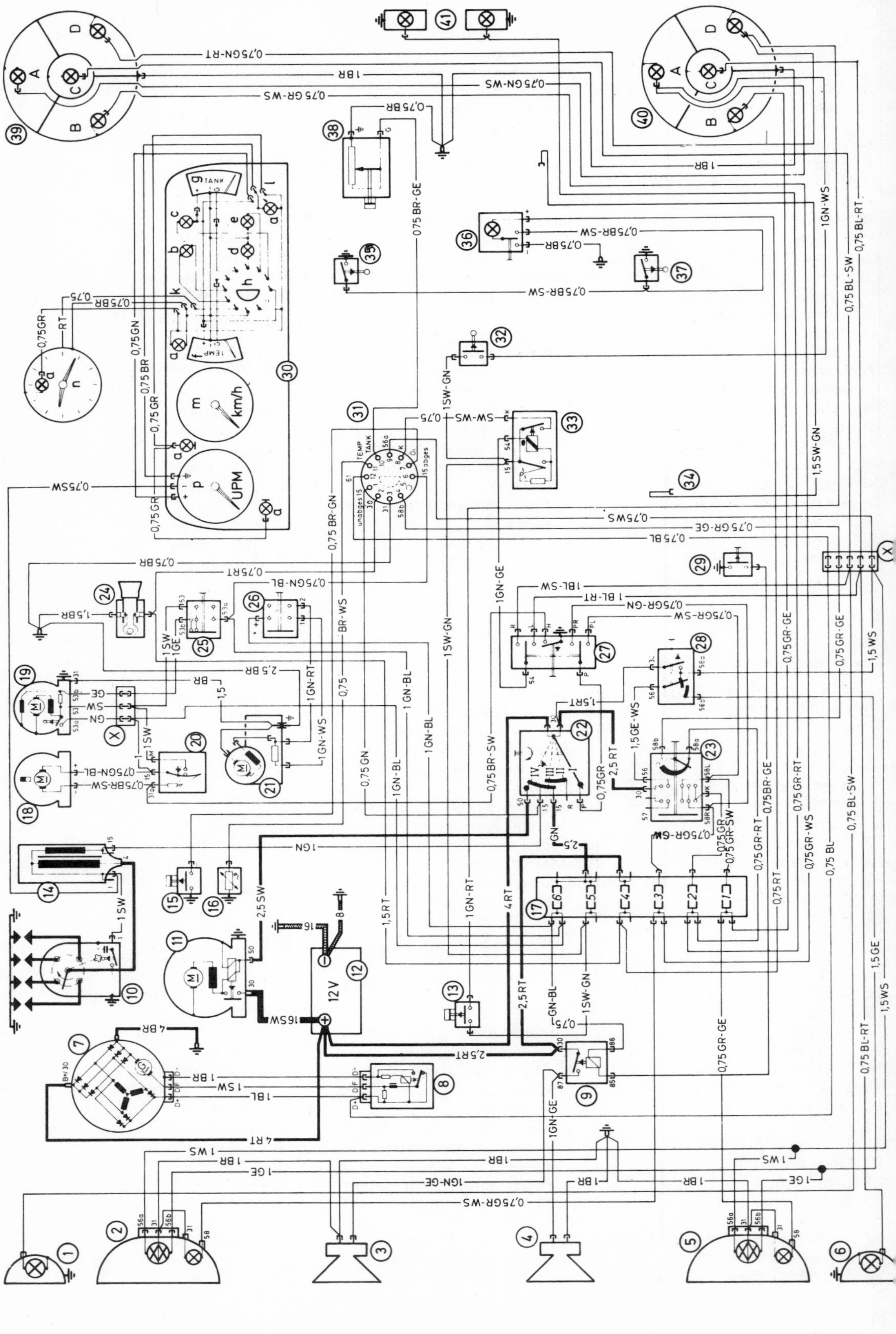
0,75GN-RT
1BR
0,75GR-WS
0,75GN-WS
0,75BR
0,75 BR-GE
0,75BR-SW
1GN-WS
0,75 BL-RT
0,75 BL-SW
TANK
TEMP
km/h
UPM
0,75GR
0,75GN
0,75 BR
0,75 GR
0,75SW
1SW-GN
SW-WS
1,5 SW-GN
0,75WS
0,75 GR-GE
0,75 BL
0,75RT
0,75GN-BL
1,5BR
2,5BR
1SW
1GE
GE
SW
GN
1GN-RT
1GN-WS
1GN-BL
0,75BR-SW
BR-WS
0,75 BR-GN
1GN-GE
1BL-SW
1BL-RT
0,75GR-GN
0,75GR-SW
1,5RT
2,5 RT
1,5GE-WS
0,75GR
0,75GR-RT
0,75BR-GE
0,75GR-WS
0,75 BL-SW
1,5 WS
1,5 GE
1,5WS
1GN
2,5SW
16SW
2,5RT
4RT
4BR
1BR
1SW
1BL
12 V
2,5 RT
GN-BL
1SW-GN
0,75
0,75 GR-GE
0,75 BL-RT
1WS
1GE
1GN-GE
0,75GR-WS

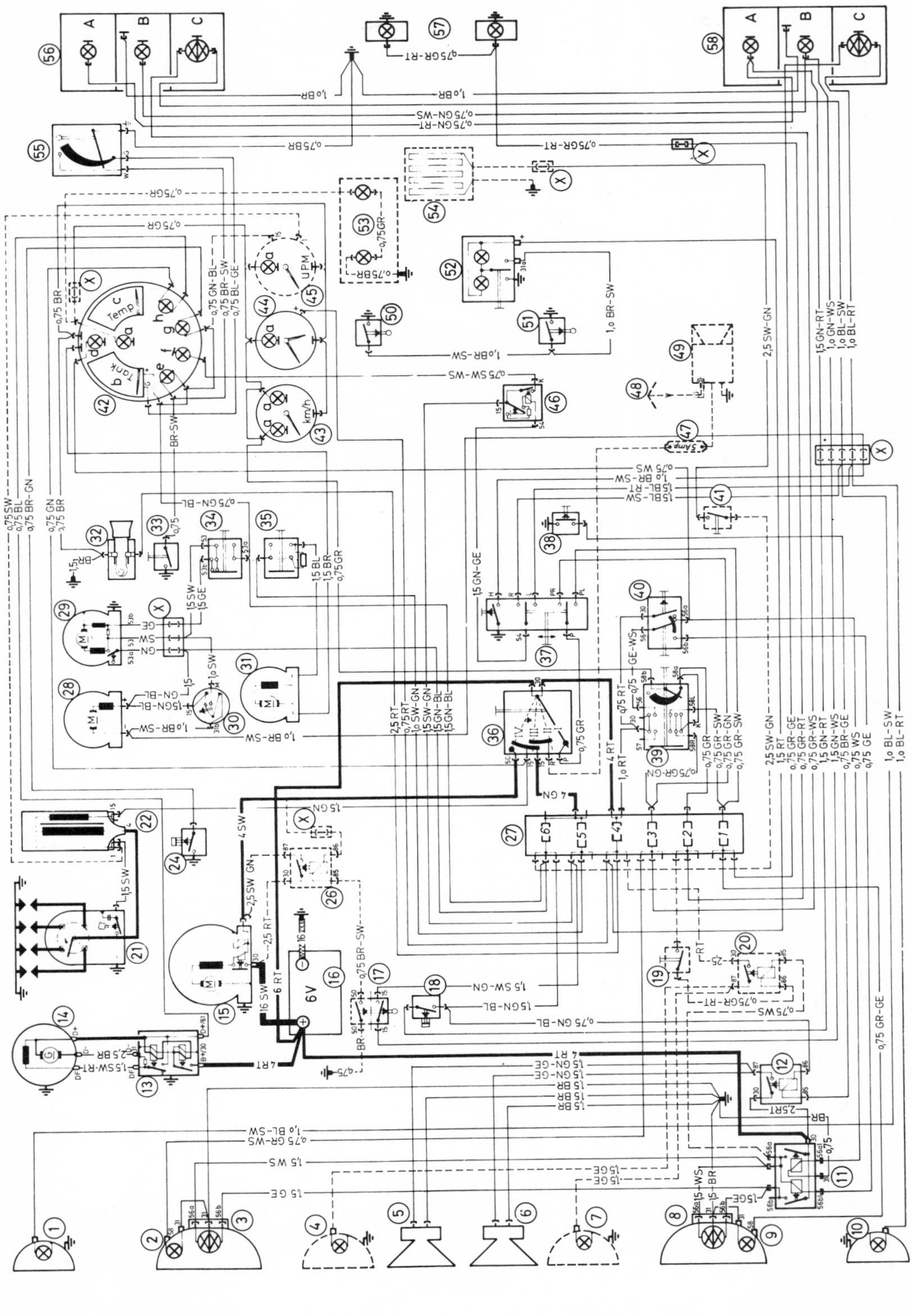

Wiring diagram, BMW 1800, 1800 A.

Key to wiring diagram, p. 81.

1 Turn indicator front RH
2 Parking light RH
3 Headlight RH
4 Foglamp RH
5 Horn RH
6 Horn LH
7 Foglamp LH
8 Headlight LH
9 Parking light LH
10 Turn indicator front LH
11 Dip relay
12 Horn relay
13 Voltage regulator
14 Dynamo
15 Starter
16 Battery
17 Reversing light and starter lock switch
18 Stop light switch
19 Foglamp switch
20 Foglamp relay
21 Distributor
22 Coil
23
24 Oil pressure switch
25
26 Starter relay
27 Fuse box
28 Screenwasher pump
29 Screenwiper motor
30 Delay relay
31 Heater blower motor
32 Cigar lighter
33 Choke cable switch
34 Screenwiper switch
35 Heater switch
36 Ignition/starter switch
37 Turn indicator/parking/light/screenwasher switch
38 Horn ring
39 Light switch
40 Dip switch
41 Switch for heated rear window
42 Combined instrument
43 Speedometer
44 Clock
45 Revolution counter
46 Flasher unit
47 Separate fuse for radio
48 Aerial
49 Radio
50 Door switch RH
51 Door switch LH
52 Interior light
53 Selector lever illumination
54 Heated rear window
55 Fuel gauge mechanism
56 Rear light RH
57 Number plate light
58 Rear light LH
X Flat pin connector

Instruments:

a Instrument lighting
b Fuel gauge
c Thermometer
d Main beam telltale (blue)
e Fuel reserve and choke telltale (white)
f Turn indicator telltale (green)
g Oil pressure telltale (orange)
h Charge telltale (red)

Rear lights:

A = Stop light
B = Reversing light
C = Stop light and turn indicator

Ignition/starter switch:

I Halt
II Garage
III Fahrt (Drive)
IV Start

Special Equipment only:

Item Nos. 4–7–19–20 (foglamps)
41–54 (heated rear window)
47–48–49 (radio and aerial)
45 (Revolution counter in place of clock)

Firing order: 1–3–4–2

For vehicles with automatic gearbox:
Item Nos. 26–53–X (2x): Starter lock switch (17) and all associated cables

Cable coding:
1.5 sq. mm cross-section
Basic colour:

BL = blue
BR = brown
GE = yellow
GN = green
GR = grey
RT = red
SW = black
WS = white

Key to wiring diagram, p. 83.

1 Starter
2 Dip relay
3 Dip switch
4 Battery
5 Flasher unit
6 Flasher telltale
7 Flasher/parking light switch with screenwasher contact
8 Stop light switch
9 Turn indicator front LH
10 Turn indicator front RH
11 Interior light
12 Revolution counter
13 Horn
14 Main beam telltale
15 Horn relay
16 Speedometer
17 Fuel gauge tank mechanism
18 Oil pressure contact
19 Rear light unit LH
A Stop light
B Reversing light
C Turn indicator/rear light/parking light
20 Rear light unit RH
A Stop light
B Reversing light
C Turn indicator/rear light/parking light
21 Heater blower motor
22 Heater switch
23 Number plate lamp
24 Combined instrument
25 Charge telltale
26 Dynamo
27 Light switch
28 Cable connector
29 Regulator
30 Reversing light switch
31 Fuse box
32 Horn button
33 Headlight LH
34 Screenwiper motor
35 Headlight RH
36 Screenwiper switch
37 Door switch LH
38 Door switch RH
39 Lock
40 Delay relay
41 Screenwasher pump
42 Coil
43 Cigar lighter
44 Ignition/starter switch
45 Distributor

Cable coding:
0.75 sq. mm cross-section
Basic colour:

BL = blue
BR = brown
GE = yellow
GN = green
GR = grey
RT = red
SW = black
WS = white

Fuses:
1–2–3–5 = 8 Amp
4–6 = 25 Amp

Ignition/starter switch:
Key positions:

I Halt
II Garage
III Fahrt (Drive)
IV Start

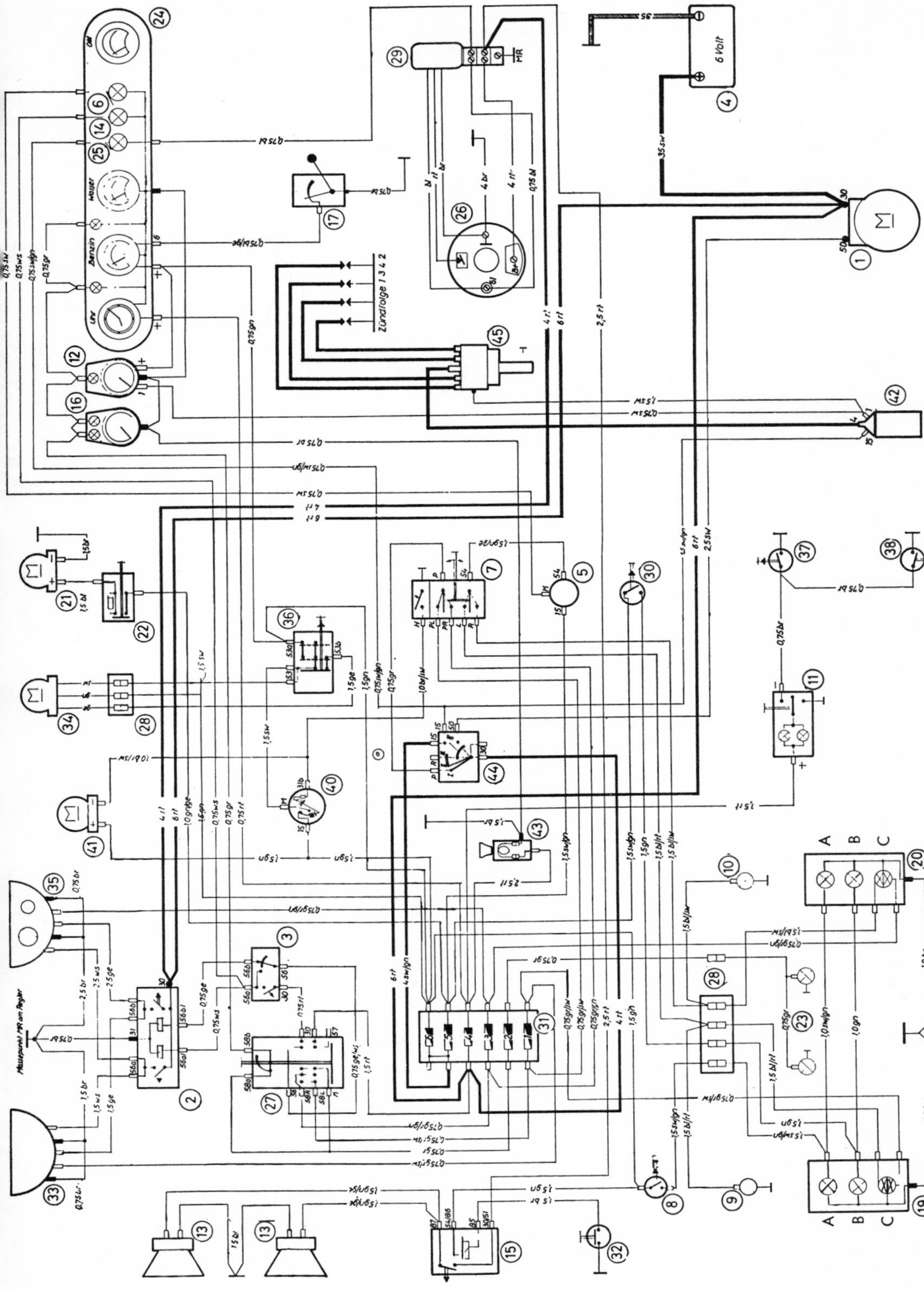

Wiring diagram, BMW 1800 TI, 1800 TISA.

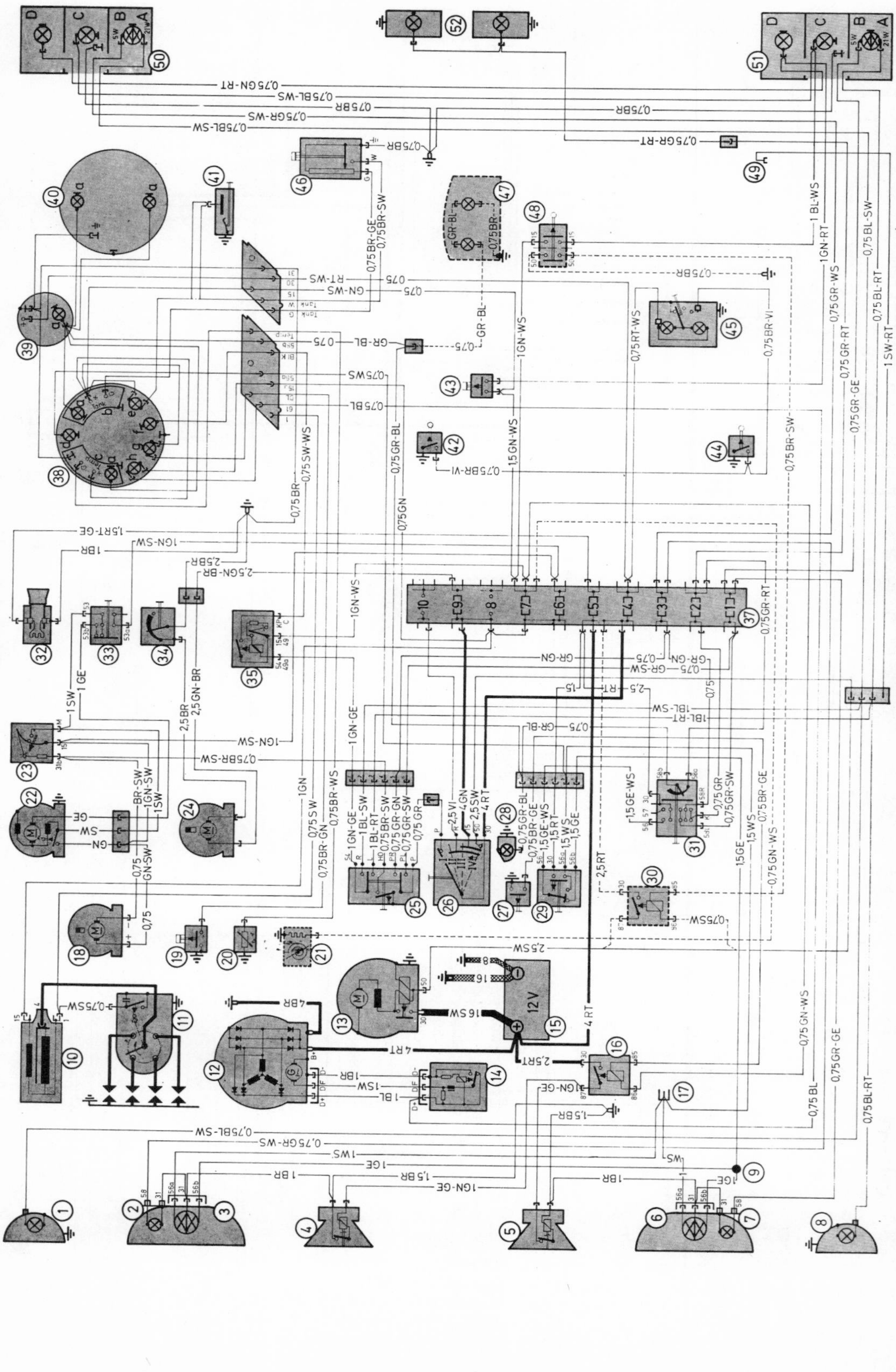

Wiring diagram, BMW 1800/69, 2000/69.

Key to wiring diagram, p. 84.

1 Turn indicator front RH
2 Parking light RH
3 Headlight RH
4 Horn RH
5 Horn LH
6 Headlight LH
7 Parking light LH
8 Turn indicator front LH
9 Solder tag
10 Coil
11 Distributor
12 Alternator
13 Starter
14 Voltage regulator
15 Battery 12 V
16 Horn relay
17 Plug for foglamp relay
18 Screenwasher pump
19 Oil pressure switch
20 Remote thermometer contact
21 Automatic choke (Automatic only)
22 Screenwiper motor
23 Delay relay
24 Heater blower motor
25 Turn indicator/parking light/screenwasher switch
26 **Ignition/starter switch:**
   I Halt
   II Garage
   III Fahrt (Drive)
   IV Start
27 Horn ring
28 Switch lighting
29 Dip switch and headlight flasher
30 Starter relay (Automatic only)
31 Light switch
32 Cigar lighter
33 Screen wiper switch
34 Blower switch (continuously variable)
35 Flasher unit
36
37 Fuse box
38 Combined instrument
   a Instrument lighting
   b Fuel gauge
   c Thermometer
   d Main beam telltale (blue)
   e Fuel reserve and choke telltale (white)
   f Turn indicator telltale (green)
   g Oil pressure telltale (orange)
   h Charge telltale (red)
39 Clock
40 Speedometer
41 Choke cable switch (not Automatic)
42 Door switch RH
43 Stop light switch
44 Door switch LH
45 Interior light
46 Fuel gauge mechanism
47 Selector lever illumination (Automatic only)
48 Reversing light switch and starter lock (Automatic only)
49 Connection for heated rear window
51 Rear light LH
   A = Turn indicator
   B = Tail light
   C = Reversing light
   D = Stop light
52 Number plate light

Firing order: 1–3–4–2
1.5 sq. mm cross-section

Cable coding:
Basic colour:
BL = blue
BR = brown
GE = yellow
GN = green
GR = grey
RT = red
SW = black
WS = white
VI = violet

Key to wiring diagram, p. 86.

1 Turn indicator and parking light front RH
2 High beam headlight (1) RH
3 Headlight (2)
4 Horn RH
5 Horn LH
6 Headlight (2)
7 High beam headlight (1) LH
8 Turn indicator and parking light front LH
9 High beam relay
10 Coil
11 Distributor
12 Alternator
13 Starter
14 Voltage regulator
15 Battery 12 V
16 Horn relay
17 Plug for foglamp relay
18 Windshield washer pump
19 Oil pressure contact
20 Remote thermometer contact
21 Automatic choke (Automatic only)
22 Screenwiper motor
23 Delay relay
24 Heater flower motor
25 Turn indicator/parking light/windshield washer switch
26 Ignition/starter switch
27 Horn ring
28 Switch lighting
29 Dip switch and headlight flasher
30 Starter relay (Automatic only)
31 Light switch
32 Cigar lighter
33 Wiper switch
34 Blower switch (continuously variable)
35 Hazard warning flasher unit
36 Hazard warning flasher switch
37 Fuse box
38 Combined instrument:
   a Instrument lighting
   b Fuel gauge
   c Thermometer
   d High beam telltale (blue)
   e Fuel reserve and choke telltale (white)
   f Turn indicator telltale (green)
   g Oil pressure telltale (green)
   h Charge telltale (red)
39 Clock
40 Speedometer
41 Choke cable switch (not Automatic)
42 Door switch RH
43 Stop light switch
44 Door switch LH
45 Interior light
46 Fuel gauge tank mechanism
47 Selector lever illumination (Automatic only)
48 Switch for reversing light and starter lock (Automatic)
49 Heated rear window connection
50 Rear light RH
51 Rear light LH
   A = Turn indicator
   B = Rear light
   C = Reversing light
   D = Stop light
52 License plate light
53 Brake fluid level switch
54 Brake fluid level telltale

Firing order: 1–3–4–2

Cable coding:
1.5 sq. mm cross-section
Basic colour:
BL = blue
BR = brown
GE = yellow
GN = green
GR = grey
RT = red
SW = black
WS = white

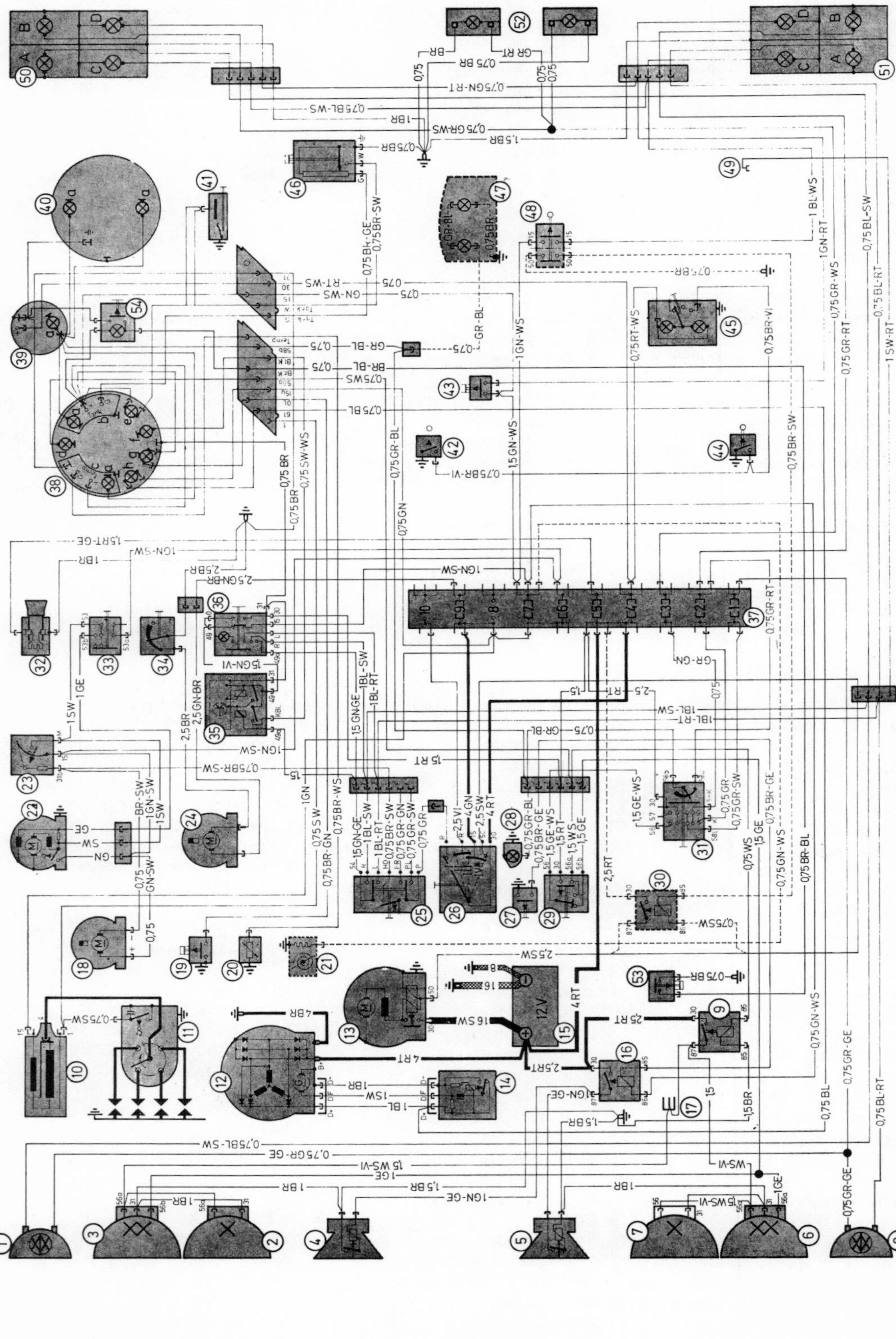

Wiring diagram, BMW 2000/69, US model.

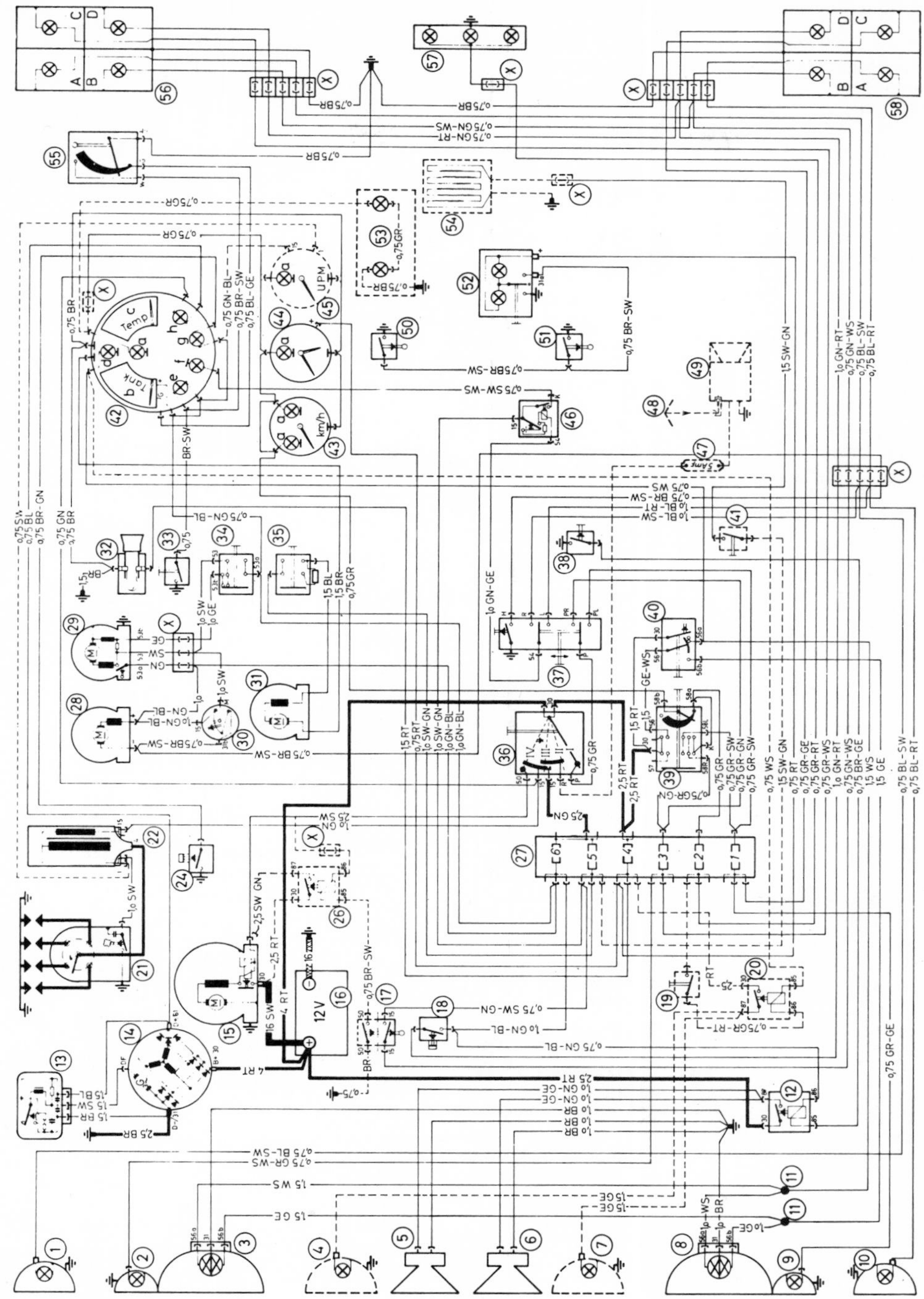

Wiring diagram, BMW 2000, 2000 A, 2000 TI.

Firing order: 1–3–4–2

For vehicles with automatic gearbox:
Item Nos. 27–53–X (2X): Starter lock switch (17) and all associated cables

For TILUX: Revolution counter and heated rear window are standard equipment (clock in combined instrument)

Special Equipment only:

Item Nos. 4–7–19–20 (foglamps)
41–54 (heated rear window)*
47–48–49 (radio and aerial)
45 (Revolution counter in place of clock)*

* Not TILUX

Cable coding:

1.5 sq. mm cross-section

Basic colour:

BL = blue
BR = brown
GE = yellow
GN = green
GR = grey
RT = red
SW = black
WS = white

Key to wiring diagram, p. 87.

1 Turn indicator front RH
2 Parking light RH
3 Headlight RH
4 Foglamp RH
5 Horn RH
6 Horn LH
7 Foglamp LH
8 Headlight LH
9 Parking light LH
10 Turn indicator front LH
11 Soldered joint
12 Horn relay
13 Voltage regulator
14 Alternator
15 Starter
16 Battery
17 Switch for reversing light and starter lock
18 Stop light switch
19 Foglamp switch
20 Foglamp relay
21 Distributor
22 Coil
23
24 Oil pressure contact
25
26 Starter relay
27 Fuse box
28 Screenwasher pump
29 Screenwiper motor
30 Delay relay
31 Heater blower motor
32 Cigar lighter
33 Choke cable switch
34 Screenwiper switch
35 Heater switch
36 Ignition/starter switch
37 Turn indicator/parking light/screenwasher switch
38 Horn ring
39 Light switch
40 Dip switch
41 Switch for heated rear window
42 Combined instrument
43 Speedometer
44 Clock
45 Revolution counter
46 Flasher unit
47 Separate fuse for radio
48 Aerial
49 Radio
50 Door switch RH
51 Door switch LH
52 Interior light
53 Selector lever illumination
54 Heated rear window
55 Fuel gauge tank mechanism
56 Rear light RH
57 Number plate light
58 Rear light LH
X Flat pin connector

Instruments:
a Instrument lighting
b Fuel gauge
c Thermometer
d Main beam telltale (blue)
e Fuel reserve and choke telltale (white)
f Turn indicator telltale (green)
g Oil pressure telltale (orange)
h Charge telltale (red)

Rear lights:
A = Turn indicator
B = Reversing lights
C = Rear lights
D = Stop lights

Ignition/starter switch:
I Halt
II Garage
III Fahrt (Drive)
IV Start

Key to wiring diagram, p. 89.

1 Turn indicator front RH
2 Main headlight RH
3 Additional headlight (main beam) RH
4
5 Horn RH
6 Horn LH
7
8 Additional headlight (main beam) LH
9 Main headlight LH
10 Turn indicator front LH
11 Dip relay
12 Horn relay
13 Voltage regulator
14 Alternator
15 Starter
16 Battery
17 Reversing light and starter lock switch
18 Stop light switch
19
20
21 Distributor
22 Coil
23
24 Oil pressure contact
25
26 Starter relay
27 Fuse box
28 Screenwasher pump
29 Screenwiper motor
30 Delay relay
31 Heater blower motor
32 Cigar lighter
33 Choke cable switch
34 Screen wiper switch
35 Heater switch
36 Ignition/starter switch
37 Turn indicator/parking light/screenwasher switch
38 Horn ring
39 Light switch
40 Dip switch
41 Switch for heated rear window
42 Combined instrument
43 Speedometer
44 Clock
45 Revolution counter
46 Flasher unit
47 Separate fuse for radio
48 Aerial
49 Radio
50 Door switch RH
51 Door switch LH
52 Interior light
53 Selector lever illumination
54 Heated rear window
55 Fuel gauge tank mechanism
56 Rear light RH
57 Number plate light
58 Rear light LH
X Flat pin connector

Instruments:
a Instrument lighting
b Fuel gauge
c Thermometer
d Main beam telltale (blue)
e Fuel reserve and choke telltale (white)
f Turn indicator telltale (green)
g Oil pressure telltale (orange)
h Charge telltale (red)

Rear lights:
A = Turn indicator
B = Reversing lights
C = Rear lights
D = Stop lights

Ignition/starter switch:
I Halt
II Garage
III Fahrt (Drive)
IV Start

Firing order: 1–3–4–2

For vehicles with automatic gearbox:
Item Nos. 26–53–X (2X): Starter lock switch (17) with all associated cables

Special Equipment only:
* Standard on 2000 TILUX-RE
Item Nos. 41–54 (heated rear window)*
47–48–49 (radio and aerial)
45 (Revolution counter in place of clock)*

Cable coding:
1.5 sq. mm cross- section
Basic colour:
BL = blue
BR = brown
GE = yellow
GN = green
GR = grey
RT = red
SW = black
WS = white

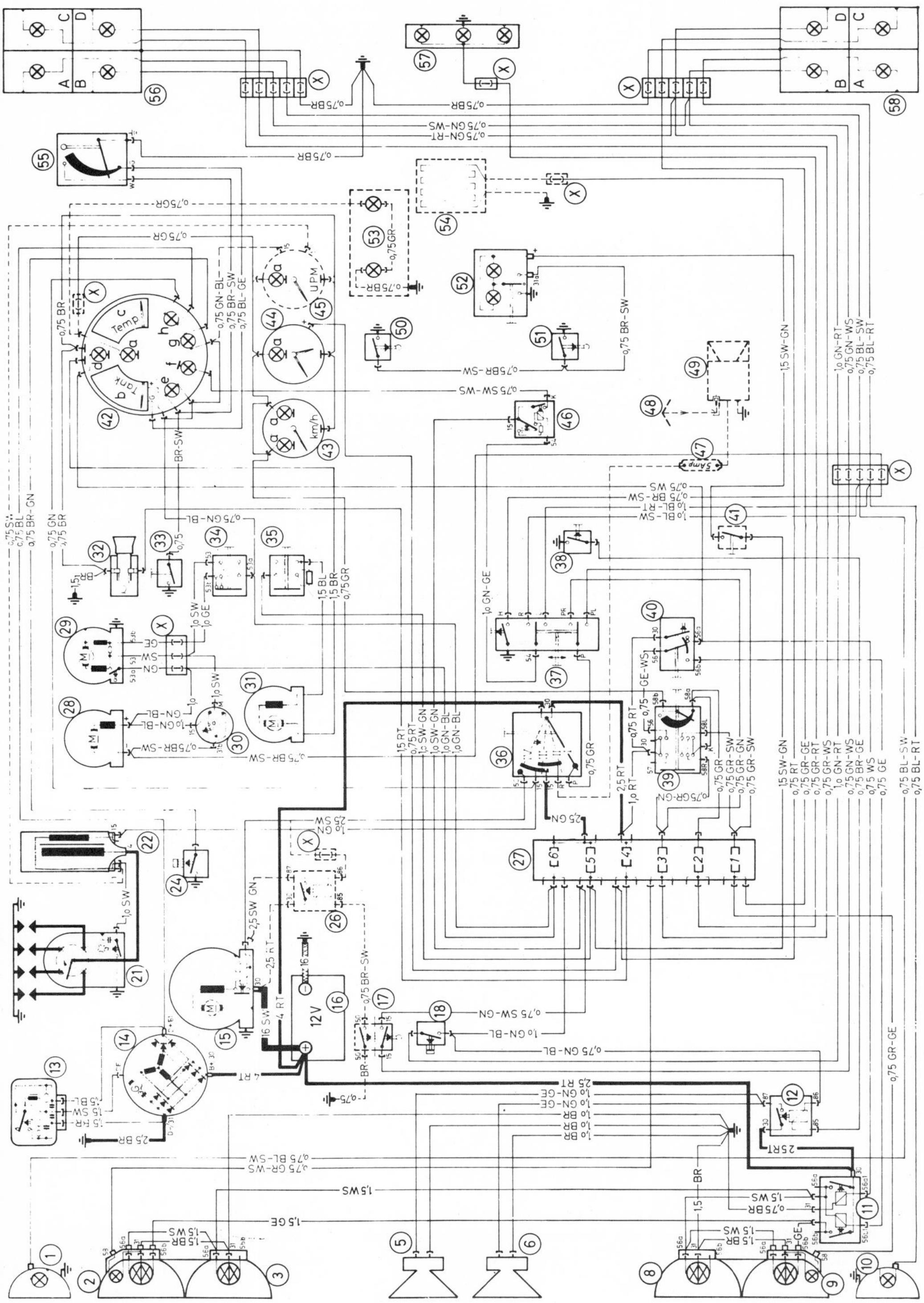

Wiring diagram, BMW 2000 RE, 2000 A-RE, 2000 TI-RE.

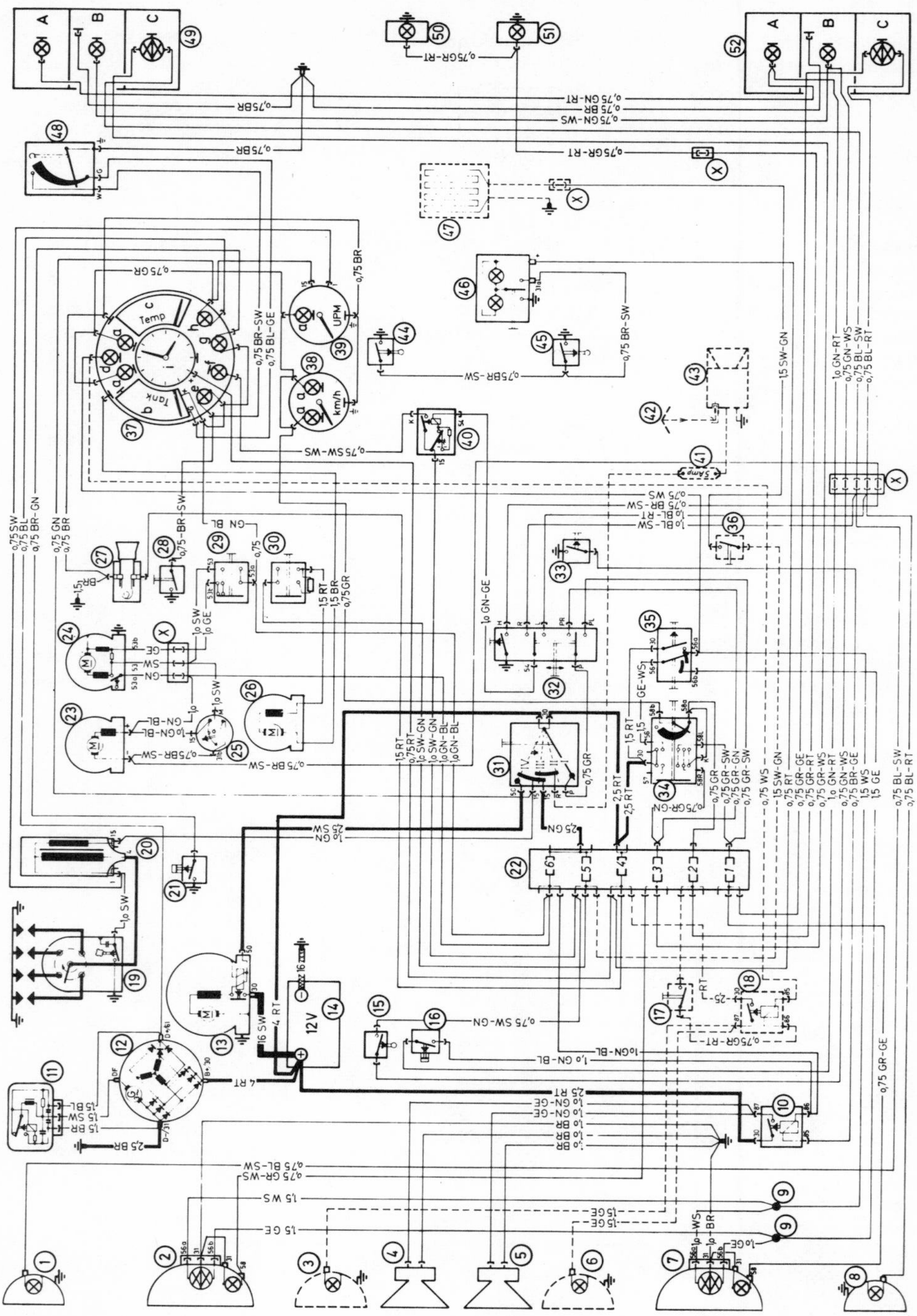

Wiring diagram, BMW 2000 TI.

Rear lights:

A = Stop light
B = Reversing light
C = Rear/parking light and turn indicator

Ignition/starter switch:

I Halt
II Garage
III Fahrt (Drive)
IV Start

Firing order: 1–3–4–2

Special Equipment only:

Item Nos. 4–7–19–20 (foglamps)
41–54 (heated rear window)
47–48–49 (radio and aerial)

Cable coding:

1.5 sq. mm cross-section

Basic colour:

BL = blue
BR = brown
GE = yellow
GN = green
GR = grey
RT = red
SW = black
WS = white

Key to wiring diagram, p. 90.

1 Turn indicator front RH
2 Headlight RH with parking light
3 Foglamp RH
4 Horn RH
5 Horn LH
6 Foglamp LH
7 Headlight LH with parking light
8 Turn indicator front LH
9 Soldered joint
10 Horn relay
11 Voltage regulator
12 Alternator
13 Starter
14 Battery
15 Reversing light switch
16 Stop light switch
17 Foglamp switch
18 Foglamp relay
19 Distributor
20 Coil
21 Oil pressure contact
22 Fuse box
23 Screenwasher pump
24 Screenwiper motor
25 Delay relay
26 Heater blower motor
27 Cigar lighter
28 Choke cable switch
29 Screen wiper switch
30 Heater switch
31 Ignition/starter switch
32 Turn indicator/parking light/ screenwasher switch
33 Horn ring
34 Light switch
35 Dip switch and headlamp flasher
36 Switch for heated rear window
37 Combined instrument
38 Speedometer
39 Revolution counter
40 Flasher unit
41 Separate fuse for radio
42 Aerial
43 Radio
44 Door switch RH
45 Door switch LH
46 Interior light
47 Heated rear window
48 Fuel gauge tank mechanism
49 Rear light RH
50 Number plate light RH
51 Number plate light LH
52 Rear light LH
X Flat pin connector

Instruments:

a Instrument lighting
b Fuel gauge
c Thermometer
d Main beam telltale (blue)
e Fuel reserve and choke telltale (white)
f Turn indicator telltale (green)
g Oil pressure telltale (orange)
h Charge telltale (red)
i Clock

Key to wiring diagram, p. 92.

1 Turn indicator front RH
2 Headlight RH
3 Long-range headlight RH
4 Parking light RH
5 Parking light LH
6 Long-range headlight LH
7 Headlight LH
8 Turn indicator front LH
9 Dip relay
10 Dipswitch with headlight flasher
11 Light switch
12 Engine compartment light switch
13 Engine compartment light
14 Horn RH
15 Horn LH
16 Horn relay
17 Horn ring
18 Fuse box
19 Alternator
20 Voltage regulator
21 Coil
22 Distributor
23 Starter
24 Battery
25 Reversing light switch
26 Stop light switch
27 Heated rear window switch
28 Screenwiper motor
29 Screenwiper switch
30 Selector gate light
31 Screenwasher pump
32 Delay relay
33 Heater switch
34 Heater blower motor
35 Cigar lighter
36 Flasher unit
37 Turn indicator/parking light/ screenwasher switch
38 Oil pressure contact
39 Water temperature thermocouple
40 Plug-in connector
41 Electric window lift front RH
42 Terminal board
43 Front window lift switch
44 Terminal board
45 Electrical window lift front LH
46 Electric window lift rear RH
47 Terminal board
48 Rear RH window lift switch
49 Rear LH window lift switch
50 Terminal board
51 Electric window lift rear LH
52 Fuel gauge tank contact
53 Interior light
54 Door switch RH
55 Door switch LH
56 Luggage compartment light switch
57 Luggage compartment light
58 Heated rear window
59 Plug-in connector
60 Turn indicator rear RH
61 Rear light RH
62 Top light RH
63 Reversing light RH
64 Number plate lights
65 Reversing light LH
66 Stop light LH
67 Rear light LH
68 Turn indicator rear LH
69 Choke cable contact
70 Ignition/starter switch
71 Radio
72 Separate fuse
73 Combined instrument
74 Revolution counter
75 Speedometer
76 Clock
77 Rear loudspeaker

Instruments:

a Instrument lighting
b Cooling water thermometer
c Fuel gauge
d Oil pressure telltale
e Choke and fuel reverse telltale
f Battery charge telltale
g Main beam telltale
h Turn indicator telltale

Ignition/starter switch:
Key positions:

I Lock
II Garage
III Fahrt (Drive)
IV Start

Fuses:
1–2–3–4–5–6 = 8 Amp
7–8 = 25 Amp
Firing order: 1–3–4–2

Cable coding:
0.75 sq. mm cross- section
Colour:

BL = blue
BR = brown
GE = yellow
GN = green
GR = grey
LI = lilac
RT = red
SW = black
WS = white

Items 27–28–59–71–72–77 = Special equipment
Item 30 only when automatic gearbox fitted
X = When manual gearbox is fitted, conected to instrument lighting; cable for selector gate light is then free.

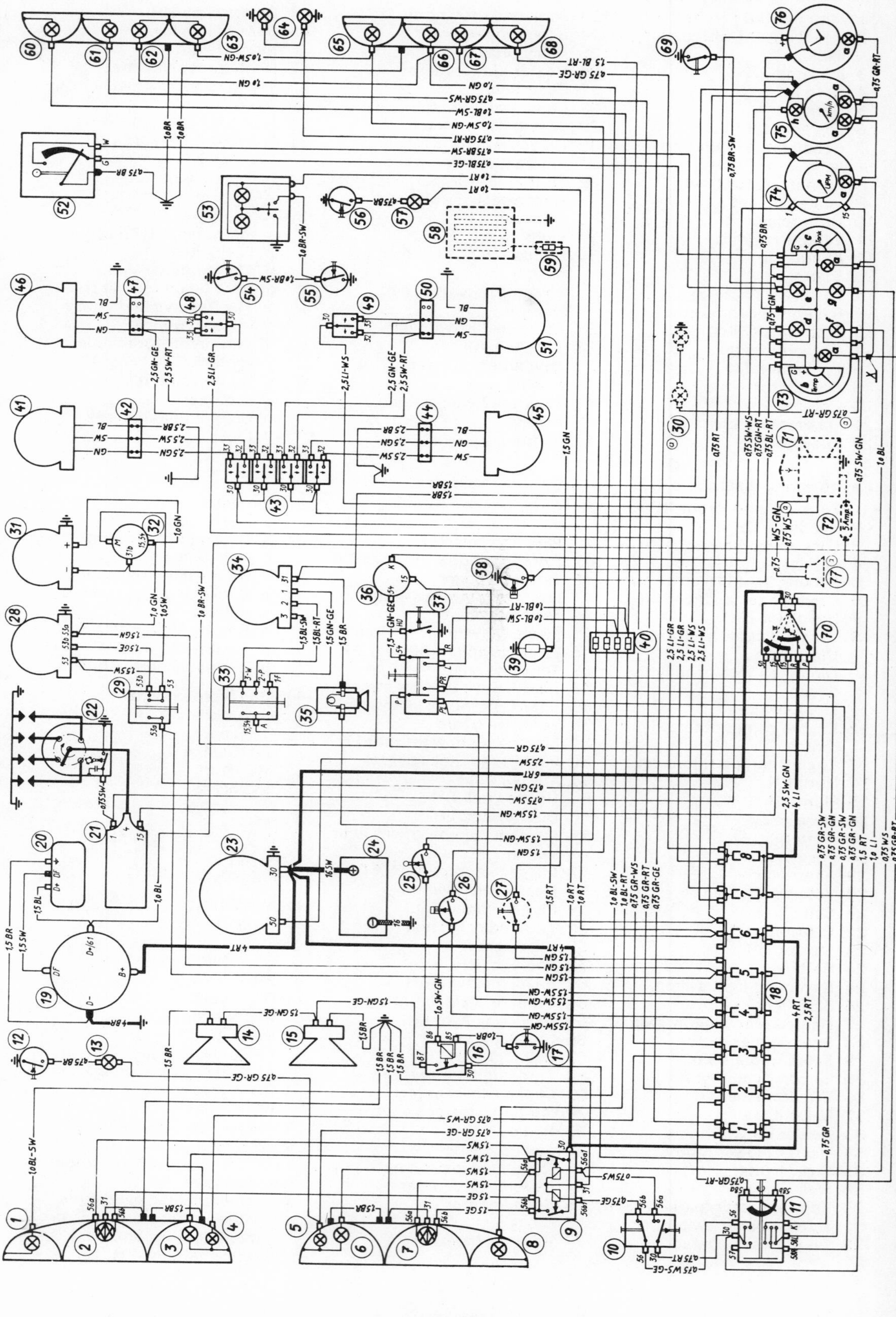

Chapter 6
Drive Train

The BMW drive train consists of the gearbox, clutch, drive shaft, differential, and rear axles.

Clutch

A single plate, dry clutch employing conventional coil springs is used on all models. It is hydraulically actuated by a slave cylinder attached to the housing and interconnected by a pushrod to the clutch throwout lever. The hydraulic clutch circuit is entirely independent of the brake circuit. A few models use a mechanically actuated clutch.

Clutch Adjustment

When fully depressed, the clutch pedal should contact the stop. Clearance between pedal plate and hornring must then be 5.7-5.9″ (145-150 mm). If clearance is less than 5.3″ (135 mm) a piston rod (1) of 4.37″ (111 mm) should be used. If clearance is 5.3-5.5″ (135-140 mm) a piston rod of 4.29″ (109 mm) is used. NOTE: *the maximum clearance of 5.9″ (150 mm) should not be exceeded or expansion orifice (3) may damage piston diaphragm (2).*

Clutch Removal

To service the clutch it is necessary to remove the transmission. Loosen clutch screws alternately, first on one side then the other. Take off clutch and driven plate. Note that the side of the driven plate with the protruding spring ends and hub faces the gearbox. The clutch plate should be replaced when thickness is .315″ (8 mm). When reassembling, center the driven plate and clutch with a suitable shaft, and tighten screws evenly and alternately. Adjust play on throwout lever to figure given in Clutch Specifications Chart.

Centering clutch disc.

Clutch Specifications

Model	Type	Spring Color Coding	Pressure Lbs. Approx.	Minimum Driven Plate Thickness In. (mm)	Clutch Lever Clearance In. (mm)	Pedal Free Travel In. (mm) Approx.
1500	KFS200K single dry plate	green/yellow/ green	880±44	.32(8)	.118-.138 (3-3.5)	.8-1.0 (20-25)
1600	KFS200K single dry plate	green/yellow/ green	880±44	.32(8)	.118-.138 (3-3.5)	.8-1.0 (20-25)
1600-2	KFS200K single dry plate	green/yellow/ green	880±44	.29(7.3)	.118-.138 (3-3.5)	.8-1.0 (20-25)
1600TI	KFS200K single dry plate	blue/white/blue w. yellow stripe	1075±33	.32(8)	.118-.138 (3-3.5)	.8-1.0 (20-25)
1800	KFS200K single dry plate	blue/white/blue w. yellow stripe	1075±33	.32(8)	.118-.138 (3-3.5)	.8-1.0 (20-25)
1800/69	KFS200K single dry plate	blue/white/blue w. yellow stripe	1075±33	.32(8)	.118-.138 (3-3.5)	.8-1.0 (20-25)
1800TI	KFS200K single dry plate	blue/white/blue w. yellow stripe	1075±33	.32(8)	.118-.138 (3-3.5)	.8-1.0 (20-25)
2002	HB225Sph single dry plate	blue/white/blue w. yellow stripe	1075±33	.32(8)	.118-.138 (3-3.5)	.8-1.0 (20-25)
2000	HB225Sph single dry plate	blue/grey/blue	925	.36(9.1)	.158-.177 (4-4.5)	1.4-1.6 (35-40)
2000TI	HB225Sph single dry plate	blue/grey/blue	925	.36(9.1)	.158-.177 (4-4.5)	1.4-1.6 (35-40)
2000CS	HB225Sph single dry plate	blue/grey/blue	925	.36(9.1)	.158-.177 (4-4.5)	1.4-1.6 (35-40)

Gearbox Specifications

Model	Speeds	Synchro-Mesh	Gearbox Ratios:1					Mainshaft End Play In./mm Max.	Counter-shaft End Play In./mm Max.	Pinion Tooth Backlash In./mm	Shaft Runout In./mm Max.
			1st	2nd	3rd	4th	Reverse				
1500, 1600, 1800, 1800TI, 1800/69	4 Fwd, Rev.	1,2,3,4	3.816	2.070	1.330	1.000	4.153	.024/.6	.0079/.2	.00236-.0059/.06-.15	.00079/.02
1600-2, 1600TI, 2002, 2000, 2000TI, 2000CS	4 Fwd, Rev.	1,2,3,4	3.835	2.053	1.345	1.000	4.180	.024/.6	.0079/.2	.00236-.0059/.06-.15	.00079/.02
2500, 2800	4 Fwd, Rev.	1,2,3,4	3.850	2.120	1.375	1.000	4.130	.024/.6	.0079/.2	.00236-.0059/.06-.15	.00079/.02
2800CS	4 Fwd, Rev.	1,2,3,4	3.850	2.080	1.375	1.000	4.130	.024/.6	.0079/.2	.00236-.0059/.06-.15	.00079/.02
1800-A, 2000A, 2000CA, 2002A	3 Fwd, Rev.*		2.56	1.52	1.0	Con-verter 1-2.2	2.0				

*Automatic ZF3HP-12/B

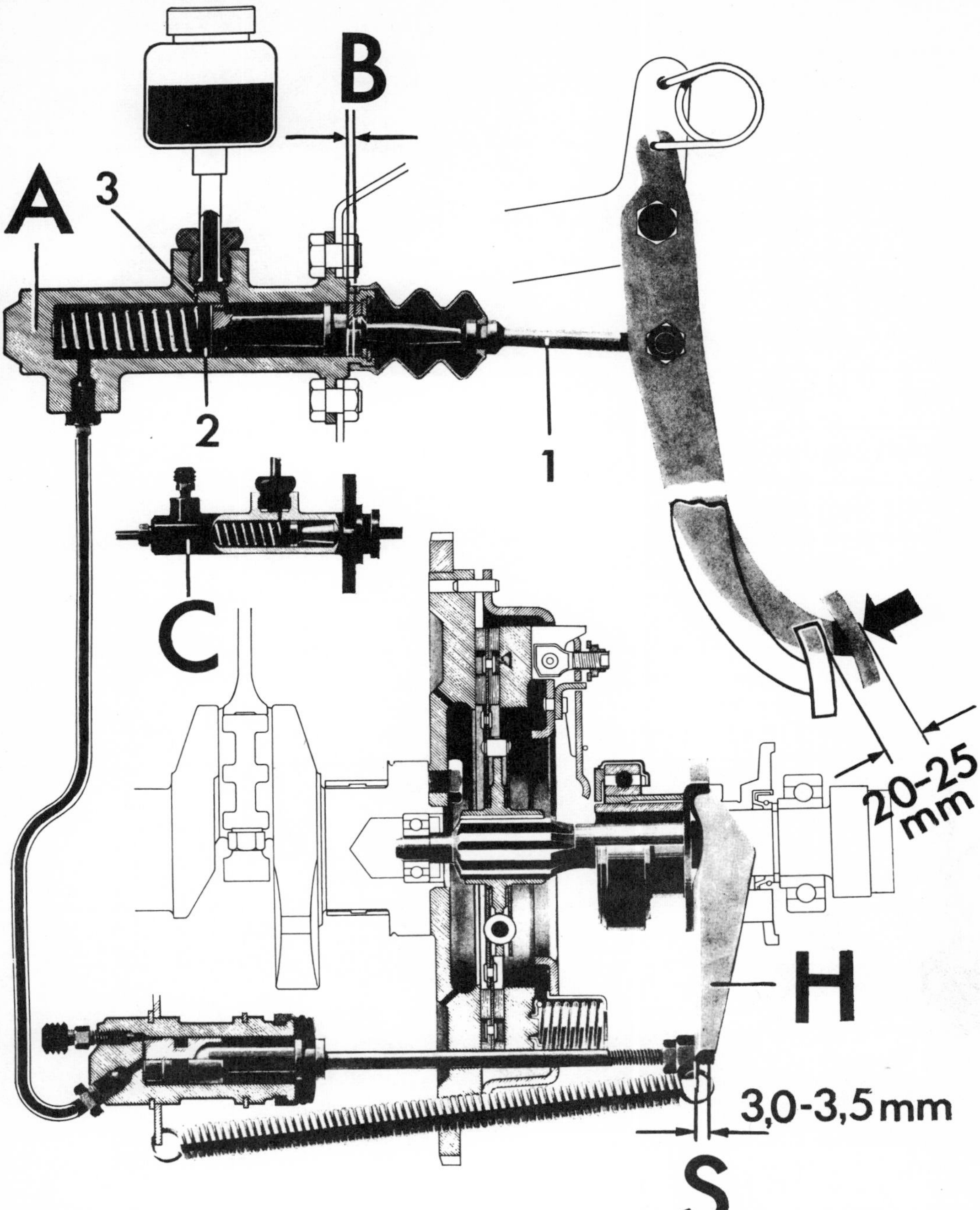

Required pedal free travel and clutch lever clearance (S) for BMW Series 1500, 1600 and 1800. See Clutch Specifications Chart for other models. Piston rod clearance (B) should be .04" (1 mm). Early master cylinders (C) have a bleed valve. Later types (A) are bled from the slave cylinder.

Type 225 Sph - Driving plate with torsional damper 228 PSD

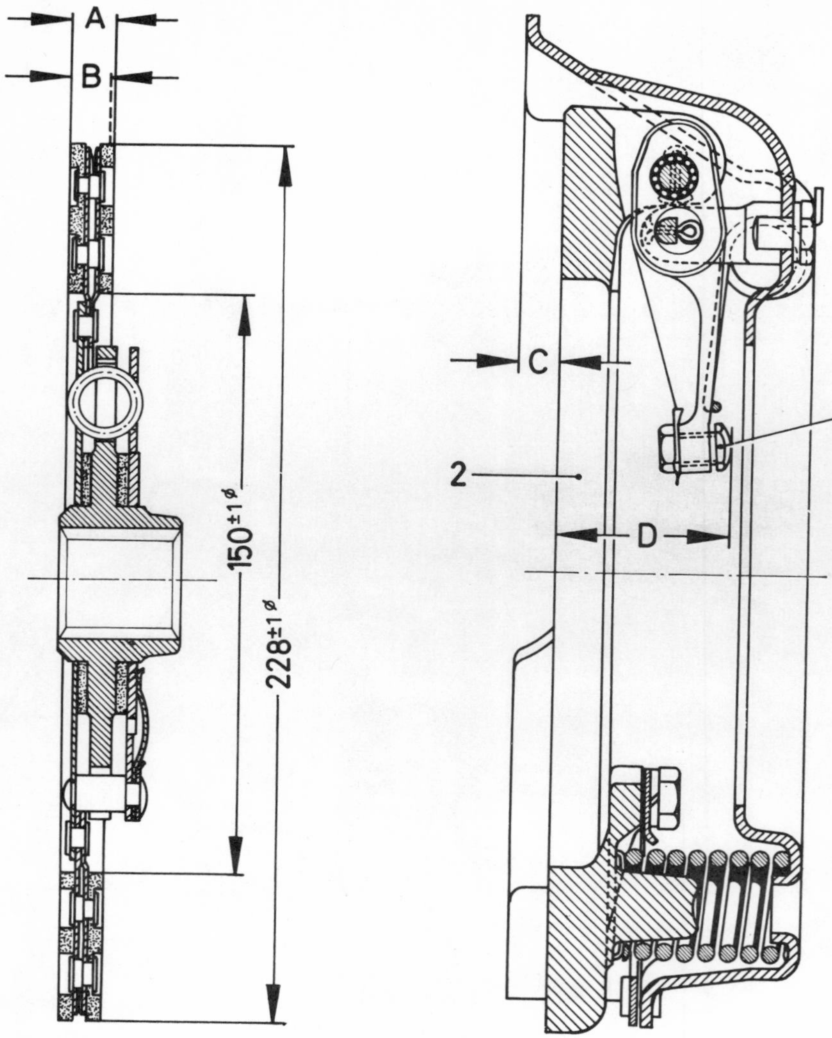

Clutch driven plate adjustments: (A) unloaded position = .398"-.414 (10.1-10.4 mm); (B) loaded with 1058 lbs. = .358-.373 (9.1-9.5 mm); (C) for adjusting clutch engagement = .374-.381" (9.5-9.7 mm); (D) correct dimension between adjusting screw (1) and pressure plate (2) = .5985"-.6615" (40.6-42.2 mm). Type 222 Sph clutch shown.

Gearbox

BMW's are equipped with two different manual gearboxes beside the automatic type ZF3HP-12 B. The manual types all have 4 forward speeds with Porsche synchronizers. Gear ratios differ slightly.

Gearbox Disassembly And Assembly — Long Neck Unit

Remove engine from its mounting and move far enough forward to allow gearbox to be dropped down at rear. Disconnect and lower steering control lever. Drain gearbox. Partially withdraw shift mechanism from housing after removing lockpin and screwing out the plug, lock bolt and spring. By rotating the mechanism counterclockwise, turn the shift finger until it is clear of the driver. Be careful not to damage seal. NOTE: *the shift mechanism cannot be pulled out completely.* Remove the throwout lever hairpin spring and remove lever.

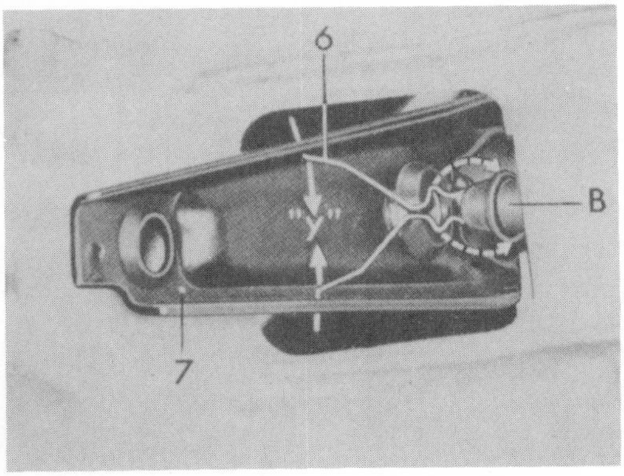

Clutch throwout lever (7), spring (6), collar (B).

Remove guide flange (11) from clutch shaft, recovering shims. Lift out snap-ring and pull off clutch shaft bearing, again recovering shims. Gently pull out shaft, being careful not to damage seal.

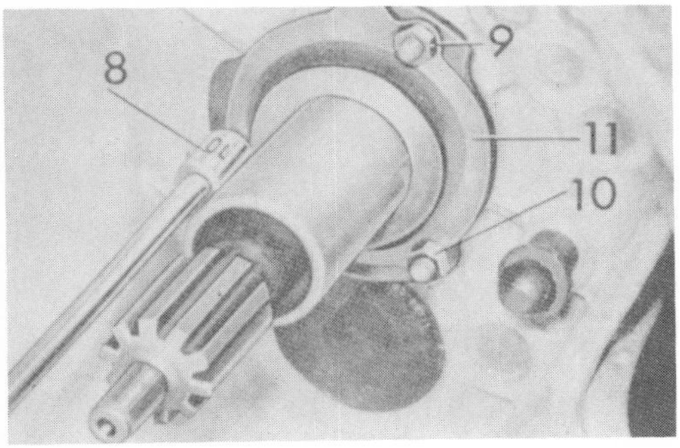

Clutch shaft drive flange (11), nuts (8, 9, 10).

Remove gearbox housing assembly nuts and warm area around countershaft seal to facilitate removal of bearing. Gently tap gearbox free and withdraw. Free spacer (Z) with complete gear train from housing extension by tapping at stud (N) and remove.

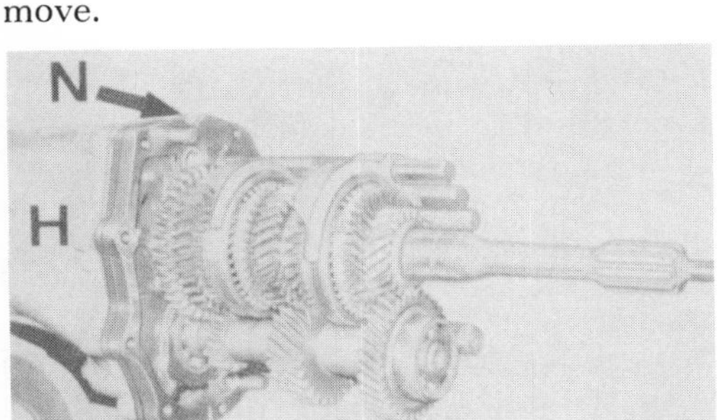

Gearbox disassembly. Housing extension (H), stud (N), spacer (Z).

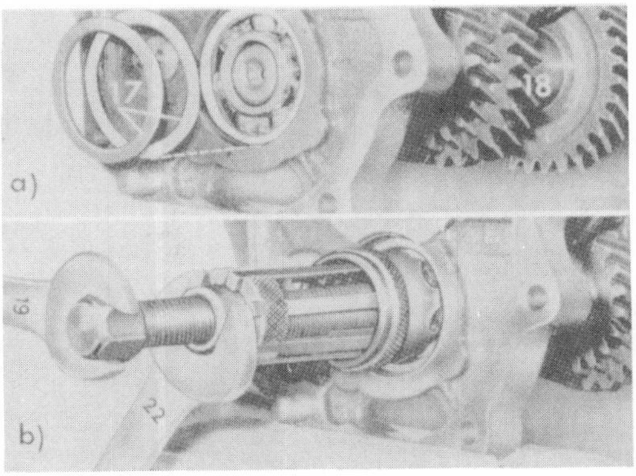

Removing shims (17) and pulling bearing from countershaft (18).

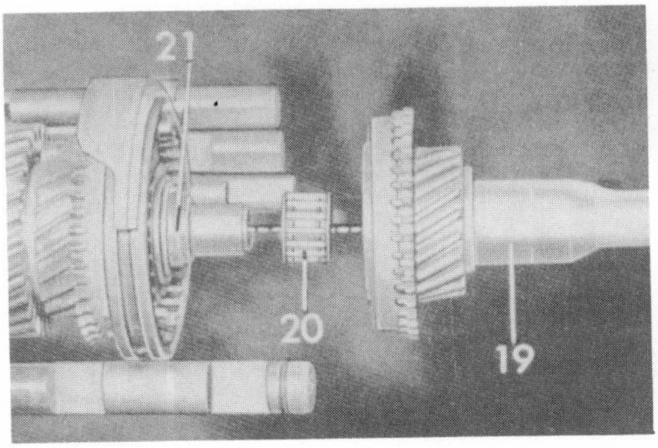

Removing clutch shaft (19) and bearing (20) from mainshaft (21).

Mount gear train together with spacer in a soft jawed vise, remove the countershaft shims (17) and pull bearing. WARNING: *be careful that the countershaft gear does not press the synchronizer out of position.*

Remove clutch shaft (19) and bearing (20) from mainshaft (21).

Remove shift forks after removing lockpins, then drive shift shafts from spacer. Mark associated parts to ensure correct reassembly. Recover balls that are released.

Bend down tabs of lockplates and remove screws from mainshaft bearing retainer. *Note position of the special lockplate for correct reassembly. This serves also as a lubricator for the odometer drive.* Drive mainshaft out of spacer.

Clamp mainshaft (36), and remove snapring, thrust washer and guide flange for 3rd and 4th gears. Remove 3rd gear (a) with synchronizer assembly. Remove spacer (b) and bearing (c). Push off spacer ring (d) and thrust washer (e). Lift off 2nd gear (f) with synchronizer assembly, bearing (g), bushing (h) and spacer (i).

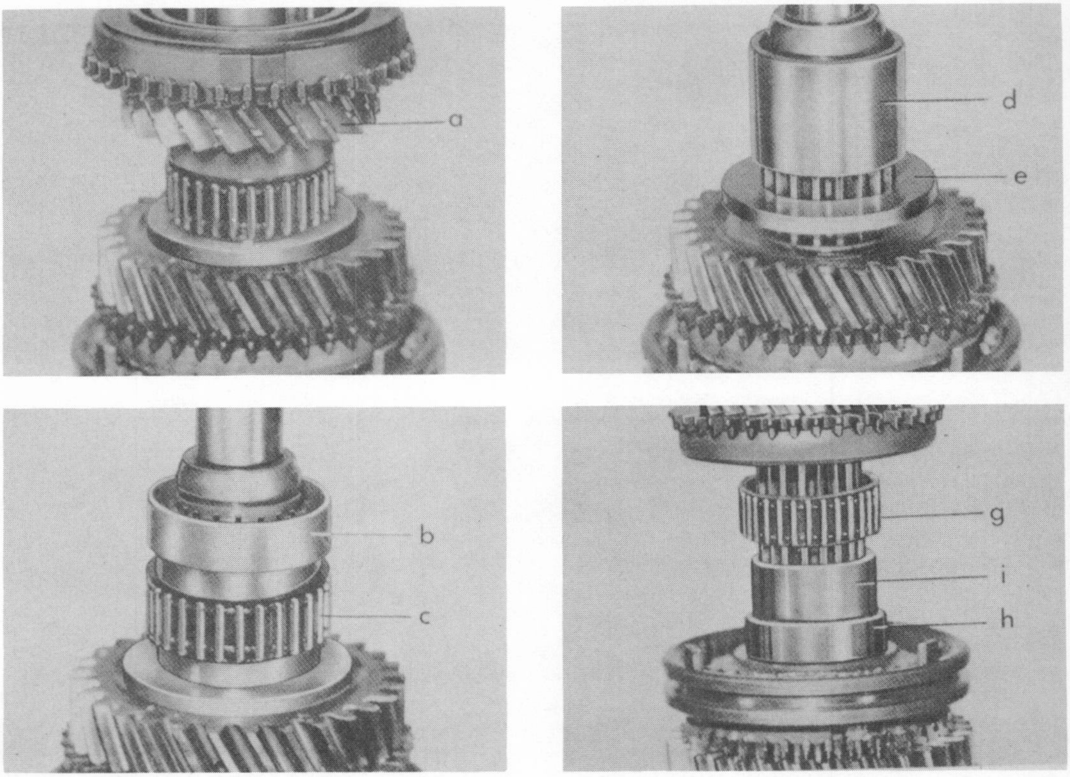

Second and third gear removed. Third gear (a), spacer (b), bearing (c), spacer (d), thrust washer (e), 2nd gear (f), bearing (g), spacer (h), spacer (i).

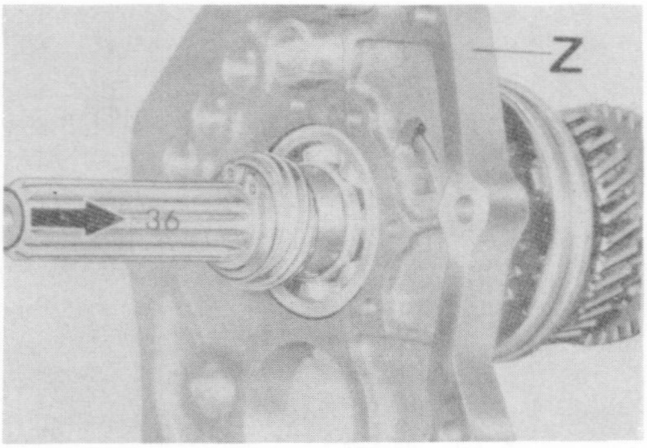

Spacer (Z) with mainshaft bearing retainer removed. Drive out mainshaft (36) in direction of arrow.

Remove shift sleeve (40), guide flange (41) and 1st gear with synchronizer assembly (42). Take off spacers (43, 44), bearing (45) and reverse gear (46). Remove coupling flange (47) and mark the side (F) facing the reverse gear for correct reassembly. Remove snap-ring (48) and washer (49). Press odometer drive gear (50) and bearing (51) off mainshaft (52).

Reassemble gearbox in reverse order from above. Assemble mainshaft so that overall dimension measured from hub of reverse gear (60) to smooth surface of guide flange (61) is:

$$5.0394''^{+.04''}_{-.08''} \text{ or } (128^{+.1}_{-.2} \text{ mm})$$

Compensate with shims in front of reverse gear.

When assembling shift shafts, and shift forks insert lockpins with their slits facing in the direction of travel of the shafts.

In adjusting gear mesh of mainshaft and countershaft, use shims (91) to adjust play between ball bearing and end seal in intermediate plate to specifications. Install gear train assembly in gearbox housing only in neutral position. Adjust mainshaft end play to specifications by installing a suitable shim on the input end of the mainshaft. Size of shim may be calculated by method shown for Universal 232 gearbox.

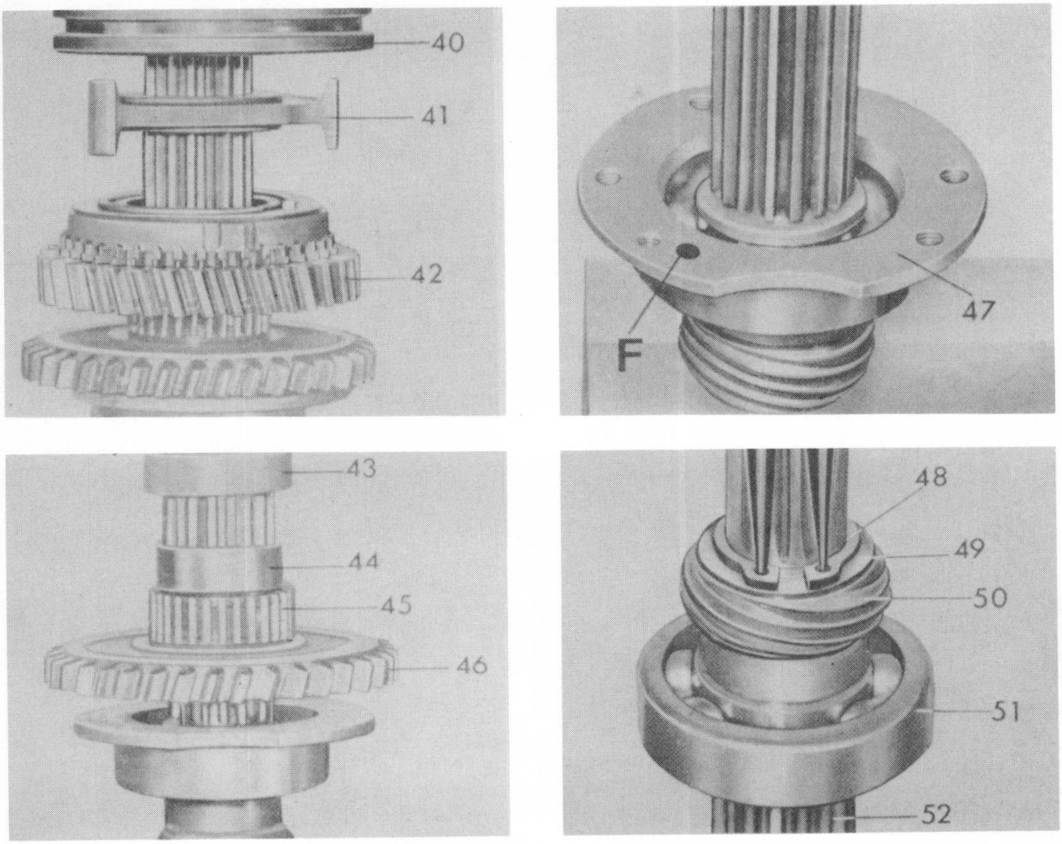

First gear, reverse gear and odometer drive removal. Shift sleeve (40), guide flange (41), 1st gear with synchronizer (42), spacers (43, 44), bearing (45), reverse gear (46), coupling flange (47), position mark (F), snap-ring (48), spring washer (49), odometer drive wheel (50), bearing (51), mainshaft (52).

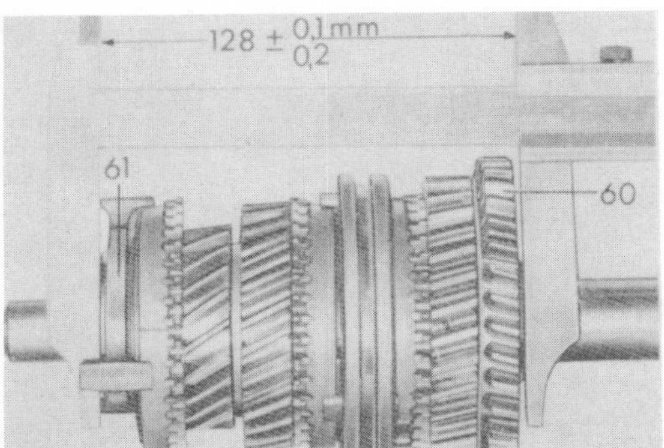

Correct length of mainshaft assembly as measured from guide flange (61) to reverse gear (60).

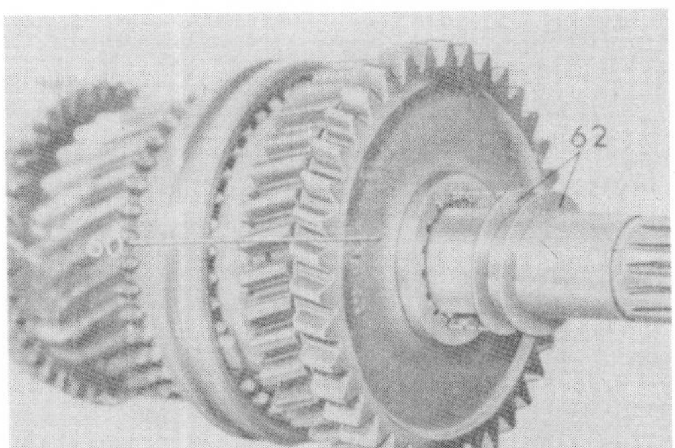

Use of shims (62) in front of reverse gear (60) to obtain correct length of mainshaft assembly.

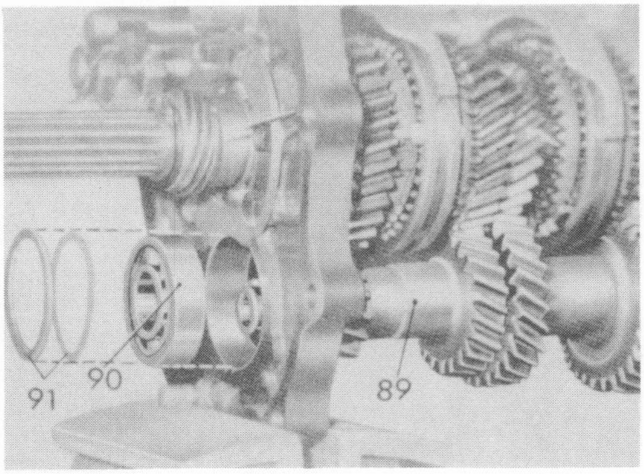

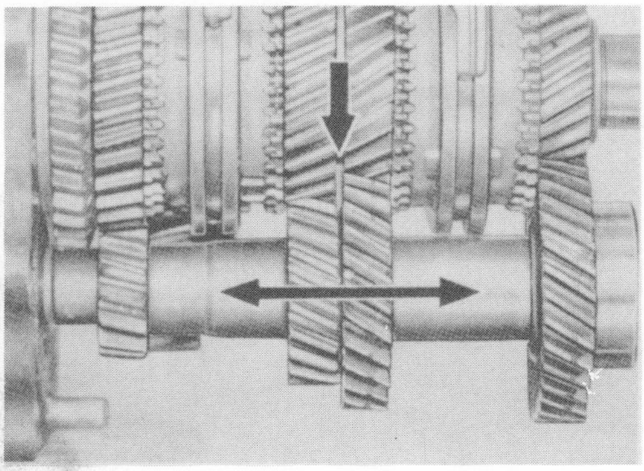

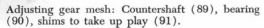

Adjusting gear mesh: Countershaft (89), bearing (90), shims to take up play (91).

Gear Box Disassembly — Universal 232

Remove engine from its mounting as described in Chapter 3 and move far enough forward to allow gearbox to be lowered out of car toward rear. It will be necessary to disconnect and lower parts of the steering linkage also.

Drive out pin and remove shift selector shaft and joint. Mount gearbox on jig, if available and drain oil. Pull bearing from clutch shaft and save shims. Remove gearbox housing cover and warm area around countershaft end-seal to facilitate removal of shaft bearing. Lightly tap to loosen housing, pull off and remove seal. Remove shift shaft (14) by sliding forward after removing lockpin from side of housing, cutting safety wire and loosening bolt from shift bar.

Place shift shaft (15) in 4th gear position. Remove lockpin (16) and pull shift shaft (15) forward until shift fork (17) can be removed. Catch loose ball bearings. Place shift fork (19) in neutral, push shift shaft (18) to 2nd gear position and drive lockpin out from shift fork (20). Pull shift

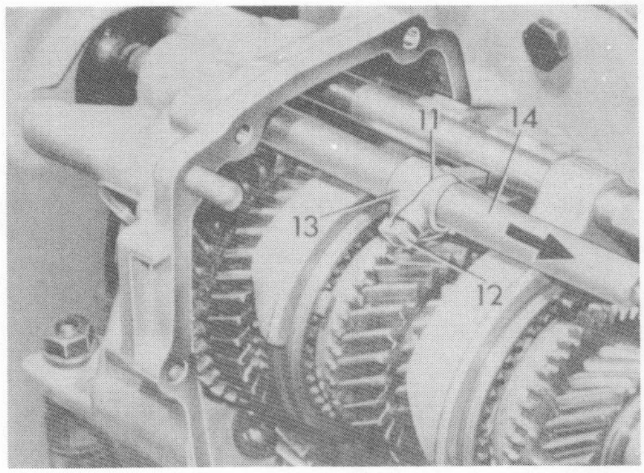

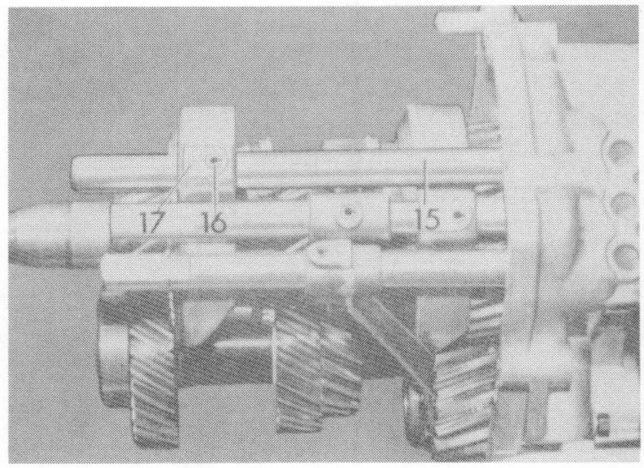

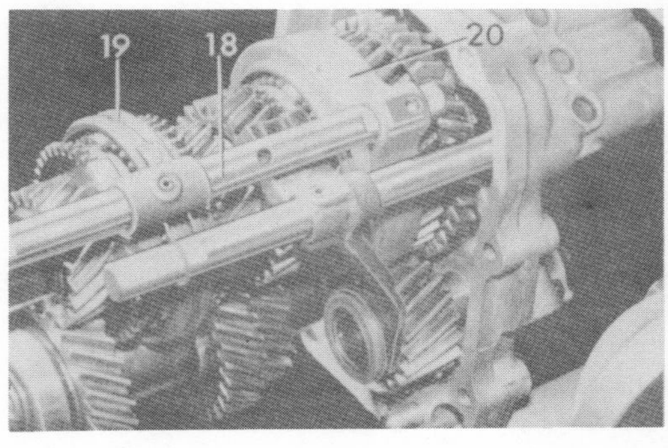

Mainshaft and countershaft assemblies: safety wire (11), lockscrew (12), shift forks (13, 17, 20, 23), shift shafts (14, 15, 18, 24), lockpins (16, 22), shift sleeves (19, 21).

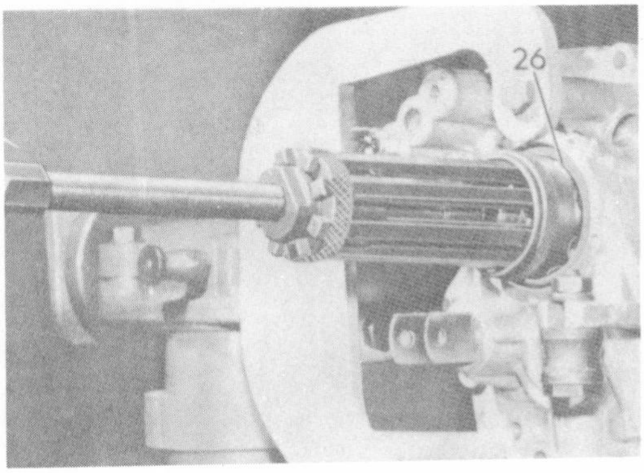

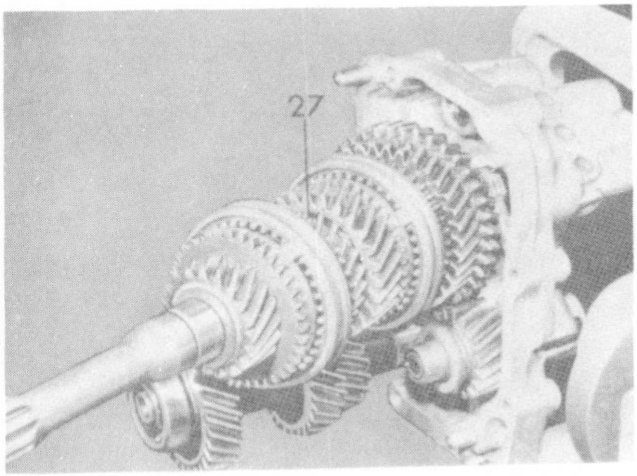

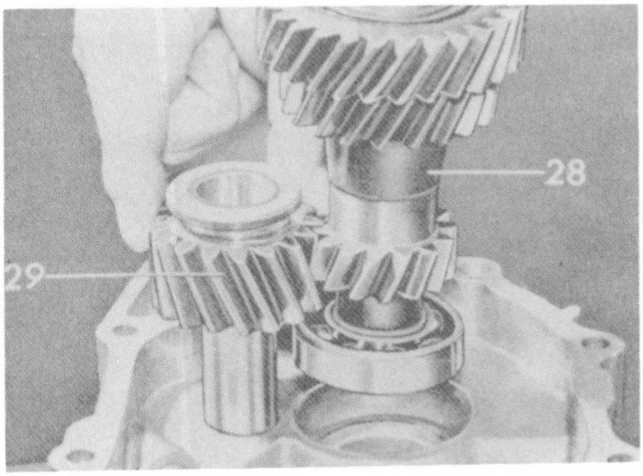

Countershaft bearing retainer (25), ball bearing (26), shift assembly (27), countershaft (28), idler gear (29).

shaft (18) forward until shift fork (20) can be withdrawn. Catch loose ball bearings. Set shift fork (21) to neutral. Drive out lockpin (22) from shift fork (23) and pull shift shaft (24) forward until shift fork can be pulled from the reverse gear. Catch loose ball bearings.

Remove bearing retainer (25) and pull bearing (26). Lift out complete shift mechanism (27).

Warm gearbox cover gently, then pull countershaft (28) and idler gear (29) from gearbox housing cover.

Pull clutch shaft (30), shift sleeve (31) and bearing (32). Remove snap-ring (33) and disc. (34). Pull off guide sleeve (35) and 3rd gear (36) with its synchronizer. Pull roller bearing (37). Press mainshaft (38) from speedometer drive gear (39), reverse gear (40), 1st gear (41) with synchronizer, shift sleeve (42), and 2nd gear pinion with synchronizer (43).

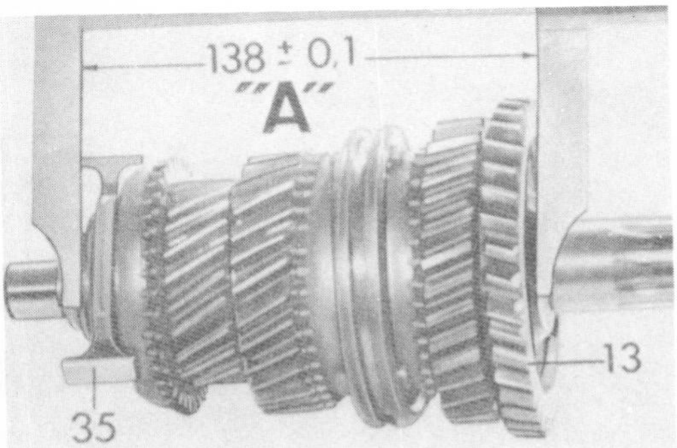

Mainshaft assembly dimension A. Reverse gear pinion (13), guide sleeve (35), shim (Y).

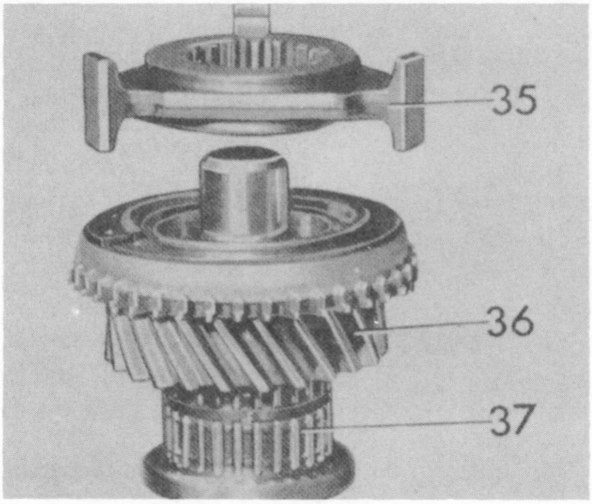

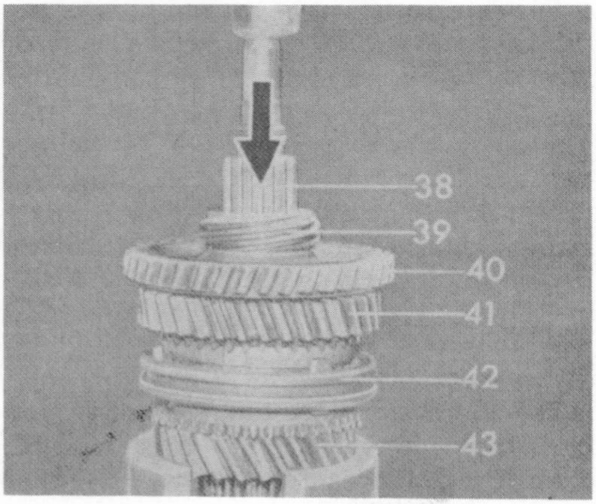

Clutch shaft disassembly. Clutch shaft (30), shift sleeve (31), bearing (32), disc and snap-ring (34, 33), guide sleeve (35), 3rd gear pinion (36), bearing cage (37), mainshaft (38), speedometer drive (39), reverse gear (40), 1st gear (41), shift sleeve (42), 2nd gear and synchronizer (43).

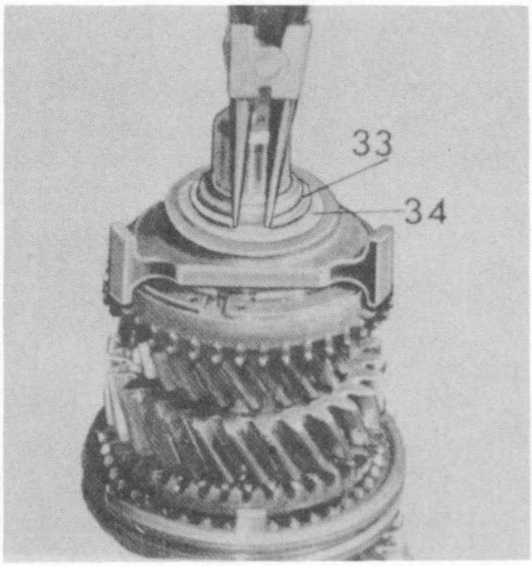

Gearbox Assembly — Universal 232

Inspect synchronizers before reassembly. Front edges of shift sleeve and synchronizer ring must be flush, and shift sleeve teeth should be perfectly sharp. If wear of synchronizer is predominately toward ends of synchronizer ring, ring should be replaced. Wear should be distributed over at least 50% of the periphery. After assembly, it should be easy to turn the synchronizer ring by hand.

The overall dimension of the assembled mainshaft, measured from the ground face of the guide sleeve (35) to the front face of the reverse gear (13) must be 5.429-5.437″ (137.9-138.1 mm). Shims of the proper thickness (Y) to obtain this dimension, if necessary, should be placed at the front of the reverse gear pinion (13). For example:

"A" ideal = 5.433″ (138 mm)
"A" actual = 5.394″ (137 mm)

"Y" (shim thickness) = .039″ (1 mm)

Drive the mainshaft bearing all the way into the gearbox housing. Then measure the distance (C) between the edge of the hous-

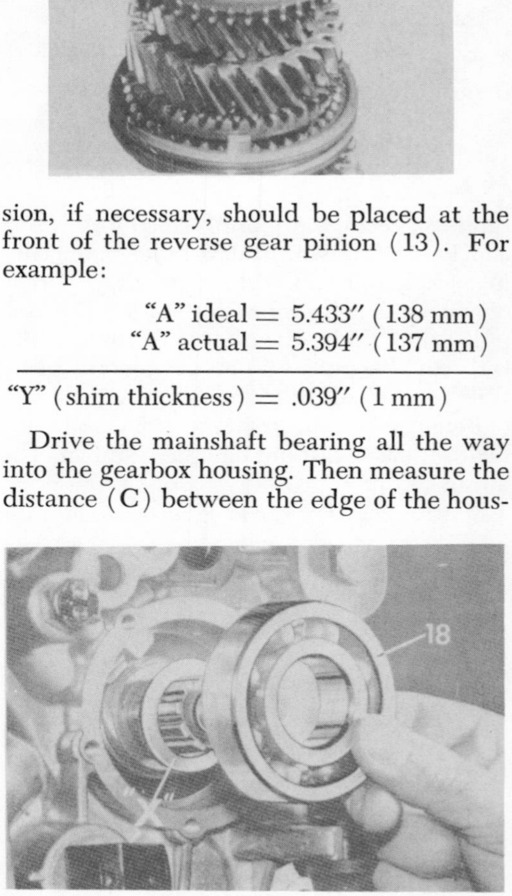

Thickness of shim (X) on mainshaft is determined as described in text.

ing surface (with gasket in place) and the bearing race. This dimension is used to calculate the correct thickness for a shim (X) on the mainshaft. Measure and note thickness (B) of speedometer drive gear. Remove bearing and calculate thickness of (X), for example:

A (mainshaft length) ideal	= 5.433″ (138 mm)
add B (thickness of speedo gear):	.583″ (14.8 mm)
	= 6.016″ (152.8 mm)
subtract C	1.457″ (37.0 mm)
D actual (shift sleeve)	= 4.559″ (115.8 mm)
D ideal	= 4.567″ (116.0 mm)
X (shim thickness)	= .008″ (.2 mm)

In fitting the countershaft, the correct thickness for shim (G) is found by first measuring the depth (F) of the housing from its edge to the snap-ring. Then install countershaft into housing cover and measure the height (E) of the shaft with the gasket in position. Find thickness of shim (G) as follows:

	F =	6.496″ (165.0 mm)
minus	E:	6.480″ (164.6 mm)
	=	.016″ (.4 mm)
minus:		.008″ (.2 mm) end play
then	G =	.008″ (.2 mm) (shim thickness)

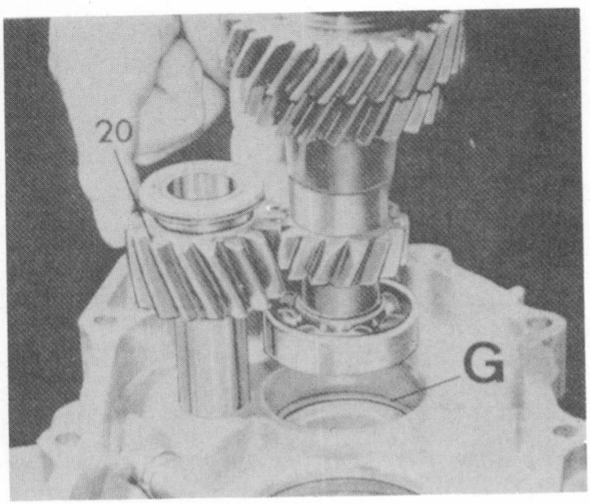

Position of shim (G) in housing cover.

Automatic Transmission

Disassembly and repair of the ZF automatic transmission requires specialized tools and techniques. It is not recommended that this work be attempted by other than an authorized service facility. Only external adjustments are covered in this book.

Throttle Linkage Adjustment

Remove kickdown stop from beneath throttle pedal (10) and adjust to basic length of 2.618″ (66.5 mm). Replace kickdown stop. When pedal (10) is fully depressed, joint (F) should not be stopped by carpet. If joint (F) hits carpet, readjust kickdown stop to suit. Unhook spring clip and ball swivel at upper end of throttle linkage turnbuckle. Open throttle butterfly fully. If butterfly goes beyond vertical position, bend stop to correct. Press throttle pedal (10) to kickdown contact position and hold throttle butterfly fully open. Adjust turnbuckle to correct length and reinstall ball swivel end and spring clip. Check adjustment by depressing throttle pedal (10) to kickdown position (13). Throttle butterfly should be fully open. If this is not the case, readjust turnbuckle.

Transmission Linkage Adjustment

Move gear selector lever to position O. Depress throttle pedal (10) to kickdown position (13). Unhook spring clip and ball swivel (15) at top end of turnbuckle (E). NOTE: *any attempt to drive vehicle with transmission linkage disconnected will result in severe damage.* Adjust length (C) of turnbuckle (E) until edge of lever (D) is aligned with index mark (B). Reinstall ball swivel end (15) and spring clip.

Adjust idling speed to approximately 800 rpm. Test drive vehicle, noting speeds at which shifts occur with throttle pedal fully depressed, but not in kickdown position. Any known speedometer error must be taken into account. Shift points should be as follows:

	1800 A	*2000 A*
1st-2nd gear shift	27-31 mph	27-34 mph
2nd-3rd gear shift	53-56 mph	53-59 mph

If shift occurs too early, lengthen turnbuckle (E); if it occurs too late, shorten

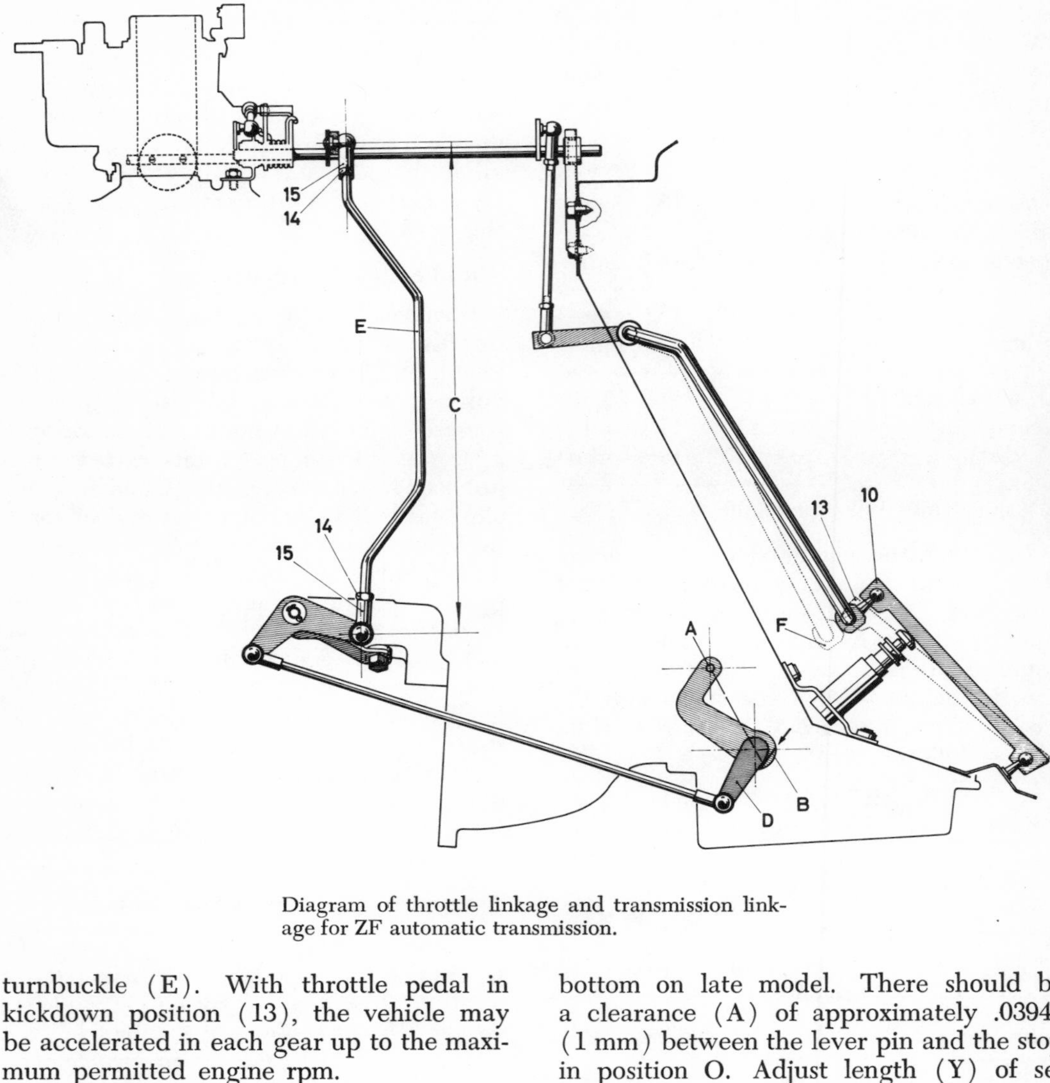

Diagram of throttle linkage and transmission linkage for ZF automatic transmission.

turnbuckle (E). With throttle pedal in kickdown position (13), the vehicle may be accelerated in each gear up to the maximum permitted engine rpm.

Transmission Shift Linkage Adjustment

There are two types of shift linkage used with the ZF automatic transmission. The first has the shift pattern P-O-A-2-1-R, and a single selector rod. The later unit has the pattern P-R-O-A-2-1 and two selector rods connected by a bellcrank mounted to the transmission extension housing. On the later model, adjustment is made at the rear selector rod.

When adjusting shift linkage, vehicle must not be raised off its wheels. Detach selector rod from hand lever; move hand lever to position O. Move transmission lever to position O, second notch from bottom on early model; third notch from bottom on late model. There should be a clearance (A) of approximately .0394″ (1 mm) between the lever pin and the stop in position O. Adjust length (Y) of selector rod (1) at shackle (3) to obtain this clearance. Reinstall selector rod to hand lever; check for proper shifting into all positions.

Final Drive Systems

BMW final drive assemblies differ with the various models. Dimensions of the one and two-piece drive shafts used with the standard long neck, universal, and automatic transmissions and long and short neck final drive units for each of the BMW models are given in the specifications.

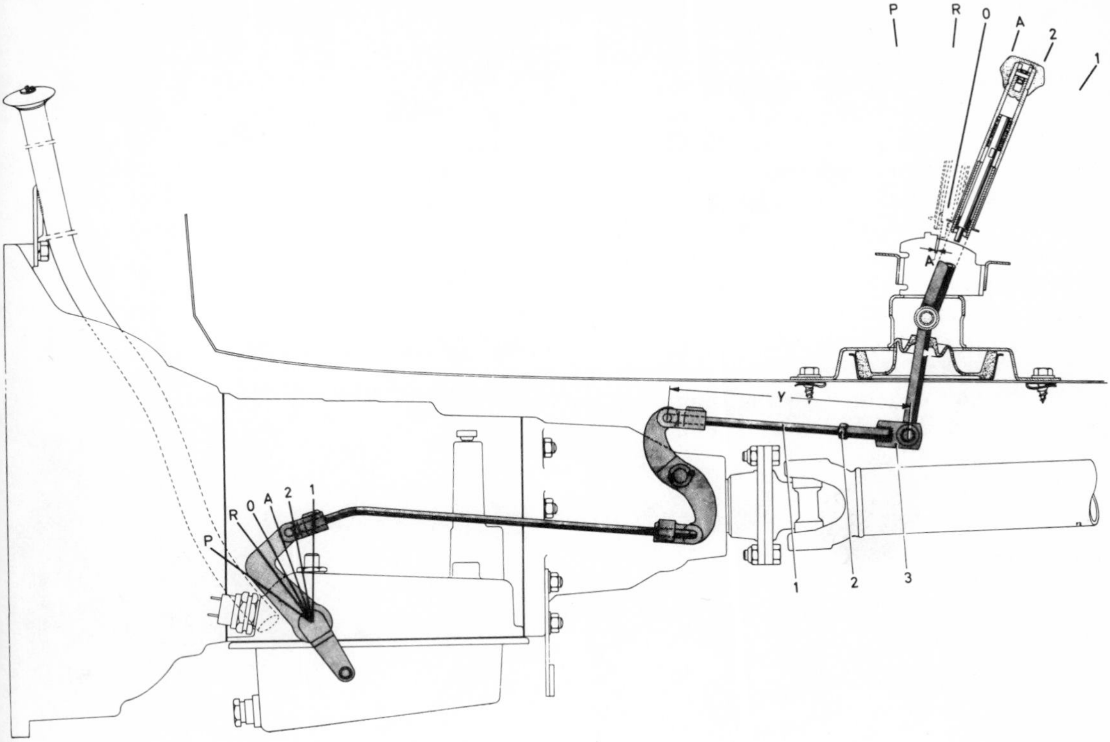

ZF automatic transmission shift linkage, late models.

Rear Axle Specifications

Model	Ratio	No. of Teeth	Basic Pinion/ Ring Gear Adj. Dim. In. (mm) Klingelnberg*	Basic Pinion/ Ring Gear Adj. Dim. In. (mm) Gleason*	Pinion/ Ring Gear Backlash In. (mm)**	Driving Flange To Axle End Play In. (mm)***
1500, 1600	4.375:1	35/8	2.068 (52.52)	2.055 (52.20)	.0028-.0047 (.07-.12)	.039-.059 (.10-.15)
1600TI, 2000TI, 2000CS	3.9:1	39/10	2.068 (52.52)	2.068 (52.52)	.0028-.0047 (.07-.12)	.039-.059 (.10-.15)
1600-2, 1800, 1800A	4.11:1	37/9	2.048 (52.02)	2.065 (52.45)	.0028-.0047 (.07-.12)	.039-.059 (.10-.15)
1600-2, 1800, 1800A, 1800/69, 1800TI, 2000, 2000A	4.10:1	41/10			.0028-.0047 (.07-.12)	.039-.059 (.10-.15)
1800/69, 1800TI	4.11:1	37/9	2.061 (52.34)	2.065 (52.45)	.0028-.0047 (.07-.12)	.039-.059 (.10-.15)
2000, 2000A, 2000CA	4.11:1	37/9	2.068 (52.52)	2.068 (52.52)	.0028-.0047 (.07-.12)	.039-.059 (.10-.15)
2000TI, 2000CS, 2000CA	3.9:1	43/11			.0028-.0047 (.07-.12)	.039-.059 (.10-.15)
2002	3.64:1	40/11			.0028-.0047 (.07-.12)	.039-.059 (.10-.15)

*Distance from face of Pinion to center of differential bearing bore in housing. For pinion heights above 1.2598" (32 mm), the basic adjusting dimension is 2.068" (52.52 mm).
**Short neck: .0031-.0051 (.08-.13)
***Long neck axle

Rear Axle Removal

Push back rubber dust cover from handbrake lever and disconnect handbrake cable. Jack up rear of car, place on stands and remove wheels. Detach muffler and rear part of exhaust system at flange and at its center. Support only one trailing suspension arm with a jack. WARNING: *the shock absorber functions as a restrainer, and should not be removed unless the trailing arm is supported. If the upper shock mount is to be disconnected before jacking the car, the half shaft must be disconnected from the half axle at the same time to prevent damage to the universal joint.*

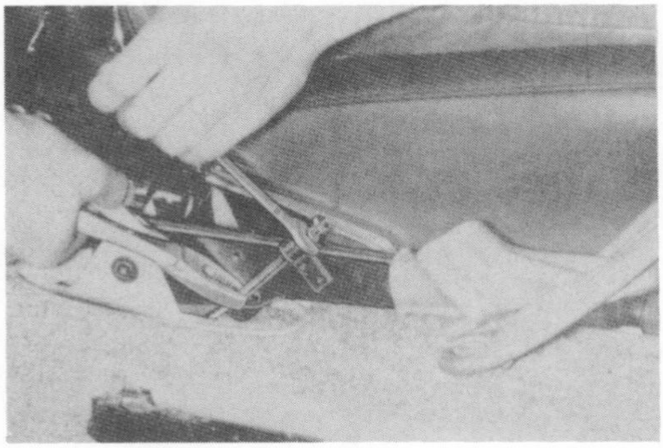

Disconnecting handbrake cable.

Disconnect half shafts from the differential and loosely wire half shafts to differential. Remove shock absorber from its upper mounting. Lower trailing arm by lowering jack. Remove the coil spring with upper plate and damper rings.

Detach rubber coupling from differential but not from drive shaft.

Disconnect flexible brake line sections from rigid feed lines and plug ends.

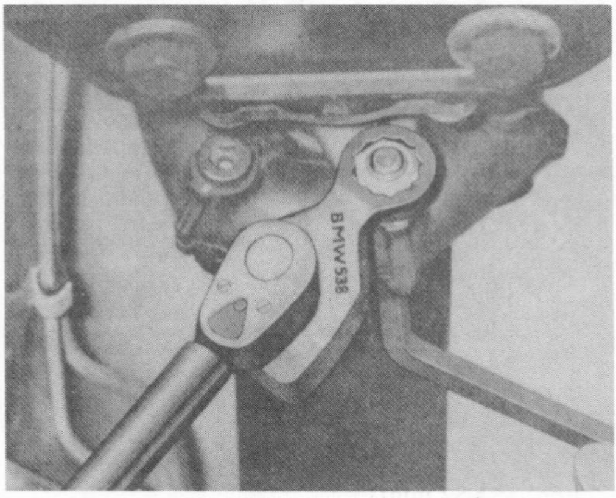

Disconnecting rubber coupling from differential.

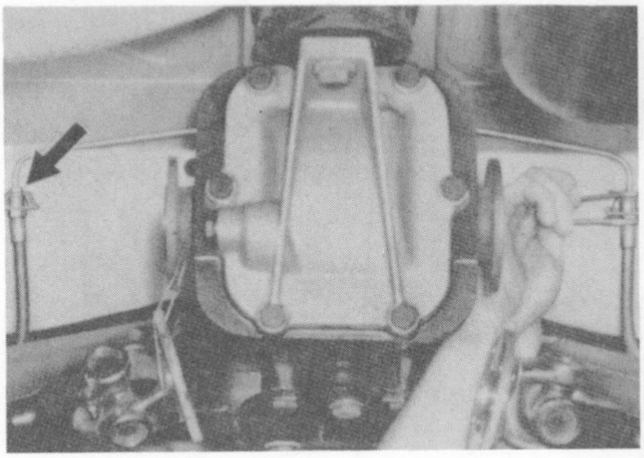

Disconnecting brake lines.

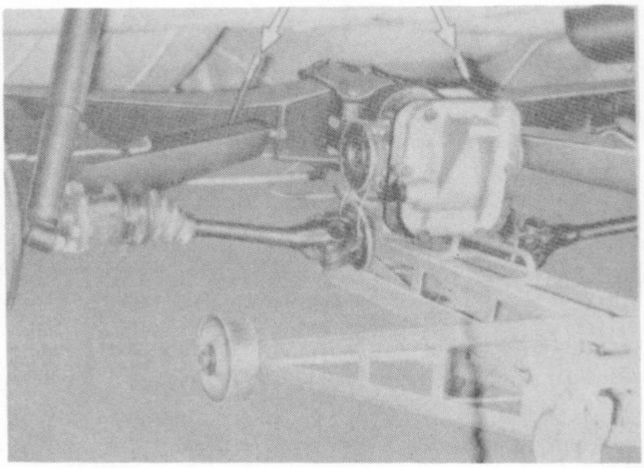

Removing rear axle assembly.

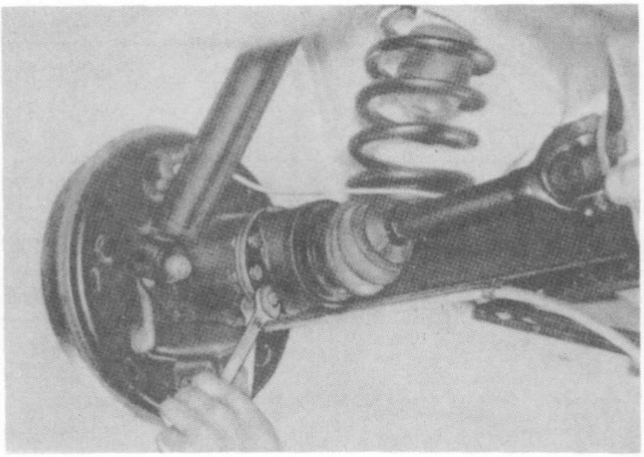

Disconnecting half-shaft from half axle.

Place a jack under differential and detach the rear axle support member from the frame. Remove rear mounting bolt of differential. Lower jack and pull rear axle assembly from under car.

Install rear axle assembly in reverse order from above, tightening bolts to the proper torque specifications. Install coil spring with smooth end up. Bleed brake system.

1 Brake drum
2 Brake lining
3 Brake shoe
4 Handbrake cable
5 Half-shaft
6 Driver flange
7 Castellated nut
8 Spacer bush
9 Grooved ball bearing 6206
10 Shaft sealing ring
11 Wheel nut
12 Knurled bolt
13 Trailing arm (Suspension arm)
14 Knurled bolt
15 Brake shoe spring
16 Driven shaft
17 Pivot housing
18 Needle bearing
19 Bearing ring
20 Sliding block
21 Collar
22 Clamp

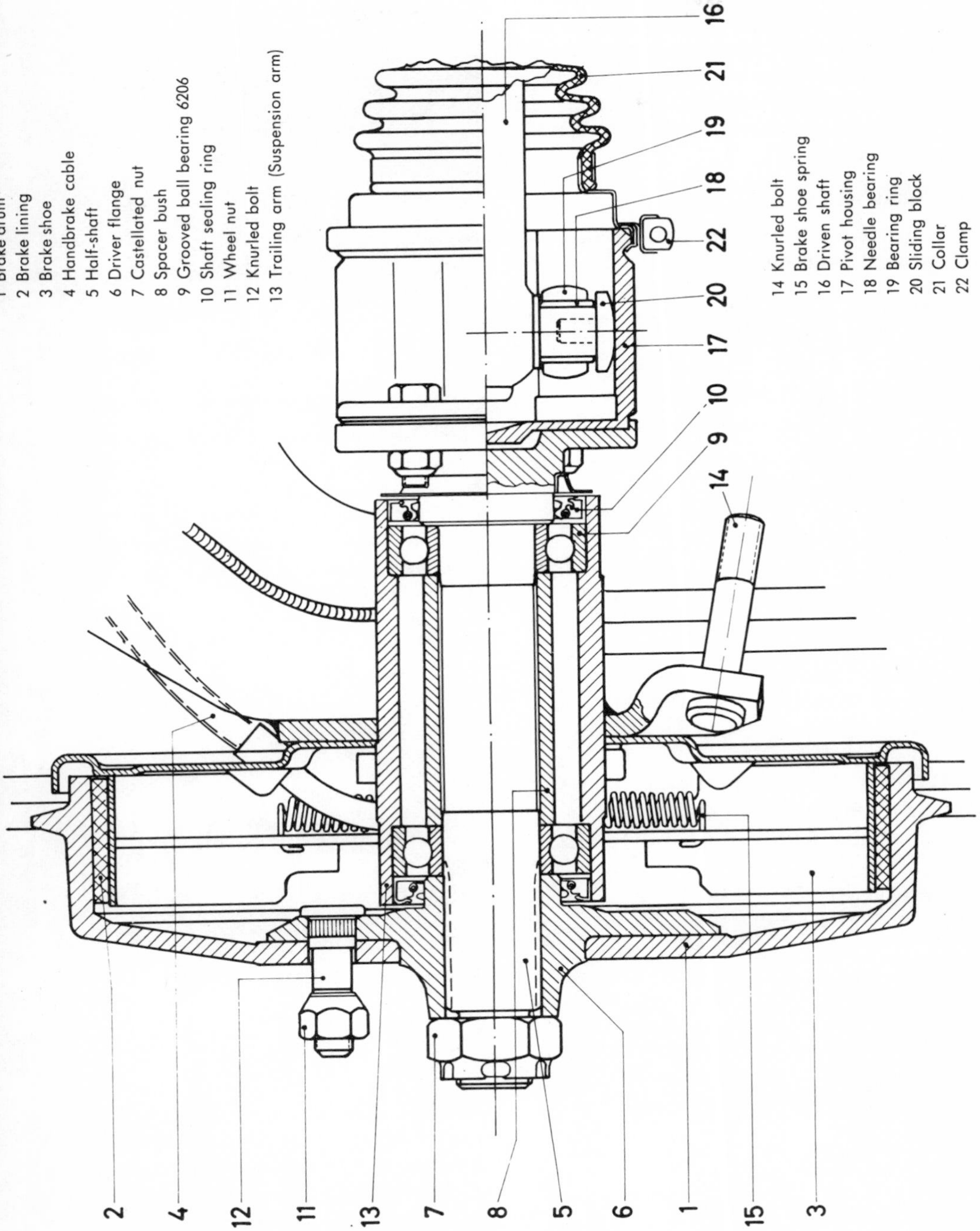

Rear wheel and axle components.

Trailing Arm Removal

To remove trailing suspension arm, disconnect handbrake, support vehicle and remove wheels. Support trailing arm with a jack, remove shock absorber, and disconnect half shaft from half axle. Lower trailing arm with jack, remove coil spring, disconnect brake line and remove trailing arm mounting bolts from frame. Re-install coil spring with smooth end up. Bleed brake system.

Drive Shaft Servicing

The drive shaft is removed by disconnecting it at both ends after disconnecting and lowering a section of the exhaust system. When installing those with a center bearing, move the bearing forward by about .08″ (2 mm). Drive shafts and splined joints are balanced pairs and must not be intermixed.

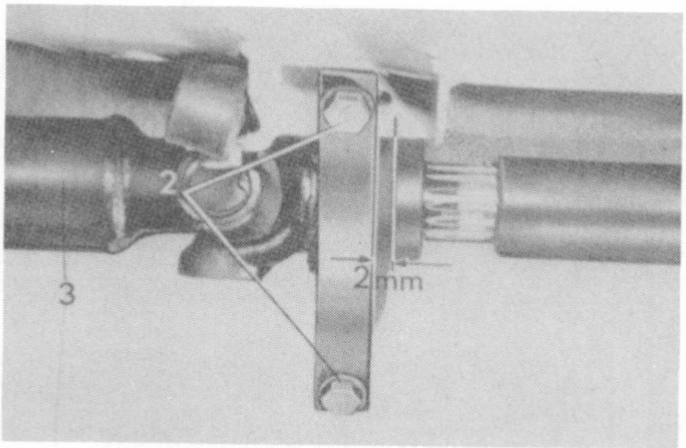

Install center bearing of drive shaft (3), .08″ (2 mm) forward, and tighten bolts (2).

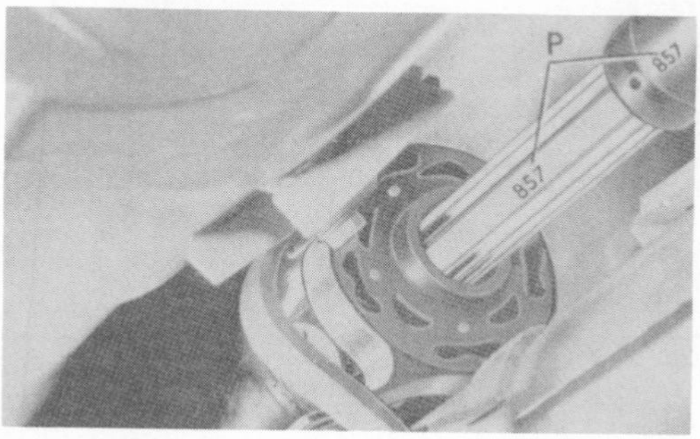

Balanced drive shaft and spline joint pairs are identified by numbers.

Rear Servicing

When disconnecting drive shaft from gearbox, tie up universal shaft so it will not slip out. Do not angle the sliding universal joints of the half shafts more than 14°.

In replacing differential bearing, heat the cap to approximately 167° F. Install cap with oil groove at bottom. The ring gear and pinion mesh must then be re-adjusted.

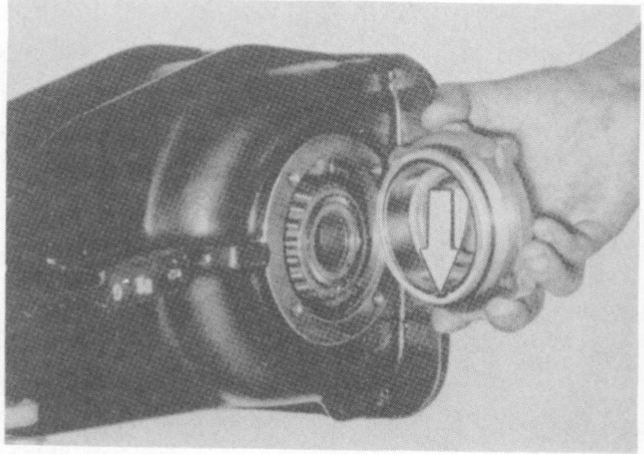

Install bearing cap with oil groove down.

RING GEAR AND PINION ADJUSTMENT

These gears are identified by a serial number inscribed on each. Another number appearing on the pinion is the deviation (±) in hundredths of a millimeter from a basic dimension (D) important to gear adjustment. (See Rear Axle Specifications Chart).

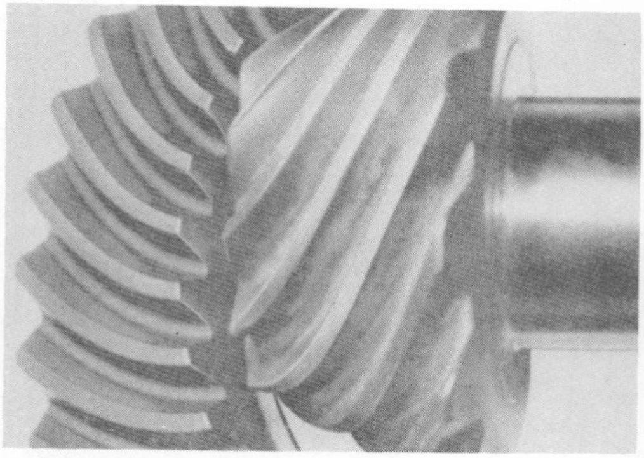

Klingelnberg (Palloid) gear teeth.

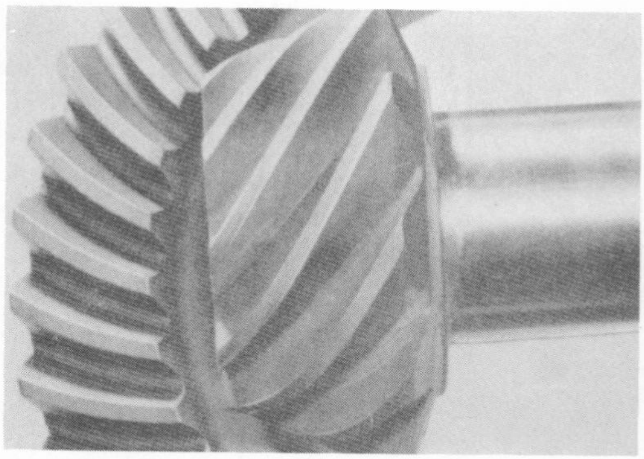

Gleason gear teeth.

Gear sets use either Klingelnberg (Palloid) or Gleason teeth. The Klingelnberg inner and outer tooth faces are identical in appearance. With Gleason gears, the outer face is broader than the inside face.

Backlash should correspond to that shown in the table. However, a more decisive test for proper gear adjustment is the tooth contact pattern. This can be altered by changing shims from one side to the other of the bearing cap.

To check tooth adjustment, cover the front and back flanks of the ring gear with blue marking dye. Turn the ring gear at least one revolution in both directions, while maintaining a slight drag on the pinion.

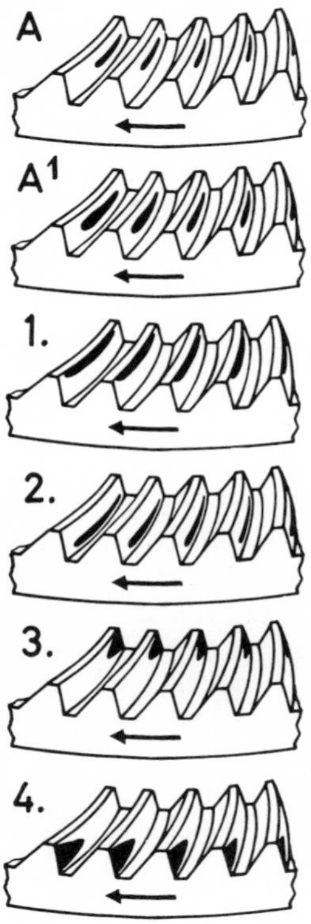

Ring gear/pinion tooth contact patterns produced by Gleason gearing.

Correct contact pattern made by Gleason teeth under no load is shown in the illustration at (A). When subjected to load, the contact pattern moves somewhat toward the outside as shown at (A1). Displacement of the ring gear primarily changes the backlash, although the pattern is displaced in the axial direction of the teeth. Displacement of the pinion moves the pattern in the direction of tooth height, and the backlash changes only slightly.

Figures 1, 2, 3 and 4 of the same illustration show the common incorrect patterns which are useful in making corrective adjustments.

1. High, narrow pattern on ring gear (tip contact). Correct by moving pinion toward ring gear, and if necessary, correct backlash by moving ring gear away from pinion.
2. Deep, narrow pattern on ring gear (root contact). Correct by moving pinion away from ring gear axis, and if necessary, correct backlash by moving ring gear toward pinion.
3. Short pattern on smallest end of ring gear tooth (toe contact). Correct by moving ring gear away from pinion, and if necessary, move pinion closer to ring gear axis.
4. Short pattern on large end of ring gear tooth (heel contact). Correct by moving ring gear toward pinion and, if necessary, move pinion away from ring gear axis.

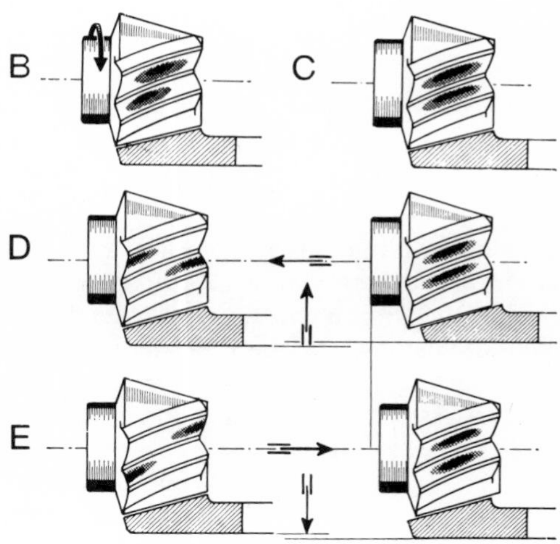

Ring gear/pinion tooth contact patterns produced by Klingelnberg (Palloid) gears.

On Klingelnberg gears, the correct contact pattern should show at about the center point of tooth length and height on both front and back flanks of the pinion.

Figure B shows a correct pattern made with no load.

Figure C shows a correct pattern under load.

Figures D and E show incorrect patterns caused by shimming the pinion in the direction shown by the arrow.

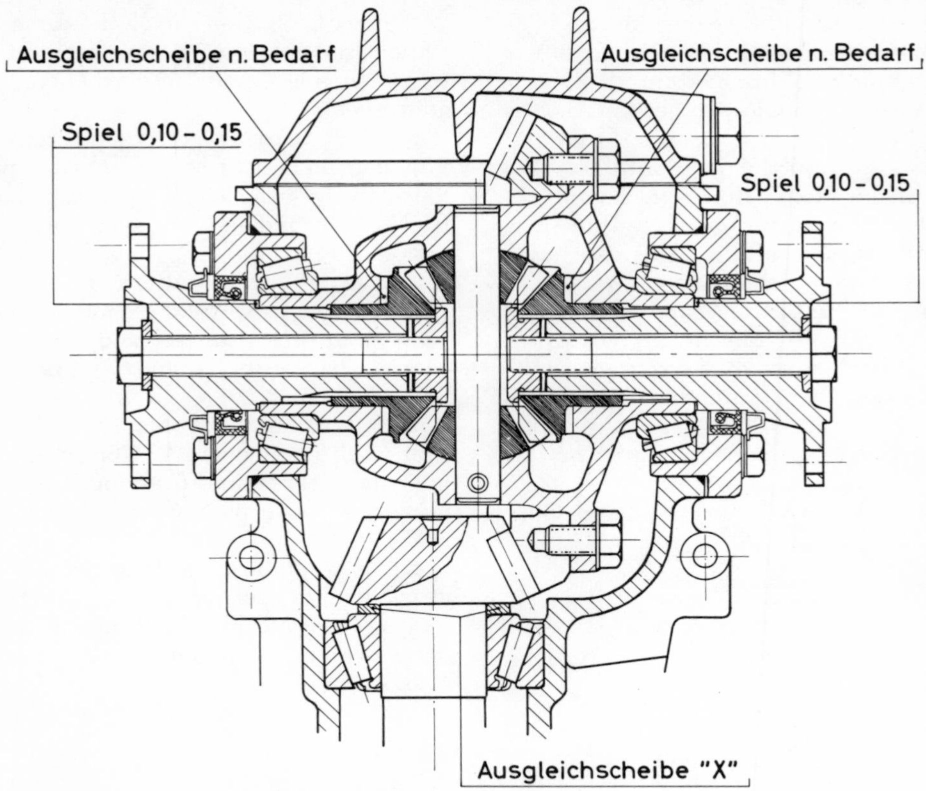

Rear assembly and adjustment shims.

Shims as required = Ausgleichscheibe n. Bedarf
Clearance = Spiel 0.10–0.15 mm (0.039–0.059")
Shim "X" = Ausgleichscheibe "X"

In assembling an overhauled rear drive assembly, the thickness of the shim (X) behind the pinion can be determined using the dimensions obtained as shown by the diagram and given by the Rear Axle Specifications Chart. For example:

1.	B	1.6338″ (41.50 mm)
	+C	1.1024″ (28 mm)
	=	2.7362″ (69.50 mm)
2.	A	4.8031″ (122 mm)
	−(B+C)	2.7362″ (69.50 mm)
	=	2.0669″ (52.50 mm) D-actual
3.	(from chart) D	2.0677″ (52.52 mm)
	+e	.0118″ (.30 mm)
	=	2.0795″ (52.82 mm) D-desired
	—D-actual	2.0669″ (52.50 mm)
	X=	− .0126″ (−.32 mm)

In this case, shim thickness must be reduced by .0126″ (.32 mm). If D-actual were greater than D-desired, shim thickness would be increased by .0126″ (.32 mm).

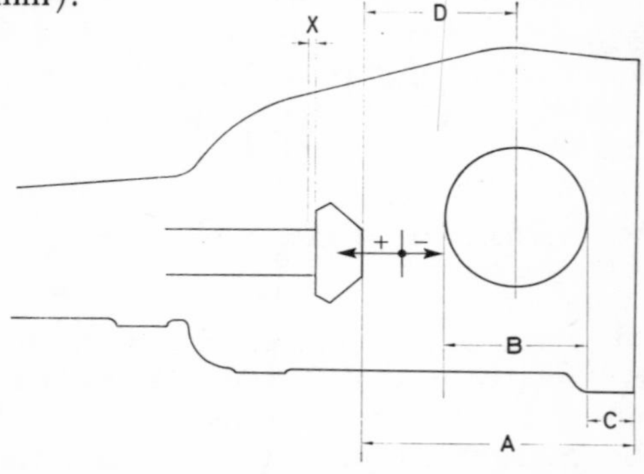

Measurements for determining shim (X) thickness.
A = distance from face of pinion to edge of housing.
B = diameter of bearing cap bore divided by 2.
C = distance from bore to edge of housing.
D = distance from face of pinion to center of bore.
e = deviation (±) from D in hundredths of a mm.
X = shim thickness.

Chapter 7
Suspension, Steering and Brakes

Front suspension is the McPherson strut type with lower wishbone, coil springs, and double acting shock absorbers. Rear suspension is fully independent with semi-trailing arms and coil springs. The differential is rubber mounted to the frame. The BMW 2002 also has a rubber mounted front stabilizer bar.

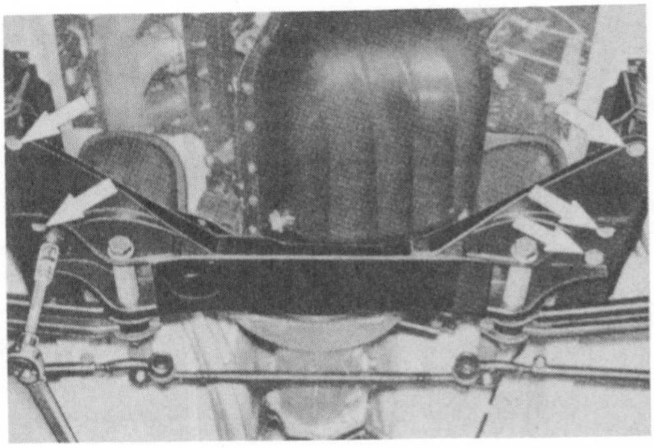

Front axle carrier mounting screws.

Suspension

Specifications for wheel alignment are given in the Wheel Alignment Specifications Chart, and are for a normally loaded vehicle. Correct tire pressures, evenly worn tire treads, and wheel bearings without excessive play are essential for proper wheel alignment. An optical measuring device must be used to obtain correct wheel alignment.

If there is reason to believe that front and rear wheels do not track, as might be caused by a misaligned rear axle, check and adjust the rear wheel alignment first.

Front Axle Carrier Replacement

jack car and place on stands. Remove wheels.

loosen nuts from guide joint.

remove steering gear from front axle carrier.

loosen steering guide lever bearing bracket from front axle carrier, and tie the bracket and steering gear to gearbox.

loosen left and right engine mounts, and hoist engine slightly.

support front axle carrier with jack and remove mounting screws.

lower jack and move front axle carrier forward and out.

Install front axle carrier in reverse order, torquing the carrier mounting bolts and steering gear to 34 ft. lbs., and the guide joint nuts to 18 ft. lbs.

Wheel Hub Removal

jack car, support and remove wheel.
loosen brake caliper from shock absorber.
remove hub cap.

Wheel Alignment Specifications

Model	*Front Caster*	*Front Camber**	*Front Toe-In* In. (mm.)*	*Front Toe-Out on 20° Turn**	*King Pin Angle*	*Rear Camber**	*Rear Toe-In In. (mm.)*
1500, 1600	3°±30′	0° 30′±30′	0–.079 (0–2)	1°±30′	8°±30′	2° negative	.039±.039 (1±1)
1600-2, 1600TI	4°±30′	0° 30′±30′	.059±.059 (1.5±1.5)	1°±30′	8° 30′	2°±20′ negative	.039±.039 (1±1)
1800, 1800A	3°±30′	0° 15′±30′[1]	.059±.059 (1.5±1.5)	1°±30′	8° 40′	2° negative	.059±.059 (1.5±1.5)
1800/69	3°±30′	0° 15′±30′	.059±.059 (1.5±1.5)	1°±30′		2° negative	.059±.059 (1.5±1.5)
1800TI	3°±30′	0° 15′±30′	.059±.059 (1.5±1.5)	1°±30′		2° negative	.059±.059 (1.5±1.5)
2002	3°±30′	0° 15′±30′	.059±.059 (1.5±1.5)	1°±30′	8° 40′±30′	2° 20′ negative	.059±.059 (1.5±1.5)
2000, 2000A, 2000TI, 2000CS, 2000CA	3°±30′	0° 15′±30′	.059±.059 (1.5±1.5)	1°±30′	8° 40′±30′	2° negative	.059±.059 (1.5±1.5)

*Vehicle loaded: 2x143 lb. (2x65kg) rear seats, 1x143 lb. (1x65kg) front seats, 66 lb. (30kg) in luggage compartment on left side, gas tank full.

[1] 0° 30′ up to 1966 model.

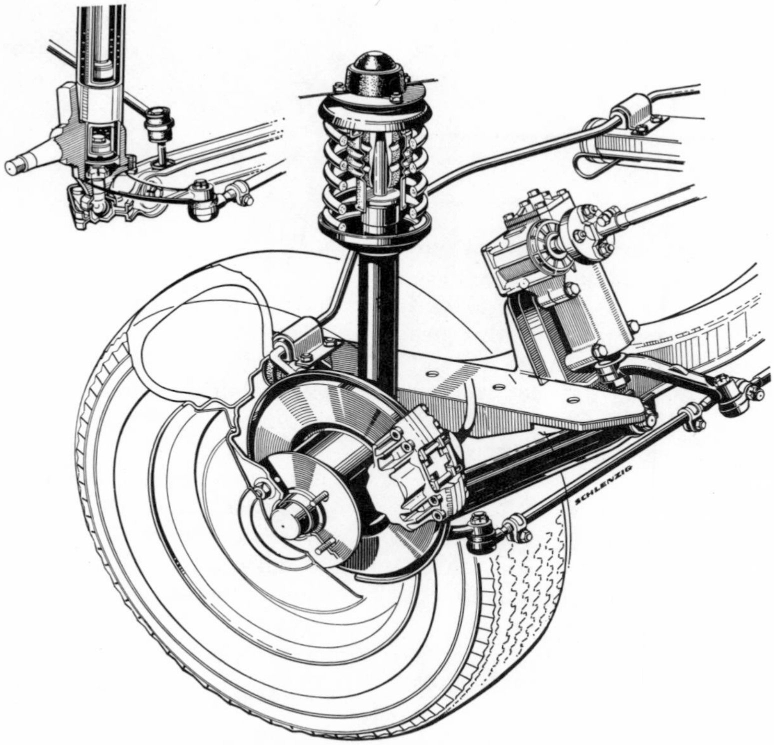

Front suspension, BMW 2002.

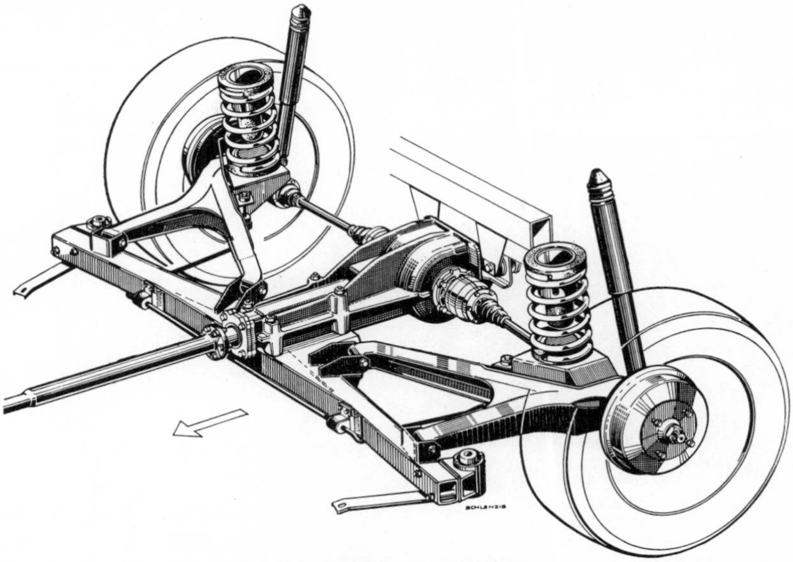

Rear suspension, BMW 2002.

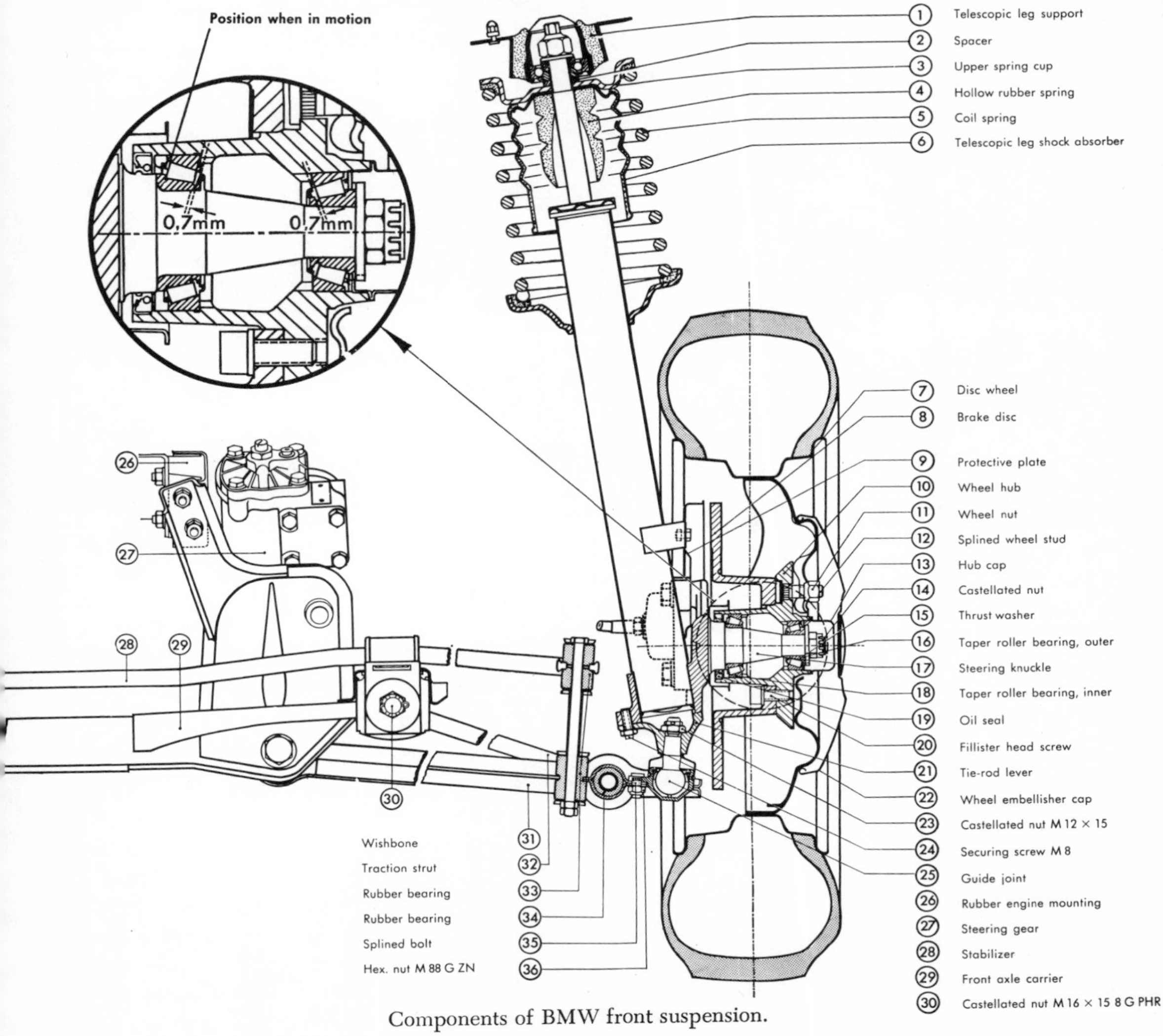
Position when in motion
0,7mm
0,7mm
(1) Telescopic leg support
(2) Spacer
(3) Upper spring cup
(4) Hollow rubber spring
(5) Coil spring
(6) Telescopic leg shock absorber
(7) Disc wheel
(8) Brake disc
(9) Protective plate
(10) Wheel hub
(11) Wheel nut
(12) Splined wheel stud
(13) Hub cap
(14) Castellated nut
(15) Thrust washer
(16) Taper roller bearing, outer
(17) Steering knuckle
(18) Taper roller bearing, inner
(19) Oil seal
(20) Fillister head screw
(21) Tie-rod lever
(22) Wheel embellisher cap
(23) Castellated nut M 12 × 15
(24) Securing screw M 8
(25) Guide joint
(26) Rubber engine mounting
(27) Steering gear
(28) Stabilizer
(29) Front axle carrier
(30) Castellated nut M 16 × 15 8 G PHR
Wishbone (31)
Traction strut (32)
Rubber bearing (33)
Rubber bearing (34)
Splined bolt (35)
Hex. nut M 88 G ZN (36)

Components of BMW front suspension.

remove cotter pin and castle nut.

remove shoulder disc and pull wheel hub.

Pulling off wheel hub.

Tie-Rod Lever Replacement

remove wheel hub as previously described.

loosen elastic stop-nuts at guide joint.

Loosening elastic stop-nuts at guide joint.

remove safety wire and loosen tie rod lever.

remove cotter pin and castle nut from ball pivot, and press out ball pivot.

force tie rod lever from shock absorber.

Install in reverse order, tightening tie rod lever screws to 18 ft. lbs. and installing new safety wire to hold cap screws.

Wheel Bearing Renewal

pull wheel hub as previously described.

pull out taper roller bearing with extractor and clean wheel hub.

press in outer rings of bearing.

place rear taper roller bearing in hub and press in oil seal. Fill oil seal with graphite grease.

install wheel hub and disc on axle.

screw on castle nut and tighten to 7.2 ft. lbs. Turn wheel backward and forward a few times to distribute grease and align bearings.

loosen castle nut one-third turn.

place screwdriver in recess of nose disc. Nose disc must be easily movable to the left and right.

attach dial indicator to wheel hub.

just touch front axle stub with dial indicator.

adjust wheel bearing play to between .00079″ (.02 mm) and .00315″ (.08 mm).

NOTE: *use of a 10-hole castle nut will allow closer adjustment, to between .00079″ (.02 mm) and .00236″ (.06 mm). The play should be adjusted as close to the minimum figure as possible.*

Loosening tie rod lever.

Steering

BMW four-cylinder models use ZF-Gemmer worm and roller type steering gear assemblies with a gearbox ratio of 15.5:1 and an overall ratio of 17.58:1. The number of turns lock-to-lock is 3.5 and the wheel turning circle is 31.5 feet. Straight ahead position for the wheels is marked on the worm and steering box. The steering box uses grade SAE 90 hypoid gear oil and has a capacity of .63 pint.

Steering Assembly Notes

when installing pitman arm, mark on steering shaft must line up with arrow on pitman arm.

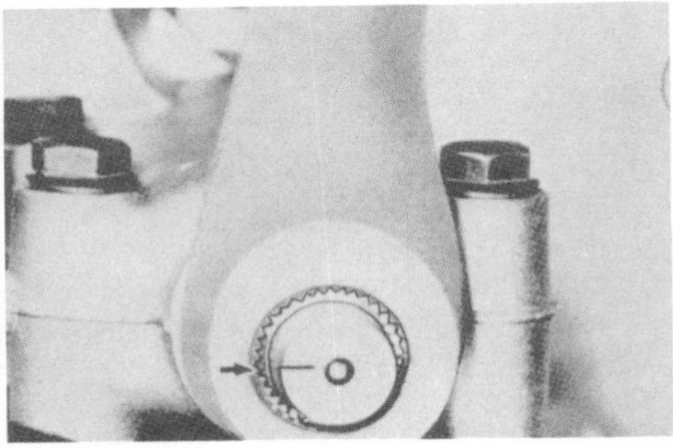

Install pitman arm so that arrow lines up with mark on shaft.

install steering shaft in case so that mark (B) on shaft lines up with mark (C) on case, and mark (A) on shaft points to the middle of the housing seam.

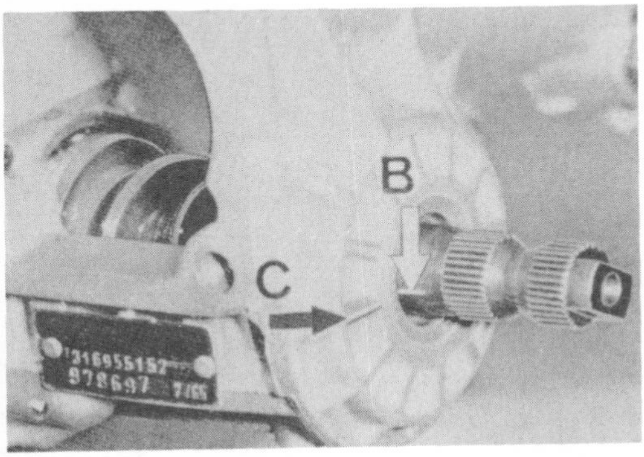

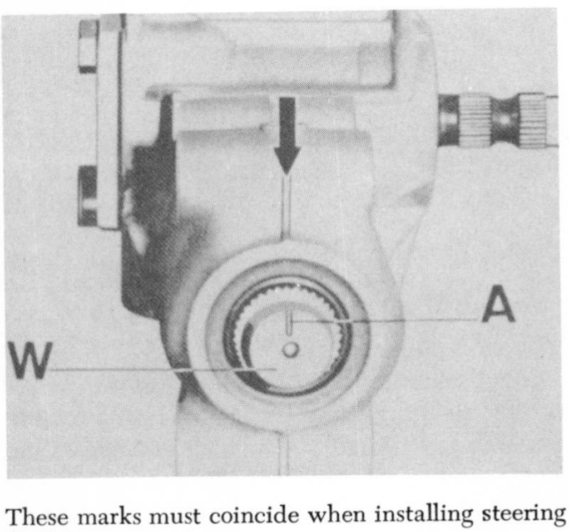

These marks must coincide when installing steering shaft in case.

with wheels straight ahead, marking on worm shaft should be aligned with marking on steering gear case.

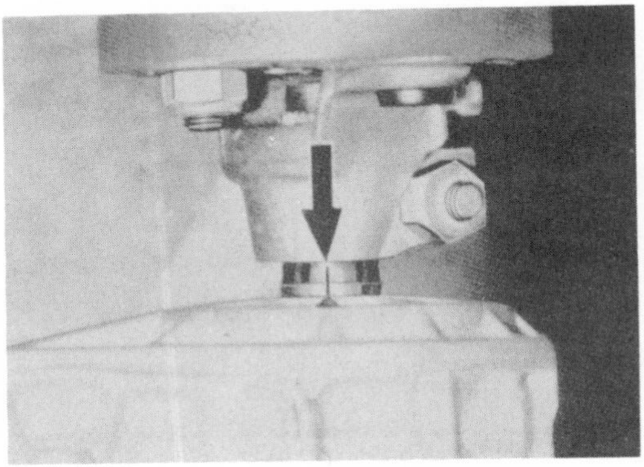

Markings should line up when wheels are straight.

Steering Adjustment

This is best made using a friction coefficient gauge attached to the nut of the steering wheel. Adjustment is correct — without play — with a friction coefficient of .72-1.16 ft. lbs.

jack up front of car with both wheels free.

remove cover cap from steering wheel.

turn steering wheel about one turn to the left.

attach friction gauge to wheel, turn friction gauge to the right beyond the straight-ahead position. Turn wheel back to the left if another test is required.

loosen locknut and turn adjustment screw while checking friction coefficient until proper value is obtained.

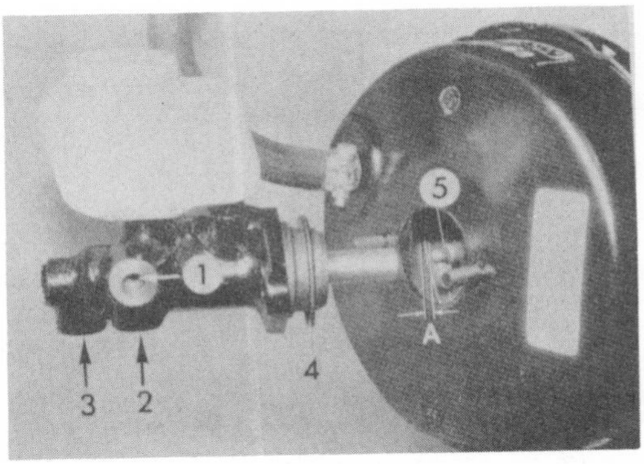

BMW 2002 master cylinder connection ports (1, 2, 3), seal ring (4), shims (5) and proper clearance (A) between pushrod and piston. (A) should be .02" (.5 mm).

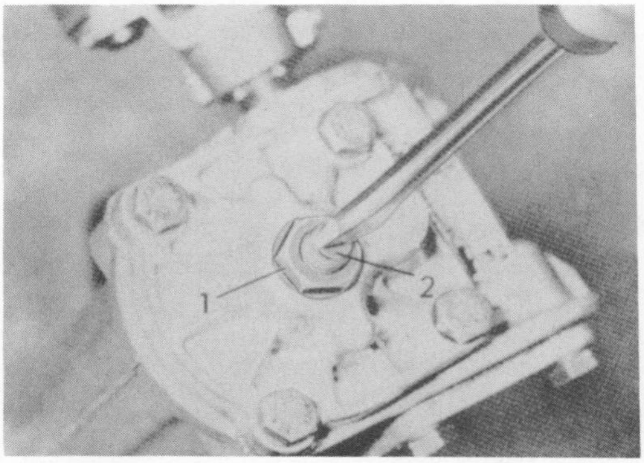

Steering adjustment screw (2) and locknut (1).

Brakes

Disc brakes are on both the front and rear wheels of BMW 2500 and 2800 cars. Other BMW models have disc brakes on the front and drum brakes on the rear. Brakes are power assisted, and the master cylinder has a tandem arrangement whereby each chamber actuates either the front or rear brake cylinders. Failure of either circuit is indicated by a warning light. The twin brake fluid reservoir is located in the engine compartment.

Warning Light Test

Warning of failure of the dual brake system is provided by a 3-watt lamp. Proper functioning of the light system can be tested by turning on the ignition switch and then pressing a small button on the instrument panel. The warning lamp should light when this button is pressed and the ignition switch is on.

Servicing Master Cylinder — 2002

disconnect brake lines: left front (1), right front (2), and rear (3).

remove master cylinder.

NOTE: *when reassembling, check rubber ring (4) which if defective will prevent vacuum formation. If renewing master cylinder, also check for proper clearance (A) between the pushrod and piston. This should be adjusted to .02″ (.5 mm) with shims (5).*

check all components and replace any that show signs of wear.

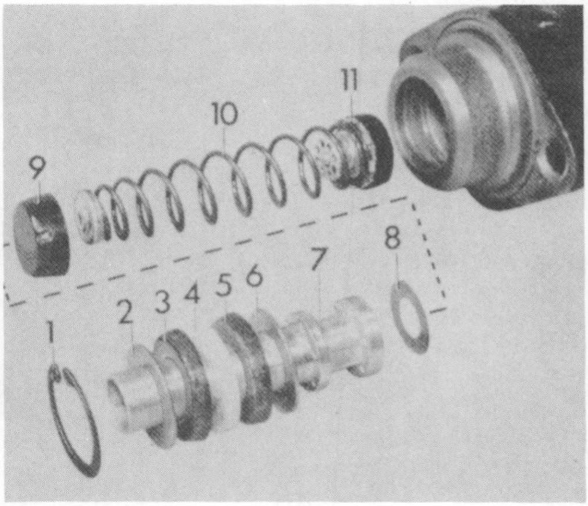

Components of BMW 2002 master cylinder: snap-ring (1), stop plate (2), secondary sleeves (3, 5), spacer (4), stop plate (6), piston (7), feeler plate (8), primary sleeve (9), pressure spring (10), bottom valve (11).

Servicing Master Cylinder — 1500, 1600

NOTE: *the master cylinder has a special bottom valve with a throttle bore (1). If the throttle bore is clogged, the brakes will drag.*

play between piston rod and piston must be .02″ (.5 mm).

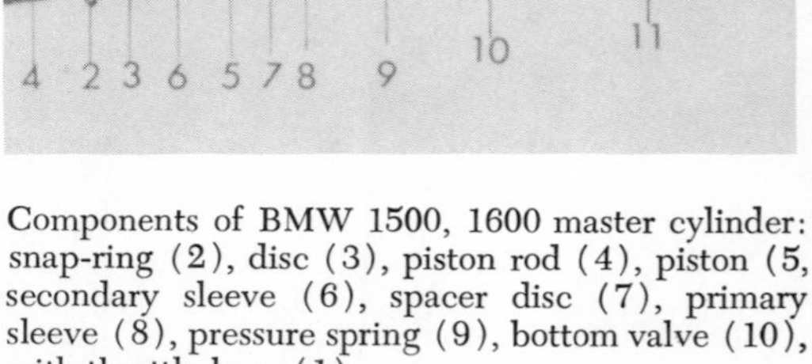

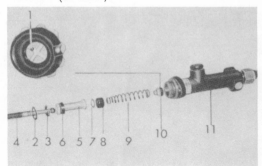

Components of BMW 1500, 1600 master cylinder: snap-ring (2), disc (3), piston rod (4), piston (5, secondary sleeve (6), spacer disc (7), primary sleeve (8), pressure spring (9), bottom valve (10), with throttle bore (1).

Servicing Master Cylinder — 1800, 1800 A, 1800 TI

check through filling opening with a wire to ensure that compensation bore is not clogged. If bore is clogged, brakes will drag.

play between piston rod and piston must be .02″ (.5 mm).

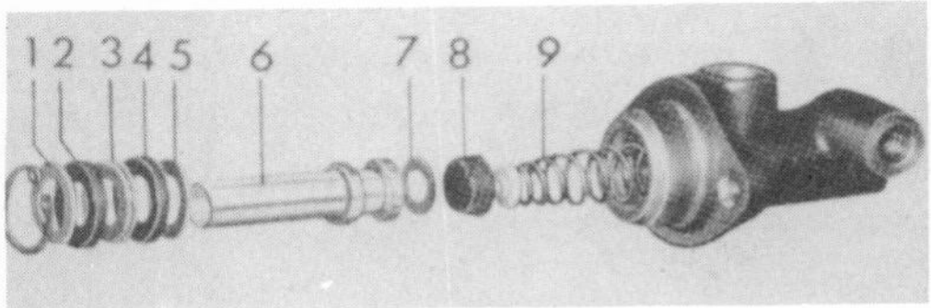

Components of BMW 1800, 1800 A, 1800 TI master cylinder: washer (1), secondary sleeve (2), intermediate ring (3), secondary sleeve (4), stop washer (5), piston (6), spacer disc (7), primary sleeve (8), pressure spring assembly (9).

Servicing Disc Brakes

Disc brakes are self adjusting and therefore require no manual adjustment, but the pad linings should be replaced when they are worn to a thickness of .7″ (2 mm). Brake discs should also be checked for maximum runout which is .0039″ (.10 mm). If the discs should have to be refinished, minimum brake disc thickness is .335″ (8.5 mm). To change pads, first remove securing lugs, if so equipped, then drive fastening pins from calipers. Remove cross spring and pull out pads with extractor hook.

When replacing cross springs, place cross spring with embossed area under the upper fastening pin. Preload the opposed section: slide it beneath the fastening pin. The cross spring eliminates undesirable movement of the brake pad linings.

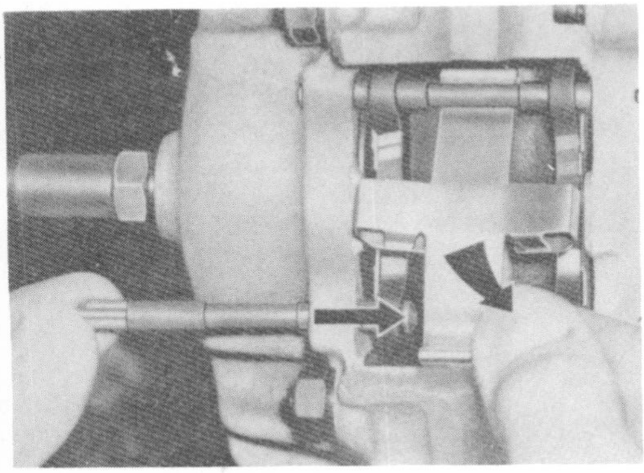

Proper assembly of cross spring.

Return piston to wheel cylinder using piston pressback pliers. Do not use any other tools to avoid damage to wheel cylinder or brake disc. Check brake fluid level in reservoir before returning to avoid overflowing.

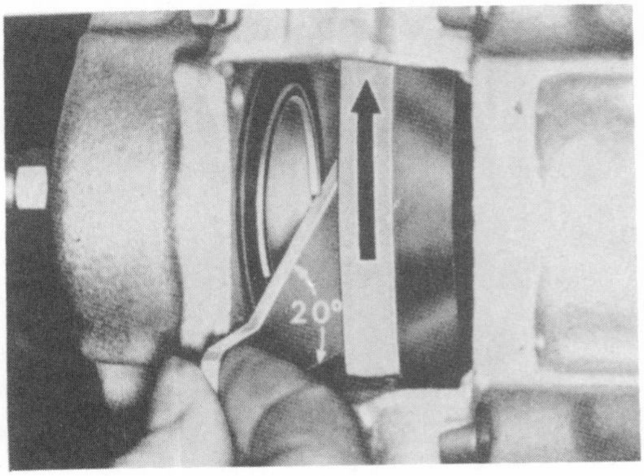

Use of piston gauge to check 20° position of piston.

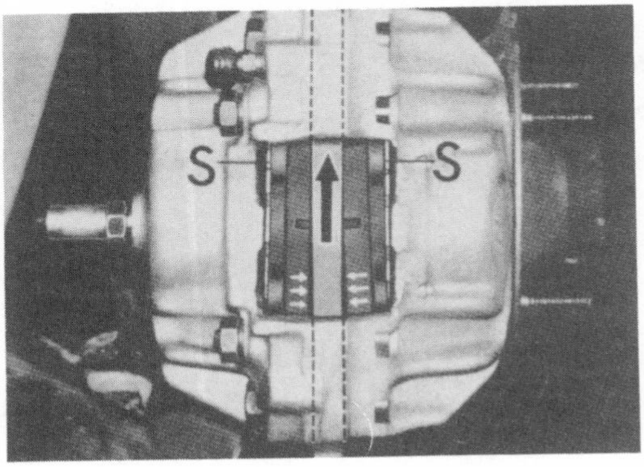

Protective cap (S) installed.

For caliper with piston without protective cap, check that 20-degree setting line of piston faces the brake disc inlet. Incorrect adjustment of the piston causes fluttering or squeaking of the disc brake and may prevent correct application of the brake lining to the disc. Installation of the protective cap (S) is recommended where possible. The cap can only be installed on pistons with a shoulder measuring .0315″ (.8 mm).

When removing pads that will be used again, mark them to be sure the inside and outside pads will be reassembled in their proper places. Make sure that each pair of wheels (front and rear) have pads of the same type as marked by the manufacturer. NOTE: *bleeding of the hydraulic system after caliper repair is made easier if calipers are filled with fluid before being installed. Remove the bleeder connector and pour in fluid, tilting the caliper.*

Drum Brake Adjustment

To adjust brake shoes, apply brakes forcefully to center the shoes, then with the pedal released, turn the adjustment cams to lock the wheels. Turn cams backward a fraction of a turn until wheel rotates freely, with no noticeable drag, with pedal released. If any brake lines have been disconnected or the pedal operation is spongy, bleed the brake system.

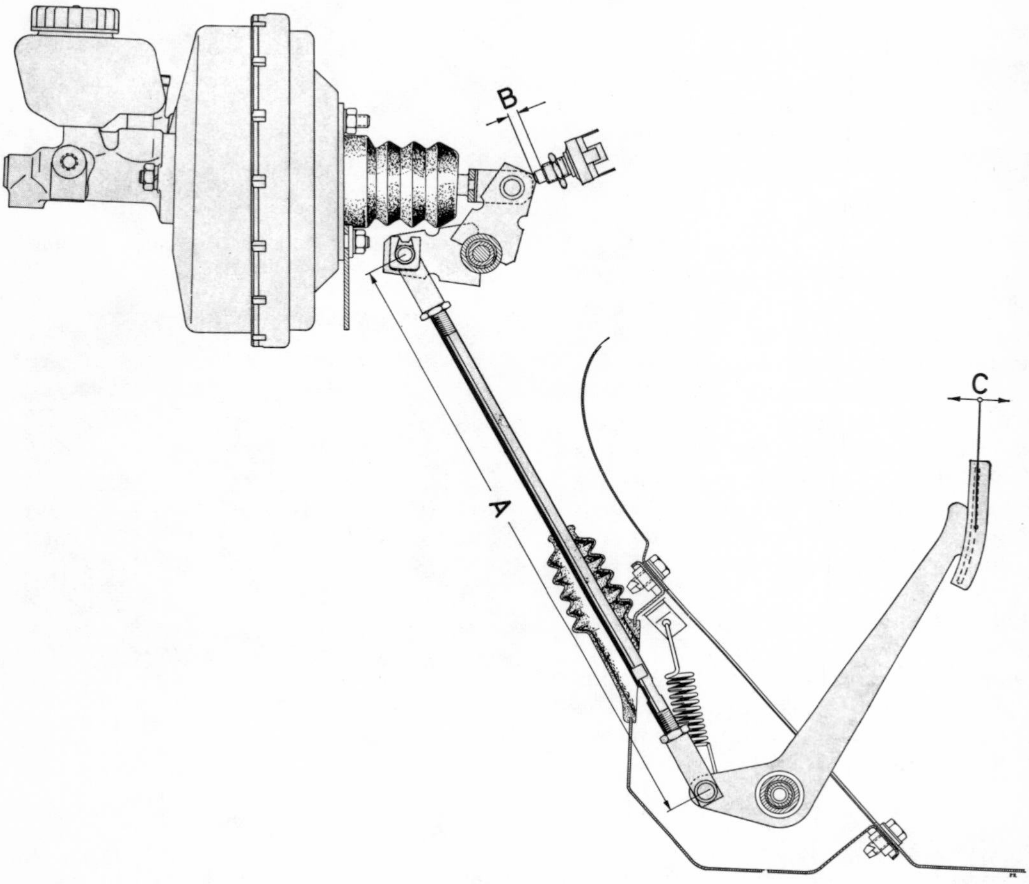

Diagram showing brake pedal, tie rod and stop light switch adjustments for BMW 1600-2, 2002. A = 14.52″ (369 mm), B = .24″-.28″ (6-7 mm), C = ± .19″ (3 mm).

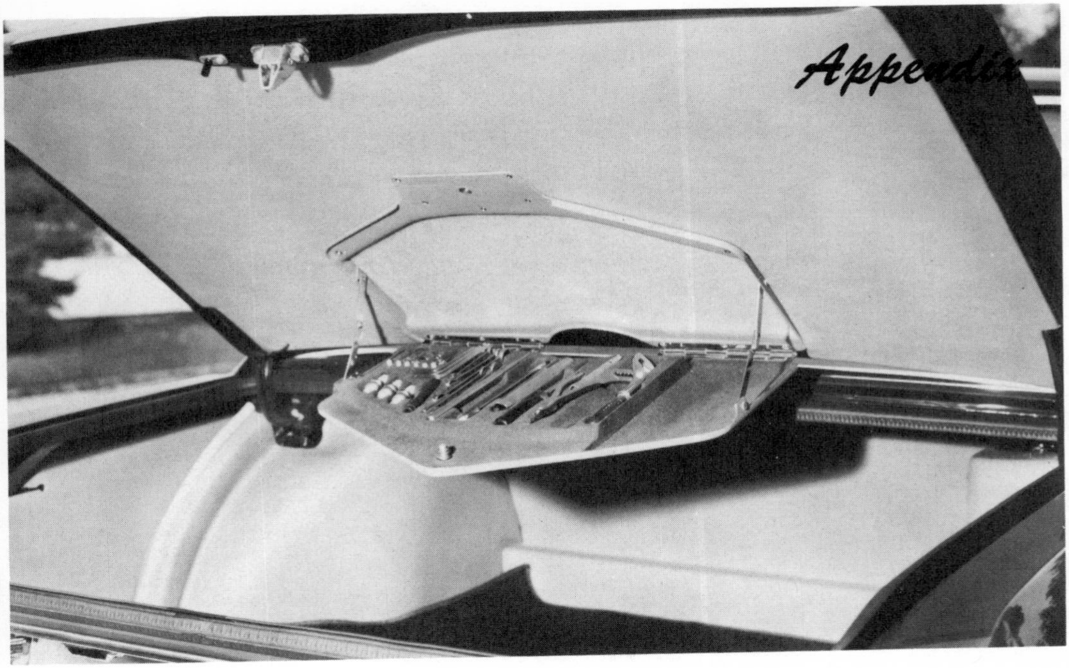

Conversion—Millimeters to Decimal Inches

mm	*inches*	*mm*	*inches*	*mm*	*inches*	*mm*	*inches*	*mm*	*inches*
1	.039 370	31	1.220 470	61	2.401 570	91	3.582 670	210	8.267 700
2	.078 740	32	1.259 840	62	2.440 940	92	3.622 040	220	8.661 400
3	.118 110	33	1.299 210	63	2.480 310	93	3.661 410	230	9.055 100
4	.157 480	34	1.338 580	64	2.519 680	94	3.700 780	240	9.448 800
5	.196 850	35	1.377 949	65	2.559 050	95	3.740 150	250	9.842 500
6	.236 220	36	1.417 319	66	2.598 420	96	3.779 520	260	10.236 200
7	.275 590	37	1.456 689	67	2.637 790	97	3.818 890	270	10.629 900
8	.314 960	38	1.496 050	68	2.677 160	98	3.858 260	280	11.032 600
9	.354 330	39	1.535 430	69	2.716 530	99	3.897 630	290	11.417 300
10	.393 700	40	1.574 800	70	2.755 900	100	3.937 000	300	11.811 000
11	.433 070	41	1.614 170	71	2.795 270	105	4.133 848	310	12.204 700
12	.472 440	42	1.653 540	72	2.834 640	110	4.330 700	320	12.598 400
13	.511 810	43	1.692 910	73	2.874 010	115	4.527 550	330	12.992 100
14	.551 180	44	1.732 280	74	2.913 380	120	4.724 400	340	13.385 800
15	.590 550	45	1.771 650	75	2.952 750	125	4.921 250	350	13.779 500
16	.629 920	46	1.811 020	76	2.992 120	130	5.118 100	360	14.173 200
17	.669 290	47	1.850 390	77	3.031 490	135	5.314 950	370	14.566 900
18	.708 660	48	1.889 760	78	3.070 860	140	5.511 800	380	14.960 600
19	.748 030	49	1.929 130	79	3.110 230	145	5.708 650	390	15.354 300
20	.787 400	50	1.968 500	80	3.149 600	150	5.905 500	400	15.748 000
21	.826 770	51	2.007 870	81	3.188 970	155	6.102 350	500	19.685 000
22	.866 140	52	2.047 240	82	3.228 340	160	6.299 200	600	23.622 000
23	.905 510	53	2.086 610	83	3.267 710	165	6.496 050	700	27.559 000
24	.944 880	54	2.125 980	84	3.307 080	170	6.692 900	800	31.496 000
25	.984 250	55	2.165 350	85	3.346 450	175	6.889 750	900	35.433 000
26	1.023 620	56	2.204 720	86	3.385 820	180	7.086 600	1000	39.370 000
27	1.062 990	57	2.244 090	87	3.425 190	185	7.283 450	2000	78.740 000
28	1.102 360	58	2.283 460	88	3.464 560	190	7.480 300	3000	118.110 000
29	1.141 730	59	2.322 830	89	3.503 903	195	7.677 150	4000	157.480 000
30	1.181 100	60	2.362 200	90	3.543 300	200	7.874 000	5000	196.850 000

To change decimal millimeters to decimal inches, position the decimal point where desired on either side of the millimeter measurement shown and reset the inches decimal by the same number of digits in the same direction. For example, to convert .001 mm into decimal inches, reset the decimal behind the 1 mm (shown on the chart) to .001; change the decimal inch equivalent (.039″ shown) to .00039″.

Conversion—Common Fractions to Decimals and Millimeters

Inches			Inches			Inches		
Common Fractions	*Decimal Fractions*	*Millimeters (approx.)*	*Common Fractions*	*Decimal Fractions*	*Millimeters (approx.)*	*Common Fractions*	*Decimal Fractions*	*Millimeters (approx.)*
1/128	.008	0.20	11/32	.344	8.73	43/64	.672	17.07
1/64	.016	0.40	23/64	.359	9.13	11/16	.688	17.46
1/32	.031	0.79	3/8	.375	9.53	45/64	.703	17.86
3/64	.047	1.19	25/64	.391	9.92	23/32	.719	18.26
1/16	.063	1.59	13/32	.406	10.32	47/64	.734	18.65
5/64	.078	1.98	27/64	.422	10.72	3/4	.750	19.05
3/32	.094	2.38	7/16	.438	11.11	49/64	.766	19.45
7/64	.109	2.78	29/64	.453	11.51	25/32	.781	19.84
1/8	.125	3.18	15/32	.469	11.91	51/64	.797	20.24
9/64	.141	3.57	31/64	.484	12.30	13/16	.813	20.64
5/32	.156	3.97	1/2	.500	12.70	53/64	.828	21.03
11/64	.172	4.37	33/64	.516	13.10	27/32	.844	21.43
3/16	.188	4.76	17/32	.531	13.49	55/64	.859	21.83
13/64	.203	5.16	35/64	.547	13.89	7/8	.875	22.23
7/32	.219	5.56	9/16	.563	14.29	57/64	.891	22.62
15/64	.234	5.95	37/64	.578	14.68	29/32	.906	23.02
1/4	.250	6.35	19/32	.594	15.08	59/64	.922	23.42
17/64	.266	6.75	39/64	.609	15.48	15/16	.938	23.81
9/32	.281	7.15	5/8	.625	15.88	61/64	.953	24.21
19/64	.297	7.54	41/64	.641	16.27	31/32	.969	24.61
5/16	.313	7.94	21/32	.656	16.67	63/64	.984	25.00
21/64	.328	8.33						

Torque Specifications

Engine and Gearbox

	KGM	*Ft. Lbs.*
Cylinder head	6.8–7.2	49.2–52.0
Chain tensioner locking bolt	3–4	21.7–28.9
Main bearing caps	5.8–6.3	42.0–45.6
Connecting rod caps	5.2–5.7	37.6–41.2
Suction pipe attachment to oil pump retainer	0.9–1.1	6.5–8.0
Expansion bolt M12X1-5	(12K)	
with Loctite	9.0–10.0	65.1–72.3
without Loctite	10.0–11.0	72.3–79.6
Flywheel shoulder stud	7.0–7.5	50.6–54.2
Crankshaft pulley	14.0	101.3
Plug on oil pump	5.0	36.2
Water pump pulley	40	28.9
Gearbox mounting		
M 8	2.5	18.1
M 10	4.7	34.0
Gearbox spacer plate	2.0	14.5
Gearbox output flange	15	108.4
Gearbox housing cover	2.5	18.1
Gearbox sealing flange	1.0	7.2
Clutch mounting bolts	1.5–1.9	10.9–13.7
Spark plugs	2.5–3	18.1–21.7
Fuel pump	1.2	8.7
Oil drain plug	6.0	43.4
Oil sump	0.8–1.0	5.8–7.2
Carburetor to manifold (single carb.)	1.0–1.4	7.2–10.1
Hollow bolt for oil supply to camshaft	1.1–1.3	8.0–9.4
Timing case cover top to bottom	0.9	6.5
Distributor flange M 8	2.5	18.1
Distributor flange M 6	1.1	8.0
Cylinder head cover	0.8–1.0	5.9–7.2

Front Axle

	KGM	*Ft. Lbs.*
Shock absorber leg, center top	8.0	57.8
Shock absorber leg, support	2.5	18
Shock absorber screw ring	12.0+2	86.8+14.5
Shock absorber piston to piston rod	2.5	18
Tie-rod lever to axle	2.5	18
Guide joint to tie-rod lever—minimum	7.0	50.6
Wishbone to front axle (under load)—minimum	15.0	108.5
Front axle to frame	4.7	34.0
Strut to wishbone and axle (under load)—minimum	6.0	43.4
Caliper to axle	9.5	68.7
Steering lever bearing	2.5	18
Steering gear to front axle	4.7	34.0

Rear Axle

	KGM	Ft. Lbs.
Drive casing to floor	9	65
Rear axle carrier mounting to floor	12	87
Thrust rod on body floor	2.5	18
Trailing arm on axle beam (under load)	7.5	54
Lower shock absorber mounting (under load)	7.5	54
Final drive attachment	9	65
Large cover on casing	5	36
3-point coupling on pinion—minimum (with Loctite AVV)	15	108
Rubber coupling at gearbox	4.5	33
Ring gear to differential body	8.3	60
Side casing cover	2.5	18
Hexagon bolt on drive flange	9+1	65+7.2
Half-shaft castellated nuts min.	30+5	217+36
Output shaft at driving flange	3	22
Output shaft at half-shaft	3	22
Drive shaft at gearbox	3	22
Rubber bearing at rear axle carrier		
M8	3	22
M10	4.5	32.5
Housing cover (short neck unit)	2.0+0.5	14.5+3.6
Ring gear to differential (short neck unit)	8.5+1	61.5+7.2
Driving flange to half-shaft pinion (short neck unit)	9.0+1	65.1+7.2
Three-arm flange to input bevel pinion—minimum (short neck unit)	15.0	108.5
Output shaft to driving flange (short neck unit)	2.4+0.6	17.4+4.3
Final drive to rear axle carrier (short neck unit)	6.5+1	47.0+7.2
Rubber mounting to body floor (short neck unit)	4.2+0.5	30.4+3.6
Final drive to rubber mounting (short neck unit)	8.1+0.9	58.6+6.5
Drive shaft to final drive (1600–2)	4.5	32.5
Cross-member to final drive (1600–2)	4.5	32.5

Steering

	KGM	Ft. Lbs.
Steering damper to clamp	4.2+0.5	30.4+3.6
Steering damper to retaining strap	4.2+0.5	30.4+3.6
Steering wheel nut	5.5+0.5	39.8+3.6
Joint disc attachment	1.5+0.5	10.8+3.6
Joint flange attachment	2.5	18.0
Steering arm to steering box	14	101.3
Castellated nut on steering guide arm—minimum	8	57.8
Retaining strap to engine mounting	1.9+0.5	13.7+3.6
Clamp to track rod	1.9+0.5	13.7+3.6
Track rod castellated nuts—minimum	3.5	25.3
Steering box to front axle beam	4.7	34.0
Guide lever to front axle beam	2.5	18.0
Track rod clamp bolts	2.5	18.0

Brakes and Wheels

	KGM	Ft. Lbs.
Caliper to kingpin pivot	9.5	68.7
Brake disc to wheel hub	6+0.7	43.4+5.0
Brake hose to caliper	1.3–1.6	8.7–11.6
Pre-pressure valve	1.9	13.7
Wheel nuts	9	65.1
Collar nut on brake line	1.3–1.6	8.7–11.6
Retainer on rear of brake unit (1600–2)	1.9+0.5	13.7+3.6
Retainer on front of brake unit (1600–2)	1.6+0.4	11.6+2.9
Brake unit holder to wheel arch (1600–2)	1.6+0.4	11.6+2.9
Caliper halves	3.4	24.6

Equipment Specifications

Type	*1500 1600 1600–2 1600T1 1800 1800A 1800/69 1800T1 2002*	*2000 2000A 2000T1 2000CS 2000CA*	*All Types*	*1500 1600*	*1600–2 1600T1 1800 1800A 1800/69 1800T1 2002 2000T1 2000CS 2000CA*
OIL PUMP (Gear type)					
Oil Pressure @ idling speed, PSI	7.1–21.3	14.2–21.3			
maximum speed, PSI	71–85	71			
Relief valve opening pressure, PSI			57–71		
Output, gals/hr.			409		
Gear tooth backlash max. in. (mm)			.0028 (.07)		
normal in. (mm)			.0012–.0019 (.03–.05)		
End play max. in. (mm)				.0028 (.07)	.0035 (.09)
normal in. (mm)				.0019 (.05)	.0019 (.05)
Free length of pressure relief spring, in. (mm)	2.68 (68)	2.70 (68.5)			
OIL PUMP (Rotor Type)					
Outer rotor—housing clearance, in. (mm)			.0020–.0079 (.05–.20)		
Rotor—housing, sealing surface,play, in. (mm)			.0013–.0033 (.034–.084)		
Inner–outer rotor clearance, in. (mm)			.0035–.0106 ±.0012 (.09–.27±.03)		
WATER PUMP					
Housing–impeller Clearance, in. (mm)			.038–.040 (.8–1.2)		
THERMOSTAT					
Opening temp.			163°–171°F 181° (optional)		
RADIATOR CAP					
Pressure, PSI			12.1–16.3		

Type	*1500 1600 1800 1800A 1800T1*	*1600–2 1600T1*	*1800/69*	*2002 2000A 2000T1 2000CS 2000CA*	*All Types*
FUEL PUMP					
Solex PE	15059	15520	15581	15517 and 15574	
Pressure @ 1000 rpm, PSI					2.99–3.56
Output @ specified rpm, GPM	11.9–13.2 @ 5500	11.9–13.2 @ 5500	11.9–13.2 @ 5500	15.8–18.5 @ 5700 [1]	

1 22.5–26.4 @ 5700–2000TI, 2000CS

Type	*1500 1600 1600–2 1600T1 1800 1800/69 1800T1 2002*	*2000 2000T1 2000CS*	*All Types*	*1500 1600 1600T1 1800 1800/69 1800T1 2002*	*1600–2*	*2000 2000T1 2000CS*
TCH						
te I.D. in. (mm)	7.87 (200)	8.50 (216)				
te I.D. in. (mm)	5.12 (130)	5.67 (144)				
ing:						
Engine side			T450W			
Transmission side			T50S			
ickness in. (mm)				.41 (10.3)	.37 (9.3)	.37±.0079 (9.3±.2)
thdrawal arm clearance, in. (mm)	.118–.138 (3–3.5)	.158–.177 (4–4.5)				
e pedal travel, in. (mm)	.8–1.0 (20–25)	1.4–1.6 (35–40)				

Type	*All Types*	*1500, 1600, 1800, 1800A, 1800/69, 1800T1, 2000, 2000A, 2000T1, 2000CS, 2000CA*	*1600–2, 1600T1, 2002*
STEERING			
Min. turning circle (ft.)		34.5	34.1
Steering box ratio	15.5:1		
Overall ratio	17.6:1		
No. of turns lock to lock	3.5		
Max. free play at wheel rim in. (mm)	.79 (20)		

Type	*All Types*
MANUAL GEARBOX	
Mainshaft end-play in. (mm)	.024 (.6)
Countershaft end-play in. (mm)	.0079 (.2)
Pinion tooth backlash in. (mm)	.00236–.0059 (.06–.15)
Shaft runout in. (mm)	.00079 (.02)

Type	*1500 2002 2000 2000A 2000T1 2000CA*	*1600 1600–2 1800 1800A 1800/69*	*1600T1 1800T1 2000CS*	*1500 2002 2000 2000A 2000T1 2000CA*	*1500 1600T1 1800T1 2000 2000A 2002 2000T1 2000CS 2000CA*
IGNITION ADVANCE DATA*					
Centrifugal, degrees:					
@ 500 rpm	2.5–5.5	0–5	0–4		
@ 750 rpm		9–11	7–9	8.5–10.5	
@ 1000 rpm		11–13	10–12	12–14	
@ 1200 rpm	14–16 (end)		10.5–12.5		
@ 1500 rpm		14–16	13–15		
@ 1900 rpm		16–18 (end)	14–16 (end)		
Max adj: range in distributor (degrees)		16–18			14–16
VACUUM ADVANCE (HG)					
Start: in. (mm)	4.72–5.91 (120–150) **	4.72–5.9 (120–150)			
End: in. (mm)	7.68–8.27 (195–210) **	7.68–8.27 (195–210)			
Adj. range (degrees)	5	5			

* To be measured from distributor shaft on distributor test stand.
** Not applicable to 2000TI.

Type	*1500 1600 1800T1 With Long Neck Gearbox and Long Neck Final Drive*	*1600–2 With Universal Gearbox 232 and Long Neck Final Drive*	*1600 1800 2000 2000T1 2000C 2000CS With Universal Gearbox 232 and Long Neck Final Drive*	*1800A 2000A 2000CA With Automatic and Long Neck Final Drive*	*2000 2000C 2000T1 2000CS With Universal Gearbox 232 and Short Neck Final Drive*	*2000A 2000CA With Automatic and Short Neck Final Drive*	*2002 With Universal Gearbox 232 and Long Neck Final Drive*
DRIVE SHAFT	1-piece	2-piece	2-piece	2-piece	2-piece	2-piece	2-piece
Length in. (mm)	78.3±.06 (1989±1.5)						
Length Front Piece in. (mm)		19.6 (497)	28.9 (735)	23.4 (604)	28.9 (735)	23.4 (604)	20.1 (510)
Length Rear Piece in. (mm)		33.6 (852.5)	30.3 (770)	30.3 (770)	38.8 (985)	38.8 (985)	32.1 (816)
Max. Play in Univ. Joints in. (mm)		.001 (.03) all models					